KONGO
IN THE AGE OF EMPIRE,
1860–1913

Africa and the Diaspora
History, Politics, Culture

Series Editors

Thomas Spear
Neil Kodesh
Tejumola Olaniyan
Michael G. Schatzberg
James H. Sweet

Kongo
in the Age of Empire,
1860–1913

THE BREAKDOWN
OF A MORAL ORDER

Jelmer Vos

The University of Wisconsin Press

The University of Wisconsin Press
1930 Monroe Street, 3rd Floor
Madison, Wisconsin 53711-2059
uwpress.wisc.edu

3 Henrietta Street, Covent Garden
London WC2E 8LU, United Kingdom
eurospanbookstore.com

Printed in the United States of America

This book may be available in a digital edition

Library of Congress Cataloging-in-Publication Data
Vos, Jelmer, author.
Kongo in the age of empire, 1860–1913: the breakdown of a moral order / Jelmer Vos.
pages   cm   (Africa and the diaspora: history, politics, culture)
Includes bibliographical references and index.
ISBN 978-0-299-30620-5 (cloth: alk. paper)
1. Kongo Kingdom—History.   2. Kongo Kingdom—Politics and government.
3. Kongo Kingdom—Foreign relations—Portugal.
4. Portugal—Foreign relations—Kongo Kingdom.
5. Rubber industry and trade—Kongo Kingdom—History.
6. Missions—Kongo Kingdom—History.
7. Catholic Church—Kongo Kingdom—History.
I. Title. II. Series: Africa and the diaspora.
DT654.V67   2015
967.51'1401   dc23
2015008826

ISBN 978-0-299-30624-3 (pbk.: alk. paper)

For
ÉRICO

Contents

Illustrations

Figures

Maps

Table

ACKNOWLEDGMENTS

Research for this book started more than fifteen years ago as I began writing my doctoral dissertation under the supervision of William Gervase Clarence-Smith. In these early stages, the University of London's Central Research Fund, the School of Oriental and African Studies, and the Royal Historical Society gave financial support. A two-year postdoctoral fellowship in 2008–9 at the Centro de História de Além-Mar in Lisbon, funded by the Fundação para a Ciência e a Tecnologia, and a Summer Research Grant from Old Dominion University in 2011 gave me a chance to collect additional materials from several repositories in Europe and Angola. Thanks are recorded to the staff of the many archives and libraries consulted over the years, especially the people at the Arquivo Nacional de Angola, the Arquivo Histórico Ultramarino, and the Sociedade de Geografia de Lisboa, on whose assistance I have relied the most.

During the academic year of 2012–13 I held a fellowship at re:work, the International Research Center "Work and Human Lifecycle in Global History" at the Humboldt University in Berlin. I want to thank the staff and my co-fellows for creating an environment that was both accommodating and intellectually stimulating, allowing me to develop many of the ideas on colonial rule in northern Angola presented in this book. Chapters 2 and 5 were first presented as seminar papers at re:work, and I thank all participants for their feedback.

The following colleagues read parts of the manuscript as draft chapters or conference papers: Mariana Candido, Frederick Cooper, Andreas Eckert, Joseph Miller, Michelle Moyd, John Thornton, Luise White, and my colleagues at Old Dominion University, Brett Bebber, Erin Jordan, Anna Mirkova, Megan Nutzman, Tim Orr, John Weber, and Elizabeth Zanoni. Their comments and suggestions have been extremely helpful. As outside readers for Wisconsin, John Thornton and Jan Vansina provided valuable commentary on the full manuscript, for which I am very grateful. Thanks are also due to David Birmingham, Samuel Coghe, Roquinaldo Ferreira, Cécile Fromont, Linda Heywood, Alexander Keese, Carola Lentz, Wyatt MacGaffey, Peter Mark, Malyn Newitt, and Hein Vanhee for providing input in one way or another.

Taya Barnett at Old Dominion University has been a wonderful help in designing the maps (one of which was originally produced by Don Pirius for the Ohio University Press). I am grateful to Dr. Joachim Piepke of the Anthropos Institute in Sankt Augustin for digitizing an old image from the institute's journal and to Dr. José Carlos de Oliveira for granting me permission to use two photographs from his private collection. Many thanks to my brother, Aldo, for preparing all photographic images for publication. Luzolo Kiala, Maria Panzo Saca, and Inês Bondo helped in translating documents from Kikongo into Portuguese. John Thornton has always been helpful in sharing archival notes. Finally, I would like to thank Gwen Walker, Thomas Spear, and the production team of the University of Wisconsin Press for their enthusiasm, feedback, and general editorial assistance.

The list of friends, colleagues, and relatives who have supported me along the road is too long to thank each individually. Still I would like to mention some by name. For their hospitality during my last two visits to Angola, in 2007 and 2011, I remain indebted to the Bondo family. Marissa Moorman and Maria Conceição Neto helped out during my first fieldtrip to Luanda back in 2000. In Berlin, I received valuable guidance on the local mores and customs from my friend Keith Allen. As I was struggling to beat the manuscript into shape and the gray skies of Berlin seemed forever closed, the friendship of our Brazilian neighbors Raquel Kritsch, Andreas Hofbauer, João Klug, and Oscar Abdounur and his family proved invaluable. Finally, I owe a tremendous debt to Inês and our son, Érico, who, even when I was away teaching for months on end, have always been with me.

Parts of chapter 1 were previously published in Jelmer Vos, "Christianity, Adaptations in Africa of," in *The Princeton Companion to Atlantic History*, edited by Joseph C. Miller, 93–96. Copyright © 2015 by Princeton University Press. Reproduced by permission of Princeton University Press. Parts of chapter 1 were previously published in Hein Vanhee and Jelmer Vos, "Kongo in the Age of Empire," in *Kongo across the Waters*, edited by Susan Cooksey, Robin Poynor, and Hein Vanhee, 78–87. Copyright © 2013 by University Press of Florida. Reproduced by permission of the University Press of Florida.

CHRONOLOGY OF KONGO KINGS UNDER PORTUGUESE RULE

Pedro V	(1860–91)
Álvaro XIV	(1891–96)
Henrique III	(1896–1901)
Pedro VI	(1901–10)
Manuel III	(1911–13)
Álvaro XV	(1915–23)
Pedro VII	(1923–55)
António III	(1955–57)
Pedro VIII	(1962)

Kongo
in the Age of Empire,
1860–1913

Introduction

This book examines how the Kongo people of northern Angola engaged the nineteenth-century expansion of European imperialism in their realm. The story begins around 1860, when a long succession dispute in the kingdom of Kongo was decided in favor of Dom Pedro Elelo, a scion of an old noble family and protégé of the Portuguese in Luanda. Five years later, the last transatlantic slaving vessel left the Congo River, destined for Cuba with a human cargo obtained from local Kongo brokers.[1] Together, these events mark the beginning of Kongo's colonial history. As abolition ushered in a new economic era based on the export of ivory and rubber, traders and missionaries from different European countries settled in Kongo's historic capital, São Salvador, while the kingdom itself was slowly integrated in the colonial state of Angola.[2]

This book argues, first of all, that the development of colonialism in northern Angola rested on the sociopolitical infrastructure of the kingdom of Kongo, as different foreign agents with a stake in Central Africa depended on the leverage of the Kongo king, his relatives, and other clients of the royal court to carry their imperial projects forward.[3] The kingdom at the time was a small polity founded on a social contract holding the king accountable to lower-ranked chiefs and their followers. While processes of European commercial, missionary, and political expansion were initially adapted to local needs and circumstances, after 1900 the Kongo found it increasingly difficult to reconcile colonial agendas with their own. Kongo's social contract was ultimately broken with the imposition, through the royal court, of colonial demands for migrant labor, causing some of the most senior Kongo chiefs to rise against the king and depose him. For the Portuguese regime, this revolt was an inconvenient setback in their quest for colonial hegemony, but for the Kongo it was a violent conclusion to a moral crisis that had consumed their political community from within.

Misguided notions of "decay" and "dissolution" have thus far shaped our understanding of what happened under colonialism to the kingdom of Kongo, famous for its longstanding engagement with Europe and its role in shaping the Atlantic world in the era of the slave trade. The general impression is that a once powerful and centralized state completely disintegrated in the seventeenth and eighteenth centuries, while the remaining territorial fragments were later divided among different European nations as the spoils of colonial conquest.[1] Considering that the later history of the Kongo kingdom has been virtually untold, such misperceptions, rooted in Eurocentric notions of what African kingdoms should look like, are understandable. In the 1960s and '70s several scholars touched on Kongo's colonial history, but they did so either from an international or imperial perspective, or within the context of a broader narrative of military encounters in colonial Angola.[5] This book writes the kingdom's early colonial history from a Kongolese viewpoint, using previously unexplored sources, many of which only became available after the decolonization of Portuguese Africa in 1975. Contradicting the standard view of a kingdom in decline, it shows how the Kongo polity survived into the twentieth century as a central node in the unfolding world of European colonialism in West Central Africa.

This book makes clear that Europeans had a smaller role than local rubber traders, mission students, and government employees in shaping the colonial world of northern Angola. Placing the traditions, motivations, and actions of these Kongo agents at the heart of a narrative about the construction of early colonial rule in Angola, this work illuminates an understudied episode in the history of the Portuguese empire.[6] Portuguese colonialism was somewhat peculiar because many of Portugal's attempts at colonial conquest grew out of the nation's older, trade-based empire in Angola, and often predated the Berlin Conference in 1885 that prompted most other European colonial regimes to claim sovereignty over African lands and peoples. Most accounts of the colonial encounter in Angola, including this one, have their starting point somewhere in the middle of the nineteenth century, when the export slave trade came to an end and policymakers in Lisbon proposed territorial expansion and white settlement as alternative strategies for developing what many considered to be Portugal's prime colonial possession in Africa.[7] The installation of Pedro V in 1860 was set in this context, as it brought Kongo within the orbit of an expansionist regime based in Luanda. Like elsewhere in Angola, however, the colonial occupation of Kongo remained limited in scope and was for a long time based mainly on the taxation of rubber and other local export products. Only after 1910 did the colonial government elaborate plans to mobilize Kongo's labor force, with devastating consequences for both the kingdom and Portugal's reputation in and outside Angola. This is not to argue that Portugal governed Angola very differently from the ways in which other European empires ruled their African territories. With regard to its reliance on local power structures, especially, colonial rule in northern Angola developed along fairly recognizable patterns, as this book will demonstrate.[8]

Colonialism in the kingdom of Kongo was different, however, not so much due to Kongo's incorporation in the Portuguese empire but rather because of the kingdom's unique relationship to Europe. Kongo's earlier "discovery" of the West profoundly influenced local responses to colonialism and made local power brokers extraordinarily receptive to foreign advances.[9] The kingdom had been involved in Atlantic commerce since the late 1400s, and many Kongo elites embraced the nineteenth-century expansion of global ivory and rubber markets into Central Africa. Over the centuries, the kingdom's rulers maintained diplomatic relations with several European polities, including the Vatican, to increase their leverage over political rivals in the region. Most significantly, they imported a Western religion, Catholicism, elements of which served the rather narrow purpose of regulating the polity's internal affairs, which were intimately tied to the export trade in slaves and ivory. Although there were occasions when the social benefits of Kongo's participation in Atlantic trade were questioned, generally local elites considered their relationship with the West as advantageous. Kongo's engagement with European imperialism took a new turn in the late nineteenth century, as different colonial agents increasingly intervened in the everyday affairs of the Kongo people, but the encounter unfolding after 1860 cannot be understood without reference to these earlier centuries of cross-cultural exchange. The new export trades in ivory and rubber grew out of the abolished slave trade, and the Christian missionaries who settled in the kingdom around 1880 built on a legacy of conversion running four centuries deep. The post–slave trade era created many new challenges for the Kongo, but the vigor with which they embraced these challenges can be explained to some extent by their long familiarity with white priests, muskets, textiles, and other things European.

Rebellion in the Kingdom

All was not well in the kingdom of Kongo by 1913. In the morning of 10 December of that year, a militia of seditious chiefs, armed with imported silex carbines and flintlock rifles, stormed São Salvador and shot their way past the few colonial troops stationed in the Kongo capital. As women and children sought shelter in the compound of the local Baptist mission while husbands tried to protect their homes, the insurgents headed for the royal palace. They had come for the incumbent king, Manuel Martins Kiditu, but when they could not find him they burned down and looted half the city before returning to their base south of the capital. In the days that followed, the rebels, led by their spokesman, Tulante Álvaro Buta, forced a frightened Portuguese administration into negotiations about colonial governance. They demanded the expulsion of Kiditu from the kingdom, a reduction of the colonial hut tax, and a stop to the forced conscription of workers for plantation labor overseas. Most demands were initially met by the colonial government, which was taken aback by mutiny in a polity whose ruling class had been dependable clients of the Portuguese empire for more than fifty years. But as a hastily arranged truce between the rebels and the government did not hold, what started as a small-scale insurrection against the king of Kongo turned into a bitter anti-colonial guerrilla war that only ended with the Portuguese capture of Buta in 1915.[10]

The fact that the revolt developed into one of the longest military conflicts in the early colonial history of Angola has somehow clouded our understanding of its causes.[11] Some historians have seen the revolt as a typical manifestation of African resistance against a colonial regime intent on exploiting the labor of its subject population. The events of December 1913 occurred, indeed, against the backdrop of a colonial program to contract migrant workers in northern Angola, and the revolt can easily be situated in a wider context of international controversies about forced labor practices in Portuguese Africa.[12] Since 1912, the colonial government had conscripted hundreds of Kongo workers for cocoa, coffee, and palm tree farms in the Cabinda enclave north of the Congo River. Then, in October 1913, it tried to contract 1,500 laborers in São Salvador for cocoa plantations in the archipelago of São Tomé and Príncipe, in the Gulf of Guinea. English missionaries were close observers of the Cabinda conscription, the government's effort to enlist workers for the infamous "chocolate islands," and the revolt that came on the heels of this failed attempt.[13] Via the British consul in Luanda, missionary reports about the violent nature of the Cabinda recruitment forced the British Foreign Office to continue looking into the issue of labor exploitation in Portuguese West Africa, which it had done intermittently since the final days of the Atlantic slave trade.[14] After colonial authorities in São Salvador arrested one of the local missionaries, Sidney Bowskill, in 1914 on the charge of instigating rebellion, British diplomatic pressure on Portugal increased, forcing the Angolan government to investigate the origins of the Kongo revolt. From this official investigation emerged a massive dossier on the colonial occupation of northern Angola compiled from official correspondence as well as eye-witness accounts, which graphically documented the atrocities committed in the conscription of Kongo workers for Cabinda.[15] These inquiries added another blemish to Portugal's already tainted colonial record, as outsiders read the

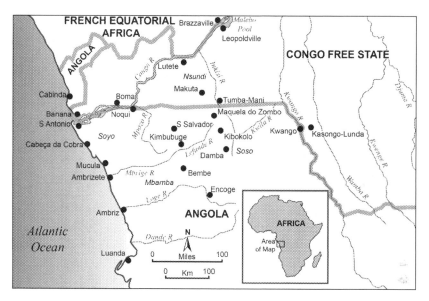

Northern Angola, ca. 1900

events in São Salvador as further evidence that Portugal's forced labor regime in Africa was analogous to slavery.

Yet from the assembled documentation it is clear that the violence inflicted upon Kongo villagers during successive recruitment campaigns came mainly from African employees of the colonial administration, many with connections to the king himself. Also a careful reading of Buta's "war palaver" in December 1913 indicates that the political motives of the rebels were more complex than the typical image of African resistance against European labor exploitation suggests. Transcripts of the war summit make clear that Kongo chiefs did not hold Portugal, the kingdom's distant overlord, directly accountable for the abuses of colonial rule in northern Angola. The occurrence of violence was instead explained as a result of the vicious and greedy behavior of some individuals within the Kongo community itself. Specifically, Buta emphasized the suffering of Kongo villagers at the hands of soldiers, policemen, and other officials from São Salvador seeking to extort taxes and manpower in the name of the king. In other words, Portuguese policies to extract tax and labor from northern Angola inaugurated a brief but intense period of state-sponsored violence, but the uprising was fundamentally a response to the corruption of a government co-opted by a foreign colonial power.

The evidence gathered in the wake of the 1913 revolt thus provides a window not just on what Frederick Cooper has called the "sordid world of labor recruitment," but also on how colonial rule was generally constructed in northern

Angola.[16] This book places the Kongo uprising within an extended time frame, starting around 1860, and argues that it epitomized a breakdown in the kingdom's long history of accommodating European colonial influences. The Kongo experienced this breakdown not as a failure of colonialism, but as a crisis within their own community. The rebel leaders aimed to resolve this crisis by restoring moral order in the kingdom and renegotiating Kongo's relationship with Portugal.

A Kongo Moral Community

In Angola, the Kongo uprising of 1913 is remembered as the Revolt of Buta, or Buta's War. It is considered a pivotal event in the history of the Kongo people, epitomizing the end of Kongo's independence and its submission to Portuguese rule. But outside Angola, few scholars have paid attention to the uprising or, for that matter, its preceding history. Historians took notice when the field of Angolan history expanded in the 1960s, but treated the event primarily as an expression of Kongo nationalism. Here was a case, they argued, that looked like a "primitive" rebellion against colonialism, while also containing elements of a popular resistance movement aimed to overthrow an oppressive colonial regime. In this interpretation, the revolt was an outburst of African discontent accumulated through decades of Portuguese rule. The articulation of long-felt anti-colonial grievances by African members of the Baptist Church, shortly before the outbreak of the war, was an early manifestation of "ethno-nationalism" in Angola. As such, the revolt could be seen as a forerunner of the Kongo insurgency of 15 March 1961, which helped trigger the war for national independence.[17] Not surprisingly, this has also been the prevailing view of the Buta revolt in Angola itself. Explaining it as a war against Portuguese rule has allowed Angolans to incorporate the event into a nationalistic discourse about the colonial past and remember Buta as a national hero.[18]

These first interpretations of the Kongo uprising were strongly influenced by contemporary theories of African resistance that tried to connect violent forms of protest in the early colonial era to later manifestations of anti-colonial nationalism. Historians have since moved away from this "primary resistance" model, as they identified several flaws in this approach to the study of collective violence in Africa. One major weakness was the teleological reasoning behind the model, suggesting an almost inevitable development from small-scale reactionary protests to large-scale movements engaged in projects of nation-building. Identifying all resisters of colonial rule as proto-nationalists, the model also built on ahistorical assumptions about what motivated rebels. African rebels, while far from being culturally isolated, did not have a bird's-eye view of the early colonial encounter as a process of gradual integration into a world of capitalism and centralized states. Instead, they "were waging political struggles within the political world they knew," as two scholars of popular protest in South Africa once put it.[19] This political world rarely corresponded directly with the realm of colonial states that Europeans were busy constructing. Early theories of resistance were furthermore criticized for concentrating too much on the confrontation between European colonizers and African subjects, while neglecting the tensions and conflicts that existed within African societies or the fact that Africans often adapted colonial influences to their own wants and ambitions.[20] Colonial intrusions in the political affairs and everyday lives of Africans still mattered, of course, but historians have become increasingly aware of "the complexity of Africans with imported institutions and constructs."[21]

My own understanding of the revolt as a crisis in Kongo's evolving relationship with colonial rule builds on several "moral economy" theories of political conflict in Africa. Focusing on the rules of social reciprocity—or mutual obligations—binding different groups in a community, the moral economy literature provides a number of basic lessons about the occurrence of violent protest in colonial Africa.[22] First, conflicts did not come about simply because "modern" European states and markets encroached on "traditional" African societies. In fact, in East Africa, rebels and individuals otherwise critical of colonial regimes often emerged from social groups who had benefited the most from participation in global commerce and cross-cultural exchange.[23] Instead, conflicts were most likely to occur when the prevailing terms of social contract between rulers and the ruled broke down; or, in the words of John Lonsdale, when people had a sense of "unmerited loss" because of the repudiation of existing social relations by those in power.[24] The causes of revolts should therefore not be sought in the European exploitation of economic or political inequalities as such, but rather in abrupt changes in the nature of colonial rule, which could happen, for example, with the introduction of direct taxation.[25] At the same time, because moral economies and the political protests they engendered were embedded in local worldviews, in sub-Saharan Africa immoral actions threatening communal survival were often cast in the idiom of witchcraft.[26]

Because conflicts over moral economies were hardly ever understood as strictly economic struggles, Jonathon Glassman has suggested using the concept of a "moral community" instead, which he defines as consisting of "people who engage in daily, face-to-face interaction, who share (and struggle over) local social institutions."[27] The kingdom of Kongo in the late nineteenth century can be seen as such a community, and the 1913 uprising as a struggle over its foundation. By this time, the kingdom was no longer the centralized political construct of earlier times, which connected peoples who were often strangers to one another, but a relatively small agglomerate of chiefdoms linked through kinship (real or imagined), religious affiliation, and commerce. For many Kongo elders, the kings at São Salvador were not distant rulers, but individuals they knew personally as fellow clan members, fellow church members, school colleagues, or from trade expeditions. If the Kongo revolt was essentially a conflict over the constitution of a moral community, however, then it should be possible to outline its contours. What did the political world of the Kongo look like in the early twentieth century?

To begin with, there were the chiefs in the countryside around São Salvador. Many of them had grown rich off the new export trades in ivory and rubber and had invested their wealth in women, slaves, and political titles. In addition, there was an upcoming class of mission-educated men, often of noble descent and sometimes with experience in the caravan trade. Residing in the capital, many used their commercial expertise and social connections to become intermediaries for European visitors to the kingdom. These older and younger elites formed the kingdom's core constituency, while some of them even held positions at the royal court as counselors, secretaries, messengers, or police agents.

São Salvador was also home to a small community of white traders, missionaries, and colonial administrators, which while limited in terms of numbers wielded extraordinary influence. Around 1900, this foreign contingent consisted of about a dozen Portuguese and English nationals. It should be noted that some strangers from other parts of Africa also resided in the kingdom at the time: a few factory workers from Lagos and Accra, who were probably employed in Noqui, on the Congo River, instead of São Salvador itself, and a dozen soldiers from Mozambique, adding to colonial troops recruited elsewhere in Angola. But as these African outsiders rarely surfaced in the colonial archives, it is difficult to document their interaction with the local population.[28] A dearth of recorded protest against Europeans dwelling in the heart of the kingdom suggests their presence was rarely considered problematic. In fact, while the Kongo sometimes ascribed special powers to the white men in their community, they also recognized their basic humanity and vulnerability. Certainly in the early period, Europeans traveling or residing in Kongo relied on Africans for supplies and protection, were dependent on local guides and translators, took black wives, smoked cannabis, and fell sick, all of which brought these whites closer to the people hosting them.[29]

European traders were not visibly involved in the politics of the royal court. For the local population, they were mainly dispensers of currency and prestige goods, which they supplied in exchange for rubber or as payment for transport services. But their factories, or stores, markedly changed the townscape, while their demand for carriers created expectations among Kongo men about work under colonialism. Missionaries tried to shape African society directly. They generally found a friendly reception among Kongo chiefs and elders who considered them fundamental to the preservation of the kingdom's Christian culture, even if the missionaries themselves tried to create distance from the old tradition. Through the provision of jobs, education, and healthcare to young men and women, including slaves, the missionaries also promoted social change. Mission stations became themselves sites of moral conflict: the missionaries were revered for renewing Kongo's tradition of literacy and Christian teaching; but some youngsters exploited their church affiliation to earn wealth and status, causing the envy of their peers, while elders were often wary of the new missionaries' intentions to educate women and their hostility to such fundamental social institutions as bridewealth and polygyny.

Colonial administrators were the local embodiment of the kingdom's distant overlord, Portugal, a benevolent patron in the eyes of many elites. Since the late eighteenth century, the Portuguese in Angola had provided the kingdom with the occasional priest, who baptized the masses and helped the governing class maintain the royal Christian cult. From 1860 to 1870, Portugal militarily supported Kongo's ruling families, the Kivuzi and the Agua Rosada, a relationship consolidated with Portugal's official occupation of São Salvador in 1888. The Kongo domesticated the representatives of colonial rule and other white men residing in their midst through naming.[30] For example, one long-serving Portuguese resident was called *lemba nsi*, one who keeps the peace in the land, a name he received for his conciliatory form of governing. Some Europeans were called *mfumu*, "big man" or chief, out of respect for their ability to generate wealth and attract followers. The Kongo sometimes added ironical twists to such naming practices. A Portuguese missionary, Father Martins, was named *padre kiaji*, a man heavy (in weight or importance) like a bunch of palm fruit. The pioneering Baptist missionary Thomas Comber was widely known as *vianga-vianga* for his "restless activity." The Dutch trader Anton Greshoff was called *mfumu ntangu*, "mister sun," a name passed on to all blond agents of the Dutch trading company as it moved upstream along the Congo River.[31] By contrast, one unpopular lower-level official, Paulo Midosi Moreira, who had a significant impact on the implementation of colonial labor laws in São Salvador, was known to everyone as just Senhor Paulo. Either way, well-liked or not, colonial officials were an integral part of the social landscape. As Clifton Crais has argued, to understand "how it was that Europeans extended control over such vast areas of the world so quickly and ruled with relatively few people," it is important to shift the emphasis from strategies of rule to the "daily relationships of colonizer and colonized." While European officials tended to operate on a fundamental belief in the difference between themselves and their colonial subjects, the "foreignness of colonial domination" becomes questionable once colonial officials are seen as part of the communities in which they served.[32]

The king was both the figurehead and the linchpin holding this community together. Elected by council, kings represented the Kongo polity externally. As they negotiated the settlement of traders and missionaries in São Salvador and communicated with the colonial government, all rulers from Pedro V (1860–91) to Manuel III (1911–13) were trusted to represent the interests of their constituency. At the same time, they were protectors of social harmony and guardians of the Christian cult, and their behavior was circumscribed by deeply rooted notions of proper political conduct. Failure to comply with this dual responsibility— protecting the community as well as representing it externally—was at the root of Kiditu's downfall in 1913.

Accommodation

São Salvador had long been a place that connected people across distances. In the five centuries prior to colonization, it was both a central node in an extensive trade network that supplied metals, slaves, ivory, and Atlantic imports to different buyers and a religious center, from which political power and prestige emanated.[33] In the second half of the nineteenth century, several European parties with different interests in this corner of Central Africa became aware of São Salvador's strategic location and were drawn to the city. Its rulers provided missionaries and explorers with the logistical support—connections, carriers, guides, interpreters—they needed for their travels. The Portuguese in Angola counted on the king's political leverage to extend their imperial reach into the northern region between the rivers Dande and Congo. Coastal traders of different nationalities opened their first inland factories in São Salvador to capture more of Kongo's growing rubber supplies. Together these exchanges constituted Kongo's first encounter with colonialism, which at the time seemed beneficial to many of the parties involved, but was fraught with contradictions from the start.

Chapters 1 through 4 examine the colonial impact on the Kongo polity before the rapid turn of events around 1910, a period in which Kongo leaders often successfully accommodated the projects of their European "collaborators" to their own agendas and the changing needs of their followers. Chapter 1 begins by analyzing the institutional structure of the kingdom around 1860. At the time, the kingdom still functioned as a traditional title association that Kongo noblemen used for organizing political and economic life in the Kongo region, albeit no longer on the same scale as in previous centuries.[31] But to see in the diminished territorial scope of the Kongo polity a sign of decadence would be unwarranted. The historian Susan Herlin Broadhead once argued that it is necessary to think "beyond decline" to understand the political processes affecting the kingdom in the nineteenth century. The continued vitality of the kingdom stemmed mainly from São Salvador's role as the center of a Christian cult through which different chiefdoms organized the political affairs associated with long-distance trading. Broadhead also assumed, however, that on the eve of colonial rule the kingdom had lost this politico-religious function and was no more than a "living memory" for the Kongo people.[35] In contrast, this book argues not only that the Christian cult was still central to Kongo politics around 1900 but also that through their association with the colonial government, as well as European traders and missionaries, Kongo elites gradually transformed the Christian kingdom into a vehicle of colonial expansion.

Subsequent chapters document this transformation of the Kongo polity in detail. Chapter 2 analyzes the influence of the post–slave trade expansion of ivory and rubber production on the economy of the kingdom and the working lives of its subjects. European trade houses were drawn to São Salvador because of its central position in the network of caravan routes between Malebo Pool (Kinshasa) and the Atlantic coast south of the Congo River. The establishment of trade factories in São Salvador in the 1880s strengthened the city's position as a market for jobs and imported prestige goods, while head carrying—the only feasible form of transport in this part of Africa—became the main occupation of thousands of young Kongo men. For these men carrying was rewarding labor, and it became their standard for working under Europeans until Portugal imposed new labor demands on Kongo in 1912.

In this era of economic change, when an increasing number of Kongo men were lured into a world of Atlantic commerce, a new generation of Christian missionaries settled in São Salvador. British Baptist missionaries pioneered what the Kongo would call the "second coming of Christianity" in 1878; two years later they were followed by state-funded Portuguese priests.[36] The local nobility saw in the near-simultaneous arrival of a Protestant and a Catholic mission an opportunity to perk up the old Christian cult. Ordinary men and women wanted baptism—a ritual Catholic priests traditionally administered—and expected missionary assistance in their everyday struggles against different maladies and evils. But for many Kongo households the attraction of these modern missions went beyond the spiritual. They associated the missionaries with the expansion of European commerce and power in the region and valued their schools for teaching students the skills they needed in the colonial era. Chapter 3 examines the motives of the first Kongo men and women to join the new mission churches, before showing how these converts helped the churches extend outward from São Salvador. The expansion of the churches into the

countryside enhanced the prestige of the kings, as elite families from all over
Kongo came to visit the capital to celebrate Christian holidays and other religious festivals.[37] But the growth of the mission churches also incubated political
tensions. These Africanized churches reshaped community life throughout the
kingdom, creating divisions between Protestant and Catholic populations that
would be articulated in the succession struggles of the early twentieth century.

Chapter 4 examines the political relations between Kongo's ruling class
and the colonial state after Portugal had secured its claims to the Kongo region
at the Berlin Conference in 1885. Portuguese rule in northern Angola resembled
constructions of colonial power elsewhere in Africa. Below a "thin white line"
of administrators and military officers, the government used local Africans as
employees and as agents to "broadcast" state power.[38] Foremost among the
Africans who helped Portugal to distribute symbols of its presence and extend
its political influence in northern Angola were members of the Agua Rosada
family, to which Pedro V also belonged. Many of the Agua Rosada had favored
Portuguese interference in Kongo politics since the late 1850s and now their
sons occupied key functions in the embryonic colonial state. Through them, the
colonial administration was able to exert some control over northern Angola's
populace, although mainly within the realm of the kingdom. In return, the
Agua Rosada received guns, capital, and new military ranks, which they used
to increase their status and power in the region. As clients of Portugal, the kings
and their courts became the true face of colonial rule in Kongo. All colonial
measures designed by the district government in Cabinda or the central government in Luanda—such as vagrancy laws or the hut tax—and those initiated by
the local administration—like police campaigns—were implemented through
the kings in São Salvador. Because the Portuguese depended on the kingdom for
influence in northern Angola, they increasingly intervened in royal succession
disputes to keep claimants critical of Portuguese patronage away from the throne.
Chapter 4 concentrates in particular on the installation in 1911 of Manuel
Martins Kiditu, a forty-year-old businessman and former student of the Catholic
mission, who was elected after a growing section of other mission-educated elites,
both Catholic and Protestant, had expressed their concerns about the increasing
corruption of the royal office under colonial rule.

Breakdown

In 1912 and 1913, Kongo witnessed its moment of "colonial meltdown," a sudden
crisis in the longstanding relationship with Portugal resulting from new colonial ambitions to deepen the structures of capitalist exploitation in northern
Angola.[39] By legally demarcating the Kongo region as a catchment area for
migrant workers for agricultural firms in Cabinda and in São Tomé and

Príncipe, the colonial government intruded for the first time directly on the African sphere of production. But the Portuguese colonial regime lacked the infrastructural capacity—the material resources and ability to penetrate African society—to implement any labor policy effectively and according to law.[40] Although the carrying trade had exposed many Kongo men to wage labor, a free labor market had not yet developed in northern Angola. With just a few colonial officials on the ground, potential recruits could be reached only through informal channels, which in early twentieth-century Kongo meant involving the chiefs, who still controlled access to the labor of their kinfolk and slaves. But the colonial government could only get to the chiefs through the king of Kongo, who in turn relied for this on his government-sponsored corpus of messengers, policemen, and soldiers. Challenged by these different colonial agents, who slickly morphed into tax collectors and labor recruiters, the problem for the chiefs was not taxation or labor recruitment per se. The chiefs had been paying taxes and there were volunteers to work for wages overseas. The question was rather *how much* or *how many*, and what happened when the king's emissaries, who showed a penchant for lawless behavior, asked the chiefs to deliver more than they were able or willing to give.

Chapters 5 and 6 focus on the violent confrontations with state agents that defined the colonial experience of the Kongo people in the early twentieth century.[41] Armed conflicts between colonial authorities in São Salvador and recalcitrant chiefs were far from new, but after 1910 state-sponsored violence intensified with the imposition of unprecedented tax and labor demands, causing widespread resistance among the Kongo populace. The violence, coercion, and abuse that people suffered at the hands of government agents during these later years represented a dramatic departure from the relative peace and prosperity of the previous period. Accommodation and violence thus formed two extreme dimensions of the early colonial experience in Kongo, although they were really two sides of the same coin. As other scholars have pointed out, the feebleness of European rule in Africa was often conducive to arbitrary violence, causing political instability in the local institutions that colonial regimes relied on.[42] Northern Angola was no exception in this regard. Limited colonial authority had allowed one faction of the Kongo aristocracy, the ruling Kivuzi and Agua Rosada families, to appropriate the local elements of state power. Because the violence associated with tax and labor collection emanated from the royal court in São Salvador, state coercion was embodied in the figure of the king, which largely explains why Kiditu became the focus of popular discontent.

Chapter 5 analyzes the impact of colonial tax and labor policies on Kongo society by focusing on the implementation of these policies at the grassroots level. In contrast to top-down views of Portuguese colonialism, which emphasize metropolitan discourses, plans, and regulations to explain the existence of forced labor in twentieth-century Angola, this chapter starts from the premise that what happened on the ground often had little to do with the laws designed by policymakers in Lisbon. It concentrates on the concrete forms of coercion that Africans were exposed to when the Portuguese government tried to put abstract labor laws into practice, showing that colonial attempts to accommodate chiefs as tax collectors and labor suppliers foundered on the social conflicts they provoked. While colonial demands for plantation labor in Cabinda impinged on existing labor relations and the kinship structures in which these were embedded, Kongo workers also found the labor contracts on offer generally unappealing, especially when compared to the earlier experience of salaried work in the carrying trade. In the end, many elders only let their sons go under the threat of violence.

Chapter 6 examines how tensions between the colonial government and its local agents, on the one hand, and chiefs and their dependents, on the other, boiled over in revolt. Trying to uncover the motives behind the 1913 uprising, this chapter analyzes a series of negotiations between Portuguese officials and Kongo chiefs about labor, colonial rule, and the role of kingship in society. Documented accounts of these negotiations make clear that colonial access to labor was negotiable for the chiefs, although labor demands from Cabinda and São Tomé often exceeded the number of workers that chiefs were able to muster. What caused chiefs to resist, in the end, was the violence with which the colonial state intruded in their villages. Since force was never prescribed by law, the causes of violence must be sought in decisions taken by authorities at the local level and the way policies were implemented by local agents who tended to operate beyond their mandate.[13] The atrocities perpetrated by the local employees of the colonial state constituted an assault on the kingdom's moral economy and were seen, specifically, as a betrayal of the community on the part of the king and his closest associates.

This study of early colonialism in the Kongo kingdom thus contributes to a larger debate about the role of African agents in the construction of colonial states.[14] By extending the analytical time frame back to the mid-nineteenth century, it shows that in Kongo, the role of African intermediaries in processes of colonial state-building grew out of their earlier, and sometimes simultaneous, forms of employment at trade houses and mission stations. It showcases several individuals, many from the Agua Rosada family and often with experience in trade, acting as interpreters for European traders, as teachers at mission schools, and as policemen and labor recruiters for the Portuguese government. In addition, if the co-optation of African authorities gave rise to "decentralized despotism," as Mahmood Mamdani has argued, then this was the result of improvisation instead of imperial design, while it also made colonial governance inherently unstable.[15] In northern Angola, to collect taxes, mobilize labor, and impose order, the colonial administration relied on the power the king of Kongo wielded through his clientage of other chiefs in the kingdom. Colonial rule was, for that reason, circumscribed by traditional structures of authority and concepts of political legitimacy. Put differently, by co-opting the kingdom as a client system, the Portuguese administration got itself involved in a Kongo moral economy that was centered on the king. Portuguese efforts to reshape relations of patronage in the kingdom in collaboration with the Agua Rosada clan backfired as it gave unprecedented power to the royal court and even to people who had little or none of it before. When the abuse of colonial power turned violent, Kongo chiefs started to question the benefits of being clients of the regime in São Salvador. In essence, the revolt of Tulante Álvaro Buta epitomized a battle fought by chiefs over political accountability in the kingdom, which originated from efforts by the colonial state to recruit a class of middlemen into its governing structures.[46]

Note on the Sources

This book is based on extensive research in archives and libraries in Angola, Portugal, the United Kingdom, the Netherlands, and Belgium, using records from the colonial government, British and Portuguese missionaries, and traders and explorers of different nationalities, only some of which are available in published form. The assembled documentation provides a broad empirical basis for a history of colonialism in the kingdom of Kongo from 1860 forward, setting this region apart from most other regions in Africa, where written sources tend to become available only from a later date. Like much written evidence from the colonial era, however, the documents used here are problematic for their bias and scope. Writing this history raised two main methodological challenges. One was to capture the voices of the laboring people: women, slaves, rubber producers, and the workers of the caravan trade, among others. The other was to gain insight into the labor relations between chiefs and dependents, with their affinities and power struggles, which profoundly influenced the expansion of the colonial economy into Kongo villages. Although some sources enabled me to document the social lives of women, slaves, and carriers in the early colonial period, the evidence was never rich enough to put them center stage. As a result, the main protagonists in my narrative are kings, chiefs, and other male notables, including members of the new mission-educated elite. If it is recognized that complex relations existed between these "big men" and their followers, and that Kongo chiefs generally represented kin groups and larger communities, a focus on powerful males might well be justified. In Kongo as elsewhere, after all, rebels were most often found among chiefs and other local authorities, who were hinge figures in the creation of colonial society, as they had been in this region's previous interaction with the Atlantic world.[17]

1

The Kingdom of Kongo
after the Slave Trade

Modern-day views of the kingdom of Kongo as a once powerful state that had all but vanished on the eve of colonial rule have their roots in the published observations of nineteenth-century visitors to Kongo, who expected to find a great king where there was none. The writings of these missionaries, colonial officials, and other travelers still hold important clues about the nature of royal power in Kongo in the late nineteenth century, although they present a confusing picture of the kingdom. These European visitors often expressed ambivalent views of the Kongo polity, resulting from a conflict between their everyday experiences and their Eurocentric notions of kingdoms as centralized states and kings as autocrats. Missionaries, for instance, could trivialize the authority of the king of Kongo and at the same time describe lesser chiefs as the king's "vassals."[1] They usually failed to understand the spiritual dimension of royal power, and therefore also failed to connect the ubiquity of Roman Catholic symbols in Kongo life to São Salvador as the kingdom's sacred capital. Thus, after first vividly describing the enduring importance of crucifixes in the management of political and commercial affairs throughout Kongo around 1900, and pointing out that resentment among one clan over the usurpation of the Kongo throne by another had barely withered, the Baptist missionary Thomas Lewis stated that the kingdom had "been reduced to all but an empty name, for the present king of Kongo is nothing more than an ordinary chief, with very limited powers, even over his own people."[2]

Some Portuguese officials in Luanda believed that King Dom Pedro V (1860–91) was politically sovereign over the lands between the river Congo and Portugal's own nominal possessions in Angola, a belief occasionally shared by

European coastal traders.[3] The Portuguese had good reasons to entertain this thought, as they hoped to employ the king in their project of colonial expansion north of Angola. Against this background, they were often frustrated with the limited influence the king was able to exert over other chiefdoms in the Kongo region, and then complained "how little this potentate is worth."[1] By contrast, William Grandy, commanding a British expedition to the Congo in 1873, called the king "the most important person in the country . . . whose influence would materially affect our future prospects." But his narrative still conveys the difficulty contemporaries had in understanding the nature of royal power. "The king of Congo commands the road from the interior to the coast, and levies contributions on all 'chiboukas' [caravans] of ivory. He was once a very powerful chief, and, being supported by the Portuguese, was much respected; but since they withdrew from Congo [in 1870] he has been gradually sinking to the level of other chiefs; and although he keeps up an outward show of authority he has very little power."[5] Grandy probably overestimated the authority Pedro V wielded under Portuguese protection, but his report exemplifies European travel accounts from the late 1800s: in their abstract depictions of the kingdom, visitors showed contempt for a perceived lack of royal power, whereas in narrating their actual dealings with the king they acknowledged dependency. In particular, it was the name of the king and the attachment of an ambassador from São Salvador that gave European travelers a chance of entry into surrounding districts. Thomas Comber, the first Baptist missionary to reach São Salvador, observed that the city was perhaps not the largest but surely "the most important, influential, and central place in the whole region round about. As visitors to the King of Kongo, and as his guests, our travelling was made much easier than it otherwise would have been."[6] So the king carried authority—but in what sense?

The work of modern scholars like Susan Herlin Broadhead, Anne Hilton, and Wyatt MacGaffey suggests that the kingdom was a kind of "collective strategy" on the part of Kongo elites to control the long-distance trade in slaves and ivory between Malebo Pool and the Atlantic coast north of Luanda.[7] Participation in the kingdom had dwindled since the late seventeenth century, as an increasing number of Kongo chiefs joined competing political networks, some of which were offshoots from the kingdom. Most historians agree that the kingdom of the eighteenth and nineteenth centuries was a product of the civil wars that ravaged Kongo in the decades around 1700, and no longer resembled the more centralized political structure from earlier times. After Pedro IV's reconstitution of the polity in 1709, Kongo noblemen with a stake in the regional long-distance trade maintained alliances under the umbrella of the kingdom, strengthening its core institution, the Christian cult, with its focus on "the king, royal insignia, royal graves, royal titleholders, royal ancestor cult, and capital city."[8] The kingdom thus became a federation of chiefdoms and the Christian cult its particular form of power management, not very different from the oligarchic alliances that ruling elites throughout the lower Congo region created through intermarriage and membership in title associations.[9]

But questions remain about the extension of this particular "trading corporation" in the late nineteenth century, and the precise role of the Kongo king in the organization of politics and trade. Broadhead suggested that new forms of Atlantic commerce since the 1860s brought on a further fragmentation of political power in the Kongo, ultimately causing the Kongo polity to dissolve. By the time Pedro V died, in 1891, "the kingdom was little more than a memory among the Bakongo, living in independent towns and only rarely, if ever, dealing with the king at San Salvador."[10] The evidence presented in this chapter only partially supports this interpretation. It suggests that greater attention must be paid to different forms of commercial change in the wider Kongo region and their variable impact on political processes. In the coastal hinterland and along the banks of the Congo River, communities switched to the production of exportable vegetable oils after the slave trade ended. In these areas, a rapid decentralization of power took place, as political leaders formed bonds of patronage with European trade houses and thus further disassociated themselves from the old kingdom. But in the Kongo heartland the expansion of "legitimate" commerce was based on long-distance trade, principally of ivory and rubber. In this commercial environment, São Salvador continued to function as a ritual center connecting different points in the trade network.

There is also a tendency in the literature to deny nineteenth-century kings much agency, as their powers seemed to be progressively reduced to their role as guardians of the Christian cult. According to Broadhead, "the king himself was not a figure of great economic and political power, but a mediator, a constitutional descendant of Pedro IV. The only power resource open to development under the circumstances was the sacred or cultic one—in this case the royal Christian cult."[11] Occupying the sacred city of São Salvador, the king made sure that Catholic priests came to sanctify the marriages and burials of noblemen, baptize their followers, and assist him with installing independently elected chiefs in the Order of Christ, a Portuguese religious-military order that Kongo elites had adopted to control access to senior titles. The king's ritual importance, combined with his secular impotence, had turned him into a living *nkisi*, a charm, whose sacred powers were rooted in the Christian cult. In Hilton's words, he was "the key symbol which legitimized the rule of the corporation."[12]

The spiritual nature of royal power in late nineteenth-century Kongo is indubitable, if only because it is impossible to distinguish between political and ritual roles in Central African kingship. But behind the appearance of the king as a "religious" object lay a world of material interests, including those of the king himself. To understand how the kingdom functioned on the eve of colonial rule, this chapter uses numerous archival and other primary sources from the 1850s to about 1880 to document and examine the agency of Pedro V. First, it describes how two closely connected aristocratic families, the Kivuzi and the Agua Rosada, plotted the accession of Pedro V at the expense of a competing faction represented by Álvaro Ndongo. Their succession dispute, which lasted from 1857 to 1860, can be read as a conflict between a powerful lobby of slave traders and a section of the elite with strong ties to the Portuguese government of Angola, which was struggling to abolish the slave trade and extend its political influence north of Luanda. After capturing São Salvador with Portuguese military support, Pedro had to exploit his duties as "Catholic king of Kongo" in order to win the consent of the Kongo aristocracy. As I explain below, Christian symbols and practices were fundamental to the politics of the kingdom, and the rituals related to the royal office circumscribed much of the authority that Pedro V wielded in Kongo. I later demonstrate, however, that the king amassed significant wealth from being chief at São Salvador and was able to use his influence for the benefit of his family and other followers. The alliance with Portugal was crucial to Pedro's success, and in many ways the negotiations between the Kongo nobility and their main European patron in the 1860s and '70s were a preamble to the refashioning of the kingdom in the colonial period.[13]

Pedro's Coup d'État

The man crowned as Pedro V first appeared in the historical record during the last years of the reign of Henrique II (1842–57) and in the succession struggle following Henrique's death. Documents from that time show Pedro and his family—Kivuzi on the one side and Agua Rosada on the other—belligerently trying to keep hold of the throne in the face of strong opposition from other factions of the Kongo aristocracy. The Kivuzi-Agua Rosada coalition ultimately relied on Portuguese military intervention to stay in power. The resulting alliance with Portugal was a precursor to a more profound collaboration elaborated under official colonial rule.

Late in 1856, the Portuguese priest José Tavares da Costa e Moura headed an expedition from Bembe, a mining town on the southern fringes of Kongo that Portugal had recently occupied, to the ailing king in São Salvador. In power since 1842, Dom Henrique II had often corresponded with the governor of Angola about his kingdom's need for white clerics. In return for priests and material rewards, the governor asked the king for help in diverting the Kongo ivory trade to Ambriz, which many African and European merchants were avoiding since Portugal had occupied the port in 1855.[14] As the expedition made its way north, the travelers were joined by Dom Pedro Elelo, the later king, who was then a thirty-year-old nobleman holding the title marquis of Katendi. The Portuguese visitors were soon made party to a lingering dispute over the future succession of the incumbent king. Pedro was explicitly presented to the Portuguese as the natural heir of Henrique II, his maternal uncle. But on the way back from São Salvador, other notables joined the group, including a "brother" of the royal family whose name—Álvaro Ndongo—escaped the record, but "of whom it was said he had to be the future king."[15]

Aware that he was not the popular choice to succeed his uncle, Pedro went in search of outside support and declared himself a "vassal" of Portugal in the middle of 1857.[16] Later that year, with Henrique II now deceased and the succession struggle intensifying, the German traveler Adolf Bastian met both contenders for the throne in São Salvador. The kingdom was briefly governed by a sister of the late king, Dona Isabel Mbamba, whose Kivuzi family was reputedly "the most powerful and wealthiest in the kingdom." Based in the Madimba region south of São Salvador, they had put their weight behind the candidacy of Dom Pedro, who was Isabel's second oldest son. Wearing a silver crucifix around his neck and carrying a sword of English make, Pedro played host to Bastian, who described him as "a stately figure, well-shaped, though slightly corpulent." Although Pedro expressed an air of confidence, it was clear that Kongo's royal council, in charge of electing the new king, leaned toward Álvaro Ndongo, who unlike Pedro had taken up his residence in São Salvador. To bolster his candidacy, Ndongo claimed to be the son of another sister of Henrique II, no longer alive but older than Isabel, so that reckoned by matrilineal descent he preceded his rival. As neither candidate showed any willingness to concede, armed conflict seemed imminent.[17]

The appointment of a new king could not proceed, however, before the deceased king had received a Christian funeral. Thus in October 1858, another Portuguese expedition, led by Lieutenant Zacharias da Silva Cruz, left Bembe for São Salvador with two priests to bury the corpse of Henrique II. They met the marquis of Katendi along the way and learned that he and his "brother" Álvaro, the duke of Mbamba, were safeguarding Kongo's royal insignia somewhere outside the capital, a politically suspect move, as it potentially undermined the sanctity of São Salvador; to silence their critics, the brothers later claimed that Henrique II had wanted it so. Twenty armed subjects of Dom Álvaro, followed by sixty of Ndongo's party, welcomed the Portuguese visitors upon their arrival in São Salvador. The city looked empty. While it still counted about three thousand homes in 1845, with an estimated eighteen thousand inhabitants, now there were perhaps no more than four hundred.[18] Many residents had abandoned the capital in fear of war and anxiously awaited the result of the succession struggle at the homes of relatives near and far. Dom Álvaro de Agua Rosada, a nephew of the former king Garcia V (1803-1830) and an "uncle" of Ndongo, warned the Portuguese that Ndongo would take the throne by force if necessary and had invested heavily in arming people to this end. Lieutenant Cruz observed that the part of town inhabited by the *escravos de igreja*—descendants of the slaves of the former Capuchin mission who, as custodians of the Catholic tradition, played a prominent role in Kongo politics— was indeed awash with guns paid for by Ndongo. In one remarkable encounter, Ndongo confided to Cruz that he knew the Portuguese were siding with his rival, but that he was the popular choice and enjoyed the backing of Kongo's ruling class. Cruz replied, however, that Portugal would accept any Kongo king who obeyed the king of Portugal, and that their only business on this occasion was to commend the soul of Dom Henrique to God.[19]

In the end it was Dom Pedro who took the city by force. In 1860, he ousted Álvaro Ndongo from São Salvador with considerable military support from the Portuguese in Angola and some Kongo allies. Despite his initial unpopularity, he held the throne until his death in 1891 and became known among his followers as "Heaven's Great One" or the omnipotent (*weni w'ezulu*).[20] John Thornton has analyzed Pedro's coup d'état in the context of Kongo's longer history of succession struggles. He has argued that, contrary to what many outsiders believed, matrilineal descent was not a guiding principle for the election of kings until Portugal began to intervene in royal successions, enabling one or two Kongo families to exploit the idiom of kinship to control the royal office. Instead of hereditary succession, about four noble families with a stake in the affairs of the kingdom had, in the early 1700s, agreed to share the throne by rotation, although in practice succession was often decided by war. Henrique II belonged to the Kivuzi family and had captured the throne in 1842 from André I, a Kinlaza, who himself had succeeded Garcia V, an Agua Rosada.[21] Pedro V was half Kivuzi and half Agua Rosada. According to an African tradition collected in the 1920s, Dom Álvaro Ndongo belonged to the Kimpanzu, the fourth family involved in the rotation system. The same source also briefly mentions Dom Pedro's successors: Dom Álvaro de Agua Rosada (1891-96); Dom Henrique Nteyekengue (1896-1901), a Kivuzi according to some; Pedro Mbemba (1901-10), an Agua Rosada by name, though possibly also Kivuzi; Manuel Martins Kiditu (1911-13), allegedly Kivuzi, who lost the throne in Buta's War; Dom Álvaro Nzingu, appointed in 1915; and Pedro Buafu, presumably Kivuzi, who ruled from 1923 to 1955.[22] This king list suggests that from Henrique II forward the throne alternated between the Kivuzi and the Agua Rosada households only.[23]

Thornton's rotation model explains to some extent why the Kivuzi clan could back the candidacy of Pedro Elelo, who was neither the oldest son of Isabel (Henrique's sister) nor the family's most senior chief.[24] In the interregnum after Henrique's death, the duke of Mbamba appeared to pull the strings for the Kivuzi in the kingdom, which suggests that Pedro represented his clan for reasons other than seniority. At the same time, both Pedro and Álvaro Ndongo evoked the principle of matrilineal descent to bolster their claims to the throne before the Portuguese and other Europeans. This suggests that matrilineality had become a significant factor in nineteenth-century succession disputes, alongside other important factors such as rotation, military prowess, and suitability for the job. In fact, matrilineality had pervaded political dynamics throughout the region and would become even more important in determining royal successions under colonial rule.

Kongo's ruling families were not identical to matrilineal clans, however. In the seventeenth century, Thornton tells us, noble households, or "houses," tied people in by descent through both the male and the female line, as well as by marriage, clientage, and slavery. This was still so in the nineteenth century, even if the language of the matriclan was increasingly used to legitimize rule within houses and even in the kingdom itself.[25] While Dom Pedro was a Kivuzi through his mother's line, he was paternally affiliated with the Agua Rosada household. This was also the family name that many of his own sons carried, though he himself never signed off any document using the name. Members of the Kongo elite hardly ever stated their matrilineal clan affiliation, but those who belonged to houses adopting patrilineal categories carried their Portuguese patronyms like European surnames. Consequently, for European outsiders it was much easier to identify an Agua Rosada than someone from the Kivuzi house, for example. The prevalence of the Agua Rosada family in the archival record is, therefore, in part a bias resulting from their own historical practice, but undoubtedly it also reflects their historically dominant position in Kongo society.

As with most Kongo chiefs, the political powers of Dom Pedro and Dom Álvaro were based on their involvement in the long-distance trade in slaves and ivory. Control of important intersections of the caravan routes enabled chiefs to tax trade or participate in commercial ventures themselves, and to purchase political titles with the wealth thus earned. Participation in the export slave trade had long since financed the political careers of Kongo aristocrats, and by 1860, noblemen in the kingdom were still supplying slaves to Atlantic markets, in particular Cuba. Shortly before his death, Henrique II had committed himself to the Portuguese campaign to abolish the slave trade and promote "legitimate" commerce in northern Angola. The fact that one of his sons was the protector of a produce trader in Porto da Lenha on the lower Congo River might suggest that the Kivuzi had some stake in the development of new export trades in the Kongo region.[26] Instead of a motivation to eradicate the slave trade from Kongo, however, abolition presented the king primarily with an opportunity to subdue powerful slave trading rivals operating along the Atlantic coast, specifically in Ambriz.[27] Outside Portugal's narrow sphere of influence, the transaction of slaves for export continued at a steady pace. Members of the diasporic Vili community, for instance, still worked the old slave route from São Salvador to Boma on the Congo River, and from there to Cabinda and Loango on the northern coast, as they had done since the early eighteenth century.[28] Records produced under a legal system of slave ransoming for contract labor in the French West Indies indicate that from an estimated fifty thousand slaves shipped from the Congo between 1856 and 1860, roughly 5 percent originated from the district of São Salvador.[29] So while the Portuguese government could control the slave trading activities of their Kivuzi allies to some extent, they were unable to stop the trade between Lusophone middlemen and "enemy people" (*gentio inimigo*), as one local officer made clear. These Lusophone traffickers, he said, "supply the group of D. Álvaro Ndongo the gunpowder, arms, textiles, and beads with which they gain the favor of all Kongo people."[30] Ndongo's popularity was thus partly based on the backing he received from Kongo's slave trading elites.

After Ndongo was defeated, the Portuguese commander of the colonial troops in São Salvador summoned several Kongo rulers to the capital to pay homage to Pedro V.[31] A document from the bishopric's archives in Luanda lists the names of thirty-one chiefs who under Portuguese pressure switched their allegiance from Ndongo to Katendi. Indicating the directions in which they traveled from São Salvador, this list suggests that Ndongo's former allies ran the trade routes from Zombo in the east, to Boma on the Congo River, and Ambrizete on the Atlantic coast.[32] The width of this commercial network corresponded to the boundaries of the constituent domains that Broadhead proposed for the eighteenth-century kingdom, although the Zombo had since stopped participating directly in the affairs of the Kongo polity. The mention of Ambrizete is also noteworthy, because this town (currently N'zeto) had just displaced Ambriz as the main slaving port on the Kongo coast.[33]

Pedro's coronation by the Portuguese in August 1859, before his effective occupation of São Salvador, suggests that he had few supporters at the time. The ceremony took place in Mbanza Mputu, a small town located a few miles south of the capital, which was governed by Dom Álvaro de Agua Rosada. Present at the coronation were the duke of Mbamba and a handful of chiefs from the surrounding region. The document by which Pedro restated his nominal submission to his adopted brother, the king of Portugal, was also signed by his secretaries, Dom Álvaro Bubuzi and Dom Garcia de Agua Rosada, and by the royal scribe, Dom José Pedro, a young man from Massangano who had been educated in Luanda and had lived in Kongo for eight years.[34] This coronation had the appearance of a family affair that received very little attention from other stakeholders in the kingdom. As soon as Pedro was effectively in power, therefore, he took measures to enhance the legitimacy of his rule. Receiving formal recognition from Ndongo's partisans was one measure. Furthermore, using visits by the parish priests of Bembe and Ambriz, he arranged Christian funerals for his uncle, Dom Henrique, his recently deceased brother, the duke of Mbamba, and a number of other noblemen. He also invested a large group of influential chiefs in the Order of Christ, for which they pledged allegiance to the king of Kongo and the king of Portugal. Moreover, Pedro had secured the royal insignia, including the staff (*mpangu*), which had been granted by Capuchin missionaries formerly residing in the kingdom and which, as Thornton explains, embodied the legitimacy of kingly rule "above the politics of lineage."[35]

In his first years in office, therefore, Pedro V immediately set to exploiting his official role as guardian of the Christian cult. Much to the disappointment of his Portuguese patrons, however, the king was unable to build on his spiritual importance to expand his military powers. Yet he would skillfully use the royal office for personal enrichment, the benefit of his family, and the extension of his own commercial interests.

A Christian Kingdom

The religious foundations of the Kongo polity received an exotic makeover as the kingdom's governing class converted to Christianity in the late fifteenth century.[36] The country at large quickly responded to an African laity, who taught local elites as well as commoners the rudiments of the faith and the main Catholic prayers. In the meantime, white missionaries—Jesuits at first, but mostly Capuchins after 1645—administered the sacraments of the Church. For the Kongo, Christianity became part of a political identity that exceeded in scale the villages and regions that had composed the fifteenth-century polity. They integrated Christianity on their own terms, according to their own needs, and drawing on the adaptability of Christian practices to their own. Of course this meant that Kongo Christianity never fully corresponded to European iterations of the faith. A Portuguese visitor to the kingdom in 1845 observed what he thought was a poorly developed Catholicism: the Kongo received baptism and they confessed, but were little interested in celebrating the Eucharist or accepting Christian marriage.[37] Baptism was always the most popular sacrament, probably because the baptismal salt was thought to deter witches. For the Kongo, confession was another form of the purification rituals they had always practiced, as breaking the consensus of the community—"sin" in Catholic terms—was believed to cause disease. Catholicism was, in African terms, a healing cult or, in John Janzen's terminology, a "cult of affliction."[38]

Elites accepted the ideal though rarely the practice of canon-law marriage, which they perceived as a special kind of blessing on the fertility of the union between husband and wife and as a way to strengthen marital alliances between noble families. The Capuchin priest Raimundo de Dicomano bitterly reflected that he married less than half a dozen noblemen during his residence in Kongo from 1792 to 1795.[39] Kongo nobility furthermore adopted the Portuguese aristocratic Order of Christ, an order of nobility symbolized by the cross, which became a cult to regulate trading contacts among people otherwise strangers to one another. They also used the Christian calendar to organize public rituals of the polity as a whole. For example, All Saints' Day, followed by Halloween, was turned into an opportunity to pay respect to the ancestors. On Saint James's Day, people flocked to the provincial capitals, São Salvador and Mbanza Soyo, to hear Mass, pay tribute, and commemorate Kongo's second Christian king, Afonso I (1509–42/43), who had overthrown a pagan brother through the claimed miraculous intervention of the warrior saint of the Reconquista in Iberia, Saint James. Christian Kongo authorities, in short, appropriated the church holidays to underwrite their political power.

Christianity in Kongo was predominantly a royal political cult.[40] From the start it was therefore rivaled by alternative cults, some of them millenarian versions of Catholicism itself, such as the Antonian movement. In the mid-seventeenth century, the central cult of Catholicism began to lose some of its attraction because of the dispersal of political and economic power. Around 1700, when warfare between rival political factions ravaged the country, a young woman named Dona Beatriz Kimpa Vita, who had been initiated as a traditional healer (*nganga*) and claimed to be possessed by Saint Anthony, started a purification movement aiming to restore the political harmony that she believed Christianity stood for. As she denied the power of the cross, she was a threat to Kongo's nobility, but large segments of the populace accepted her for promising not only to bring peace but also to cure infertility. Although Beatriz was burned at the stake and peace was restored without her, the civil wars of the late seventeenth and early eighteenth centuries seriously undermined the allure of the Kongo Christian cult. Nevertheless, by 1850, crosses still signaled chiefly authority along the trade routes to the historic seat of Christianity, São Salvador, where the *mani* Kongo was the only mediator of the highest spirit, called Desu (from the Portuguese *Deus*, God).[41]

After 1800 few white priests passed through Kongo, or stayed very long if they did, but Kongo elites kept the Christian tradition alive by themselves. Nineteenth-century travel accounts from the Kongo picture an African society that was still deeply Catholic.[42] In 1816, for example, the British expedition of Captain James Tuckey received a visit from an ordained priest from Soyo, who was "qualified to lead his fellow negroes into the path of salvation. . . . This man and another of the Christians had been taught to write their own names and that of Saint Antonio, and could also read the Romish litany in Latin. All these converts were loaded with crucifixes, and satchels containing the pretended relics of saints, certainly of equal efficacy with the monkey's bone of their pagan brethren." Tuckey found a similar display of crucifixes higher up the river in Noqui.[43] Almost half a century later, the explorer Richard Burton found "a lot of old church gear, the Virgin (our Lady of Pinda), saints, and crucifixes" at a church in Soyo.[44] A few years before Burton's visit, the local Solongo had welcomed a Portuguese priest, taken baptism, and also shown him their Christian apparel. In 1872, the missionary António Castanheira Nunes baptized close to a thousand men, women, and children in the area around São Salvador, at the same time administering the sacraments of Extreme Unction, Penance, and the Eucharist. The inhabitants of the city itself, he said, still knew the main Catholic prayers in the Kikongo language.[45]

When Boaventura dos Santos traveled from Noqui to São Salvador in 1876, again hundreds of villagers made use of the opportunity to get baptized. In and around the capital, people used the cross for protection and worshipped Marian images. In 1879, the Baptist missionary William Holman Bentley noticed condescendingly that one house in the king's compound kept crucifixes that were "carried round the town" when "the rains were insufficient," while the king himself received the English visitors with royal scepter and crucifix in hand. Christianity remained a part of everyday life even in areas relatively far away from São Salvador. For instance, a Portuguese official traveling from Ambriz to Bembe in 1885 was asked by the local population to send for a cleric to baptize children and adults. Along the banks of the Congo, chiefs wore rosaries to symbolize their power, while in eastern Kongo, among the Zombo, the crucifix functioned as a symbol of ancestral power and large wooden crosses were erected to protect local markets. Christian charms were, therefore, integral to Kongo beliefs about the intervention of invisible agents in the physical world. Discussing how flat, portable wooden crosses called *santus* were thought to confer skill in hunting, Bentley noted how their effective possession was associated with the restraint of malevolence. "It is said that a *santu* loses its power if the possessor is guilty of any immorality; in such case a fine has to be paid and a ceremony gone through before its power can be restored by a doctor of *santu*."

In short, long exposure to Catholic teaching and technology had helped the Kongo recast their ideas about witchcraft and proper moral conduct in Christian terms.[16]

While Catholicism was an integral part of Kongo's religious outlook and politics, in regions that were only loosely connected to the kingdom Christian and non-Christian religious tools often coexisted. In 1856, according to one observer, the king was still able to ban the use of "idols and fetishes," that is, non-Catholic images, within the polity.[17] But the further out from São Salvador, the stronger was the competition from rival cults and charms. Along the banks of the lower Congo, for instance, traders organized in the Nkimba society, which created bonds among separate communities and protected its members against witchcraft. Around 1880, the cult was effective along much of the route from the lower river to São Salvador, though in the capital district the king still offered protection to trade caravans in return for the payment of tolls.[18] The Dembo society provided Zombo initiates with protection, and while it was particularly strong in eastern Kongo, the Baptist missionary John Weeks observed a manifestation of the cult at a two-day walking distance south of São Salvador.[19]

All cults promised to protect their elite members and their followers from evil in matters of commerce, agriculture, and general health. The royal Christian cult was in this respect not different from others. For many of its rituals, however, it was dependent on white priests. Nineteenth-century kings frequently petitioned Portugal for a missionary presence in the Kongo capital, which they argued was vital for the well-being of the kingdom and its subjects. Thus Henrique II wrote to the governor of Angola: "Twice I have asked the bishop to come to this kingdom, but he does not want to, and therefore I now just ask that . . . you will send me one [priest] to baptize, take confession and instruct my noblemen [*fidalgos*] and all of my people, in accordance with the second commandment of the Holy Mother Church, which says, 'Every Christian has to confess at least once a year, in the certainty that by not doing so he will go to hell.' As I have sent this request several times, I will not bear the responsibility that might fall on me before God as the ruler of the people of this kingdom, and as such the one seeking spiritual remedy for the salvation of their souls."[50]

Endemic diseases, caused by uncontrolled malicious spirits, could have a particularly damaging effect on the reputation of the cult. Efficacy mattered. In the early 1870s, a smallpox epidemic spread rapidly along the trade routes connecting Angola and the lower Congo region. Although Pedro V was not yet personally affected, in June 1873 he told the governor of Angola that "I am not fine here as an epidemic disease runs through all my people, a bladder illness, for which there is no remedy, so I am calling out to Your Excellency . . . send me a surgeon to help me cure this illness [as] the people are suffering a lot."[51] A few months later, Grandy returned to São Salvador from his travels north and found "the King very ill, half the town dead, and everything looking very desolate."[52] It must have been no coincidence that around this time the Kiyoka movement emerged in the hinterland of Luanda and spread north throughout Kongo, causing its followers to burn charms currently in use with the intention "to suppress the lawlessness then prevalent throughout the country," as one missionary later put it. To root out the bad magic that was causing sickness and death, the movement imposed a system of government that forced chiefs to sit on a carpet (*nkuwu*) for the daily exercise of rule, although its influence never reached São Salvador.[53]

Whereas baptism was for most Kongo the key sacrament, noble families gained prestige and respectability through Christian funerals and marriages. In 1855, Henrique II asked the governor of Angola "in the name of Jesus, Mary, [and] Joseph" for a priest to bury Dom Manuel, the marquis of Wembo.[54] Three years later, south of São Salvador, Padre José Agostinho Ferreira interred the mummified bodies of chief Dom Cristóvão and his son.[55] In the absence of priests, Christian marriages became increasingly rare, although for kings they were essential. Thus in August 1861, the parish priest of Bembe, José Gavião, married Pedro V to Dona Maria José in the presence of "all the kingdom's big men."[56] Twenty-seven years later, the bishop of Luanda came to São Salvador to sanctify Pedro's two-year-old marriage to Dona Ana de Agua Rosada, the wife of his late brother, who had her home in the northern town of Pangala.[57] Pedro had numerous other wives, none of whom were officially recognized as such by the Catholic Church. Their alleged number ranged from as high as forty in the late 1870s to a minimum of twenty-five in the 1880s. Some were slaves; others were the daughters or sisters of local headmen and neighboring chiefs. In other words, bonds of patronage between the royal court and surrounding districts were also created through marriages that went without a Christian blessing.[58]

The pinnacle of the Christian cult was the Order of Christ, an originally Portuguese religious-military order that African elites had adopted to control access to senior titles. Investiture was conferred by the king with the support of a Catholic priest. Membership entitled chiefs to use the cross to protect people from evil and establish tax collecting stations in the countryside. Kongo knights (*cavaleiros*) demonstrated their standing by donning the order's habit, typically a robe with an embroidered cross, or incorporating the cross in their haircuts.[59] Investment required wealth on the part of the chief as fees had to be paid and a periodic contribution of tribute and military assistance was expected, although the latter obligations seem to have weakened in the nineteenth century. In this period, many Kongo elites, both upcoming and established, still gave political importance to membership of the Christian cult, but investitures were increasingly hampered by the absence of priests. Thus on those rare occasions that a Portuguese priest visited the kingdom, several noblemen were usually waiting to be invested. Padre António Francisco das Necessidades reported that in less than fifteen months during 1844 and 1845 he knighted seventy chiefs in and around São Salvador, while also administering more than one hundred thousand baptisms and four hundred confessions. A decade later, Moura had only a day in the capital to bestow the Christian habit (*hábito de Cristo*), "which all Kongo aspire to [receive]," he said.[60] Missionaries who came later were mostly amazed by the order's existence. On his way to São Salvador in 1876, a number of chiefs asked Boaventura dos Santos for a *hábito*; quite puzzled, he promised to give them one on his way back to Noqui. When Padre António Barroso first arrived in the capital, in 1881, the king surprised him with a request to install some individuals in the Christian knighthood. Two years later, Barroso bestowed membership on several noblemen in Madimba, this time with the assistance of Dom Nicolau, a local chief and nephew of the king. In Kimbubuge, just south of Madimba, a new line of chiefs was waiting to be installed as Christian knights (*cavaleiros de hábito*) by a visiting missionary in 1889.[61] If the Order of Christ provided the ideological bedrock of the kingdom, the available evidence of the geographical range of investitures suggests that by 1890 São Salvador's political influence only reached as far as Madimba in the south.

Despite its limited range, however, the Christian ritual of investiture continued into the twentieth century. Padre Daniel Simões Ladeiras, residing in São Salvador from 1902 to 1913, recounted how at the king's request he invested two royal counselors. "On their knees, with their hand stretched out as a sign of oath, they pronounced the formula used on such occasions which was, more or less:—I promise to keep and defend the Catholic faith, always obey the orders of the priests and the laws of the government: God punish me if I don't comply." Then the noblemen received three touches on their backs with a large iron sword, while Ladeiras offered them bead necklaces to pray the rosary.[62] In the Portuguese translations of the oath sworn by invested knights, the content changed somewhat from 1856 (Sarmento) to 1881 (Barroso) and the early 1900s (Ladeiras). By the time of Barroso, witchcraft was no longer mentioned and obeisance to the priests and the king of Portugal was more strongly emphasized than in Sarmento's time; by the time of Ladeiras, the oath also called for respect for the colonial government. Perhaps the vows had not significantly altered, but the Portuguese simply heard them differently. For the Kongo, after all, effective governance was always about eradicating witchcraft (*kindoki*) from politics and public life in general.[63] It seems more likely, however, that the order's pledge had been adapted to a new political environment. In other words, an established patron-client relationship between Portugal and the Kongo chiefs, centered on the Order of Christ, was changing its exclusively religious focus to respond to the presence of the colonial government.

The King as Entrepreneur

The historian Jan Vansina has argued that African kingdoms were generally "built in the mind first, and were grounded on faith" rather than territorial control. As an institution that united chiefs through religion—a Christian cult—instead of centralized coercion, the kingdom of Kongo was effectively a "state of mind."[64] In this light, it is understandable that the rituals, rules, and prohibitions attached to the royal office severely restricted the secular power of the king of Kongo and could even turn him into a "living charm," as some have suggested. As the case of Pedro V demonstrates, however, Kongo kings were always capable of advancing their own agendas, even if that meant corrupting the authority granted by their constituencies.

As ruler of São Salvador, Pedro V was able to amass considerable wealth by taxing trade, judging political disputes, and being on the payroll of the Portuguese government in Luanda. The position of chief gave Pedro the capacity to tax, but as a king, he had few powers to levy tribute. The only tribute he could demand from the Kongo populace based on his title was a contribution for the right to hunt or burn the fields at the start of the agricultural cycle. He also received a share of the agricultural production of his own dependents and of the profits they made in trade. But only a narrow circle of sons and nephews who had been invested in the Order of Christ paid tribute on a regular basis and provided military support when necessary. The king had no standing army, and collecting tribute from subjects outside his own household was beyond his power. The main source of his income was, therefore, the taxation of trade.[65]

São Salvador was a key node in a network of trade routes that extended hundreds of miles inland from the Atlantic coast north of Luanda. Most caravans from the northern Kongo districts of Nsundi and Makuta and the eastern district of Zombo used to pass through São Salvador as they brought slaves, ivory, and rubber to European buyers on the coast. Being chief of São Salvador, Pedro had the right to tax these caravans. Tolls were determined according to the number of carriers in a caravan and the value of the commodities they transported. Payments were generally in high-value goods, though sometimes glass beads were also exchanged; in return for these taxes, traders expected safety on the roads. The king's influence sometimes reached surprisingly far. In 1885, for example, Pedro obtained the collaboration of chiefs south of Bembe in the capture of a local bandit who disrupted the rubber trade to Ambriz. To gain this kind of loyalty from chiefs, the king used to redistribute part of the collected taxes among them. "No chief ever visits him without getting a good present of cloth," a British missionary commented in 1880.[66]

São Salvador was also a place from which power and prestige emanated. Even in regions that had long since stopped participating in the affairs of the kingdom, political leaders still saw the Kongo capital as the ultimate source of spiritual and judicial power. As one observer put it, "The king of Congo is now only the chief of San Salvador and a few other small towns, and does not receive the least tribute from any others, nor does he possess any power in the land. Among the natives of Angola, however, he still retains a certain amount of prestige as king of Congo, and all would do homage to him in his presence, as he is considered to possess the greatest 'fetish' of all the kings and tribes."[67] The king's position as highest judge was an important source of revenue for Pedro and his council. Crimes like theft, adultery, and homicide tended to be resolved among village chiefs and elders, but undecided cases and conflicts between communities were often brought before the king of Kongo against the payment of hefty fees.

The trials or "palavers" (*fundações* in Portuguese) held at the court of São Salvador usually concerned questions of rank and affiliation, which plaintiffs articulated through narratives of migration, settlement, and slavery. In 1890, for example, Pedro judged the case of a chief who claimed authority over his neighbor's lineage, whose ancestors had purportedly settled in the area as slaves.[68] Despite Portuguese protestations, these tribunals (*nkanu*) continued under early colonial rule. As late as 1896, the royal council decided to reopen an old dispute over seniority involving the chief of Mbanza Mputu, which had probably started in 1883 if not earlier.[69] Throughout these trials, which could last weeks, representatives from both parties used to lodge in São Salvador, sometimes bringing hundreds of followers along. The procedures followed at the court were a model of protocol for other Kongo chiefs, who used to send their sons and nephews to the capital to observe the court's ceremonies, its etiquette in receiving visitors, and the royal way to settle palavers. For instance, late in the century, the chief of Lemba, near Malebo Pool, still remembered how he was educated at the "king's knee."[70]

The distribution of aristocratic titles to powerful clans was a further source of revenue for the king. Noteworthy examples of such titles were *tulante*, which was inheritable, although fees had to be paid when the title was transferred; *mfutila*, traditionally bestowed on the holder of the right to collect tolls in the capital district; and *noso mpidisipi*, the second in line after the king, derived from the Portuguese *príncipe*, which might have been a recent introduction to placate the clans sidelined by the Kivuzi's monopolization of the throne. Symptomatic of its devaluation under colonial rule, there were at least three chiefs within the kingdom who carried the *noso* title by 1913. The prefixes *dom* and *dona*, followed by a saint's name, were not chiefly titles but elite distinctions that parents usually bestowed on their children upon birth. Political titles were officially conferred in the town of the recipient by a court officer, *kapitau*, who was the king's highest representative. There were also several other officers at the royal court with distinct functions, including the chamberlain, the royal messenger, and the bearer of the king's staff (*mpangu*).[71] Some of these court officers were instrumental in disseminating royal authority outside the capital, which would soon imply the "broadcasting" of colonial power, too.

If Pedro's authority outside São Salvador was circumscribed by chiefs whose military prowess often exceeded his own, in his function as king, his power was checked by several advisors. Whatever decisions the king took, therefore, he rarely made on his own. As in most Kongo chiefdoms, executive power in São Salvador resided with a council, which in the nineteenth century typically consisted of five to six members elected from elite families in the kingdom. These counselors were "the true rulers in San Salvador," as one visitor put it in 1885.[72] While usually anonymous in European sources, in the 1880s, three counselors were identified as they converted in the Baptist Church, of whom two were related to the king. The chief counselor at the time was Dom Manuel Matengo, an elder "son" of Pedro V, who had been educated in Luanda for seven years. He resided in Madimba, where he combined the function of chief with that of Portuguese language instructor. Counselor Dom Miguel Ndelengani, a blacksmith, had a sister married to Pedro V. Shortly before his death in 1890, he became a school teacher for the Baptist mission, after a life trading brass ankle-rings and hoes welded from imported hoop iron. The third known counselor was Dom Álvaro Matoko, a wealthy businessman from São Salvador, who had assisted Lieutenant William Grandy and missionaries Thomas Comber and George Grenfell on their travels through Kongo in the 1870s.[73]

In addition to the counselors, royal secretaries also exerted considerable influence on the king, not least because they were in charge of his correspondence with neighboring rulers, including the governor of Angola. For a long time, a former slave controlled the administrative affairs of Pedro V. Born around 1830 in Mbangu, on the west side of the Zombo plateau, Dom Garcia was enslaved in childhood to Dom Álvaro de Agua Rosada, chief of Mbanza Mputu, whose surname he received. Sent to school in Luanda, Garcia learned Portuguese and was instructed in the rituals of the Catholic Church. Around 1860, he disengaged from his master and settled in São Salvador, where he became Pedro's confidant and secretary. He also took care of a Catholic mission school set up in 1878, and in the royal district people respected him as the "source of all education."[74] After Dom Garcia's passing, Pedro appointed two of his sons, Dom Pedro de Agua Rosada and Dom Álvaro de Agua Rosada, as his new secretaries.[75]

These examples also demonstrate how much the Kongo ruling class valued European education. In fact, instruction in the Portuguese language had long been an instrument of social distinction for Kongo elites.[76] Many African traders who had regular contact with Europeans used Portuguese as a lingua franca, but only a few knew how to read and write the language. Literacy was important in the political sphere, as rulers in Kongo and Angola generally corresponded in Portuguese. At the court in São Salvador, Kikongo was the dominant language and Pedro V himself was apparently illiterate, but his secretary and several sons had mastered reading and writing skills during years of education in Luanda. As will be shown in later chapters, these skills not only enabled them to serve at the royal court but also made them suitable candidates for jobs in commercial establishments and the colonial administration.[77]

Pedro V owed his accession to the Kongo throne and also much of the wealth he subsequently earned from this position to his alliance with Portugal. But the ensuing relationship with his Portuguese benefactors never proved straightforward. To begin with, the Portuguese found it difficult to figure out how powerful their protégé in São Salvador really was. In 1863, shortly after Pedro had finished his initial campaign to appease the Kongo nobility through the performance of investitures and funerals, the governor of Angola believed that the threat of an uprising against the king was sufficiently doused to start removing troops from the capital.[78] Only in 1870, however, did Portugal dismantle its military base in São Salvador, followed by a withdrawal from Bembe in 1873.[79] Had the government in Luanda changed its opinion about Pedro's authority in Kongo? Two years prior to pulling out, Governor-General Francisco Cardoso predicted that "right from the moment our forces retire the king will be killed; such is the aversion against him not just among his people, but principally among the neighboring rulers."[80] Contrary to such gloomy forecasts and despite occasional attacks on São Salvador in the first decade of his rule, Pedro would not be killed.[81] In fact, Pedro's marital record suggests that he was either a competent builder of political networks or a successful entrepreneur who invested his riches in the acquisition of women, or both.

While Dom Pedro was enjoying the privileges of rule, the Portuguese became increasingly doubtful of the king's usefulness for their project of imperial expansion north of Angola. They had conceived Pedro's clientship as an important step in their efforts to control the local export trade in ivory and vegetable oils, which was dominated by foreign merchant houses whose agents were nestled on the banks of the Congo River and the Atlantic coast north of Ambriz. But they had understood the Kongo kingdom in European terms, as a centralized political structure instead of a loose federation of chiefdoms, and expected too much from their local protégé. In 1867, Governor Cardoso reported to Lisbon that "the choice of this individual as king was awful, not only because he has never had any influence in Kongo, but, on the contrary, enjoys a general and manifest antipathy to which his awful habits have only contributed."[82]

Colonial officers knew of several chiefs in the vicinity of São Salvador over whom the king had no power.[83] One of Pedro's greatest rivals was Dom Rafael Caluga, brother of the late Álvaro Ndongo (who died around 1862). Rafael was based in Kunga, two hours southwest of São Salvador, where Ndongo had relocated after he lost possession of the capital in 1860. Rafael never accepted the kingship of Pedro V. He allegedly kept the mummified corpse of his brother wrapped in textile for decades, insisting that Ndongo had to be buried in the royal cemetery in São Salvador. Rumors of the Kunga clan plotting a coup against Dom Pedro spurred the colonial government to reoccupy the capital in 1888; ten years later, the Portuguese were finally able to reconcile Rafael with the king at São Salvador.[84] Also within a day's march from the capital was the town of Mbanza Mputu, where chief Dom Garcia Mbumba represented the clan of the deposed king André I.[85] This faction renewed its claims to the throne upon Pedro V's death in 1891, but then Mbumba proved unelectable because of his association with the Baptist mission. To his own satisfaction, he was granted the title of *noso*, the second highest in the kingdom.

Portuguese officials criticized Pedro V for provoking conflicts with neighboring chiefs and even residents of São Salvador. Some of the complaints against him were related to extortion and kidnapping. On more than one occasion, the king was accused of plotting the abduction of slaves of locally stationed troops to gain a ransom for their release. In December 1869, for instance, the female slaves of two African soldiers went missing, but were later reported to be in the king's village on the road to Bembe. Pedro alleged that his rival Garcia Mbumba had sold the women, so he demanded thirty thousand coral beads from the soldiers to redeem their slaves. After it was shown that Pedro was unable to retrieve the women, but also unwilling to return the money, José Ribeiro Guimarães, the Portuguese commander in São Salvador, told his superiors to cut the monthly salary the king received from Luanda as punishment for his corrupt behavior. "He does not have to do any of this, because the income he gets from taxing the rebel people who pass through [São Salvador] with their trade to the Zaire is more than enough."[86] According to Guimarães, there was no financial reason for Pedro to abduct people and then sell them or demand ransom, as he was sufficiently rich from taxing trade alone.

While Portugal took away Pedro's stipend and withdrew their troops from São Salvador, the government in Luanda continued to rely on the king to gain influence in regions north of Angola. In 1872, for example, the Portuguese turned to the king for help in appeasing the coffee producing Dembo chiefdoms on the southern fringes of the Kongo region. Many Dembo chiefs had political ties with Portugal through vassal treaties, which regulated the exchange of tribute for protection, but many also recognized the king of Kongo as their nominal overlord, often bolstering the legitimacy of their rule by claiming Kongo descent and receiving their insignia from the king. These ritual bonds between the Dembos and São Salvador had been formed in the era of the Atlantic slave trade, when the Dembo region was an important corridor in the trade between Kongo and Angola. While the Kongo kings had lost prestige since then, conflicts among Dembo chiefs over rights of seniority, which were ultimately about the control of land and trade routes, were brought before the Kongo court into the early twentieth century.[87]

In 1854, some Dembos began to resist payment of the colonial *dízimo* tax as well as a recently introduced tax on ransomed slaves. In the 1860s, both Álvaro Ndongo and Rafael Caluga, claiming to represent the "royal estate" of Kongo, tried to influence this anti-colonial rebellion and gain support among the Dembos for their own political cause. Pedro V responded by more vigorously asserting his position as the true guardian of the Christian kingdom, and at least one of the principal Dembo rulers, Ngombe Amuquiama, occasionally paid tribute to him.[88] Aware of the tributary ties between the Dembos and the Kongo kings, the Portuguese dispatched Padre António Castanheira Nunes to São Salvador in October 1872 to ask Dom Pedro to negotiate a settlement with Ngombe Amuquiama and two other rebel chiefs, Caculo Cacahenda and Namboangongo. The priest tried to intimidate the king by telling him that he knew exactly why he, Nunes, was there. "The rebellious Dembos say . . . that they fight us and will continue to do so, even if it lasts ten years, because you support them!" Insulted by the emissary of his Portuguese overlord and not in a position to help politically, Pedro and his secretary used the opportunity of the priest's visit for their own benefit. Using Nunes as their messenger to Luanda, they demanded monthly salaries and new European clothes for themselves, and education in Angola for the king's sons. They also advised Nunes not to return home through the independent western Soyo province, where the king was unable to send ambassadors and carriers and Nunes would have to travel alone "with his sexton, cook, and servants as a poor white man and miserable priest." The road south via Bembe to Ambriz was where the king's name was respected and Nunes would be a fool not to take it. Nunes still tried other channels to appease the Dembos, but to no avail, as the rebels made clear they only recognized the king of Kongo.[89]

Conclusion

What did the kingdom of Kongo look like in the years between the end of the Atlantic slave trade and the onset of colonial rule? In terms of territorial scope, it was a large chiefdom at best, with a center—the sacred city of São Salvador— that remained small in size until Christian missions and trade factories arrived in the 1880s. By 1868, São Salvador counted about a hundred homes and maybe four hundred inhabitants, many of whom were outsiders seeking the king's protection from enslavement somewhere else.[90] In 1876, the Portuguese priest Boaventura dos Santos found the city not much larger. It then consisted of two major sections (*sanzalas*); one was the Santo António quarter inhabited by the *escravos de igreja*, and the other the part where Pedro V lived together with his followers.[91] When the Baptist missionary William Holman Bentley first came to São Salvador in 1879, he counted about two hundred homes and another fifty in a village, Kilongo, on the southwest side of town.[92] So perhaps São Salvador had grown a little, but its overall size reflected poorly on King Pedro's power and popularity as well as on the town's economic importance before 1880.

Was the king then no more than a great *nkisi* that big men from all over Kongo used as "a bargaining chip in local power struggles," as Susan Herlin Broadhead has suggested?[93] Settling disputes was certainly one of Pedro's main political functions. In addition, he successfully performed his role as protector of the Christian cult, obtaining missionaries from Portugal to administer the sacraments among the kingdom's subjects. But in the end, his rule was about more than just being a mediator. From his office he maneuvered on behalf of himself, his family, and his clients in ways that foreshadowed the functioning of the kingdom in the later colonial era. Pedro collected taxes on trade and received tribute for distributing titles and playing judge in the conflicts of other chiefs; part of this income he shared among his peers. He also received a handsome stipend from the Portuguese government in Luanda, deposited in a personal account at the Banco Nacional Ultramarino.[94] He successfully petitioned for a government salary on behalf of his secretary, Dom Garcia, while one of his sons residing in Luanda, Dom Miguel, was another recipient of a monthly government stipend.[95] Many of Pedro's dependents had access to European education in Luanda. This was one of the main assets that the Agua Rosada family would later use to occupy key positions in the colonial administration. But some members of this prominent family were already employed in the Angolan government before Portuguese rule was formally established in São Salvador in 1887. Dom Nicolau, the son of Henrique II who was tragically murdered in Quicembo, is only the most famous example.[96]

Under Pedro's reign, the kingdom became a channel for positioning clients in the expanding world of Portuguese colonialism. Greater changes were to come in the late 1870s, when Pedro began to negotiate the settlement of trade houses and missionaries in São Salvador. The Agua Rosada and other notable families were quick to embrace the religious and commercial opportunities these different European agents presented. Together, Africans and Europeans would breathe new life into the ancient kingdom.

2

Carrying Trade

Soon after the closing of the Atlantic slave trade, in the 1860s, the kingdom of Kongo was caught up in the wave of wild rubber production engulfing many parts of West and Central Africa in this period. The African rubber boom of the late nineteenth century has long been associated with the atrocious exploitation of human and natural resources that took place in the equatorial rainforests. But in contrast to French Congo and the Congo Free State, where European colonizers granted concession companies the right to collect rubber, in Angola, Africans generally maintained control of production.[1] Since Raymond Dummett's pioneering article on the free marketing of wild rubber in the Gold Coast, more scholars have begun to pay attention to African-controlled rubber economies, albeit from different standpoints.[2] According to some, the rubber trade was mainly a disruptive force, as it opened previously isolated economies to Atlantic commerce, a process that not only upset existing social relations but was also marred by violent confrontations with European traders.[3] By contrast, several historians have interpreted the impact of the rubber boom as constructive rather than destructive, highlighting innovations within African systems of production, transportation, and trade.[4] Evidence from Kongo supports the latter rather than the former view. The Kongo rubber trade grew out of the earlier long-distance trades in slaves and ivory, keeping a traditional barter economy and its monetary values in place. As the discovery of rubber expanded the social basis for participation in the export economy, the rubber trade transformed rather than disrupted existing social relations.[5]

In Angola, rubber was generally collected and processed in regions far beyond colonial control, often several hundred miles inland from the coast, after which African trade caravans carried the rubber in cubes or balls to European merchants located on the coast or at isolated spots in the interior. In the northern region, the export trade was dominated by a handful of European firms whose home ports—Rotterdam, Liverpool, and Marseille—were supplied by several local agents based in factories along the Atlantic seaboard and the south bank of the Congo River. This chapter examines the transfer of some of these factories to São Salvador and how this movement influenced working lives in Kongo's capital. For many Kongo, the decades around 1900 were a time of opportunity. In different ways, the rubber economy created riches for different groups of people: for chiefs and entrepreneurs who carried out or otherwise controlled the trade, for caravan porters, and for women selling foodstuffs to carriers along the busy trade routes. Widespread participation in the export trade resulted in a leveling of power, as many young upstarts gained the means to create their own households, settle, and purchase political titles. This chapter focuses in particular on the expectations that the rubber economy created among young men and their elders about work under colonial rule. These expectations were mainly built on the experience of porterage, as thousands of male Kongo were employed as carriers first within African trade caravans and later by European factories. Porterage was honorable and rewarding labor, in contrast to the low-paid plantation work that was offered many of the same men after rubber disappeared from São Salvador around 1910. In order to understand the experience of the carrying trade, however, this chapter begins by setting rubber in the wider context of economic change after the end of the Atlantic slave trade.

Ivory, Rubber, and Slaves

The rise of "legitimate" commerce, as the post-abolition expansion of commodity trade in Africa is commonly described, changed the lives of many Kongo families after 1860.[6] Before delving into the details of this new export trade, it is important to remember that agriculture and production for domestic consumption remained the most important economic activities for most Kongo households into the early twentieth century.[7] The labor of women was central to this internal economy, as they planted and harvested crops, sold food at local markets, and carried the burden of domestic work and child-raising. Besides manioc, Kongo's staple crop, women cultivated peanuts, sweet potato, yam, maize, beans, pumpkin, plantain, and banana. They usually worked alone on small clearings (one or two hectares in size), though they sometimes received help from a child, a relative, or a slave, if the husband could afford one. Contrary to the occidental obsession with African polygyny, induced in part by the missionary experience with elite converts, one wife was the rule in Kongo.[8]

While young girls usually assisted their mothers in the field or at home, boys learned hunting skills and were sometimes employed by their elders as helpers in long-distance trade expeditions. Men's role in agriculture was generally limited to clearing the fields at the start of the rainy season. They also tapped palm wine and collected the fruit of the palm tree, from which women subsequently extracted the nuts and the oil.[9]

As the demand for vegetable oils increased in Kongo after the effective abolition of the export slave trade in the mid-1860s, many families, particularly in coastal areas, started cultivating peanuts and collecting palm produce for sale to Europeans. On the southern fringes of Kongo, labor was diverted from agriculture to the cultivation of wild coffee shrubs, until prices collapsed toward the end of the century and many farmers disengaged from coffee production. High transportation costs excluded most peasants from central and eastern Kongo from the trade in low-value vegetable oils, but some entrepreneurial men found other ways to participate in the new export economy.[10] They invested the revenues of surplus production and small-scale trading in two high-value export commodities that became available on regional markets: ivory and rubber. Whereas in general the production and sale of foodstuffs were female activities, men tended to dominate the export trade and with it access to imported prestige goods. This was particularly the case with the commercialization of ivory and rubber. The production of rubber was family-based, but its transport and sale were entirely male activities.[11]

In the 1850s, ivory caravans became a common sight on Kongo trade routes, as old slave trading elites and their young protégés began to invest part of their capital in alternative commercial ventures.[12] In the next two decades, ivory came to dominate the local export economy and, therefore, to define the avenues to social and political power. Coastal caravans obtained most of their ivory from Tio middlemen at Malebo Pool (Mpumbu), a commercial hub at the end of the vast interior Congo basin, where navigation halts as the river tumbles through a series of cataracts. Zombo merchants from eastern Kongo seem to have been the first to carry the ivory trade southbound from the Pool, but several chiefs controlling segments of the trade routes to the coast soon also participated in the export business.[13]

Caravans of up to five hundred carriers—often divided in different segments, each headed by a so-called *capata*—transported ivory to different locations on Kongo's Atlantic coast, before part of the trade was diverted to the tidal lower Congo River in the late 1870s. On their return from the coast, carriers were loaded with a variety of European imports, whose values were measured in different amounts of guns, gunpowder, and "longs" (textile measuring units). The tusks themselves were valued according to their weight and quality. They were typically measured in categories of less than ten pounds (*escravilhos*), over twenty pounds (*lei*), and in between (*meão*), with most tusks weighing between thirty and forty-five pounds. The caravans transporting them usually departed from the Pool in the dry months between April and October, and sometimes arrived at the coast when the rainy season had already started.[11]

São Salvador was an important station for many of these coastal caravans. Since the era of the slave trade, the Kongo capital had been a crucial node in the network of trade routes connecting the Atlantic coast between Luanda and the Congo estuary with Malebo Pool and the eastern interior. In 1878, British missionaries noticed that almost every day groups of carriers from the northeastern Zombo and Makuta regions passed through São Salvador loaded with ivory and rubber.[15] Dom Pedro V gained immensely from taxing these caravans, but he also participated directly in the long-distance trade, buying ivory inland or obtaining it from others in the form of tribute.[16] Using the diaries of Portuguese traveler Henrique de Carvalho, the historian Beatrix Heintze has been able to reconstruct a number of trading expeditions to the Lunda heartland commanded by Dom Paulo, a caravan leader from southeast Kongo who was a commercial agent of Pedro V. According to these accounts, Pedro first expedited a caravan with European manufactures to Lunda in 1874, which returned with a cargo of elephant teeth toward the end of the decade. Soon thereafter, the king dispatched a caravan with thirty loads of goods to the Mwaant Yaav, the Lunda ruler at Mussumba. As this caravan also returned successfully with ivory and slaves, Pedro decided to organize a larger expedition, composed of two hundred carriers and several noblemen, which left for Lunda around 1883 with beads, guns, powder, textiles, and hard liquor (*aguardente*).[17] By this time, one or two European trade houses had already set up shop in São Salvador and the king probably acted as their agent, too. But the expedition was a disaster, as Dom Paulo and many of the king's carriers were harassed on their return from Mussumba.[18] They might have fallen victim to a situation of growing insecurity in the Lunda commonwealth at the time. In any event they lacked the protection that Dom Paulo used to enjoy on his long-distance travels. Kongo traders traditionally operated within a commercial network extending some 250 miles inland from the Atlantic coast up to the Kwango River. At Kasongo-Lunda, a central hub near the Kwango, they usually traded with the local title-holder, who cultivated kinship with the king of Kongo as well as with the Mwaant Yaav.[19] On his way to Lunda, however, Dom Paulo decided to head south from Kongo to join a group of caravan traders from Angola, with whom he then traveled eastward, crossing the Kwango far south of Kasongo-Lunda and circumventing the broker services of the Mwene Puto Kasongo. In the end, this unconventional entry of a Kongo merchant into foreign lands across the Kwango proved catastrophic.

When the International African Association, sponsored by King Leopold II of Belgium, began to buy up ivory at the Pool and at its stations near the cataracts in the early 1880s, many traders from eastern Kongo shifted their business to purchasing and selling wild rubber.[20] By the end of the century, the ivory trade had practically disappeared from Kongo while rubber had become the only major export commodity.[21] The switch from ivory to rubber increased the demand for carriers in Kongo. While the annual volume of the ivory trade from the Pool to the coast stabilized at around a hundred tons in the 1870s and 1880s, rubber exports from Angola's Congo District quickly exceeded that number, peaking at eight hundred tons in 1893. Most of this rubber was of the *Landolphia thollonii* type—also known as *Landolphia lunda* or "root rubber"—which was extracted from the roots of latex-bearing shrubs that grew in the savanna regions east of the Kwango River, which in the colonial period was part of the border between Angola and the Congo Free State.[22] Like ivory, but in contrast to vegetable oils, rubber had a high value per unit of weight and could therefore be transported profitably from regions relatively far inland, even by caravans of bearers carrying thirty-kilo loads on their heads.

The extraction of rubber, a natural resource that had no economic value before Europeans started buying it, provided ordinary men and women with a rare and easy opportunity to gain wealth quickly. Bentley described how one African employee of the Baptist Missionary Society set to work after he discovered rubber vines near the mission station at the Pool: "On Sunday, in his own time, he would start early in the morning and go, with a number of empty milk-tins, to the wood where the rubber grew. He would cut a gash in a vine, and set a tin to catch the milky sap, and do the same everywhere, until all the tins were receiving the white drops; now and then he had to freshen a cut, and so he watched them all day. In the evening he would return with the accumulated sap, and boil it over a fire; the water would thus evaporate, and a lump of india-rubber would remain, nearly as large as his head."[23] The coagulated rubber was then cut in little cubes and sold to a trader or chief with access to carriers and money required for organizing a long-distance trading venture.

Rubber tapping of the latex-bearing sap of woodland creepers seems to have started in the hinterland of Ambriz in the late 1860s.[24] Ivory traders carried the knowledge of rubber tapping and an awareness of its value inland, and soon added small quantities of rubber to their loads of elephant tusks on their return journeys to the coast. A frontier of rubber tapping swiftly moved inland, reaching the eastern parts of Kongo by 1873.[25] According to the missionary John Weeks, people around São Salvador got caught up in the commercialization of rubber around this time. "As soon as they found it was saleable, they tapped the vines, boiled the sap, and carried it, at first secretly, to the trader."[26] But as the rubber frontier moved further east, populations closer to the coast stopped producing

Rubber factory in Kongo, ca. 1912 (Arquivo Histórico Militar, Veloso e Castro collection,
PT/AHM/FE/CAVE/VC/A10/Álbum A10/1833; © AHM)

it. Visitors to São Salvador in the 1880s observed that rubber creepers grew
along the banks of nearby rivers, but they were left untapped as Kongo traders
preferred to go out and buy rubber in eastern districts or buy it from Zombo
traders frequenting local markets.[27]

Long-distance traders traveled between regional markets that were held
throughout Kongo at regular intervals based on a four-day week. The four
days gave their names to smaller markets, in which mostly local produce was
sold. Regional fairs, held every other week, served as sites for the transaction of
ivory and rubber. At Kongo's biweekly markets, rubber was exchanged in small
pieces, known as "thimbles," which for Europeans were only a raw material,
but for Africans served as currency for internal transactions as well as for the
purchase of luxury imports. A Kongo trader who had collected enough rubber
could organize or join an expedition in order to sell his product at a coastal
factory or at a marketplace along the way to the coast. A caravan (*kibuka*) of
three hundred carriers, each bearing a bundle (*mutete*) of about thirty kilograms,
could deliver almost ten tons of rubber to a single factory.

The Zombo, who dominated the long-distance trade through São Salvador,
searched markets in eastern Kongo and even traveled across the Kwango
River to collect rubber. On their way to the coast, they usually stopped at a
regional fair near Kilembela, northeast of São Salvador, which was part of a

string of markets connecting traders north and south of the Congo River. There they would encounter traders from Makuta, who not only brought ivory from the Pool but also sold local manufactures, including pottery, pipes, mats, and grass-cloths.[28] South of São Salvador, there were two great fairs in the Kimbubuge district, which were important sources of rubber for European traders based in Ambrizete. In the eighteenth century, Kimbubuge was one of several Christian chiefdoms linking São Salvador to the hinterland of Luanda, but in the post-abolition era, it was important mainly for its location in the caravan trade from east to west.[29] Here the Zombo would meet another prominent trading group, the Soso from southeast Kongo, who normally circumvented São Salvador as they traveled to the coast from their homes in the Damba district.[30]

Thus many different Kongo groups participated in what was essentially a relay trade, although apart from the Zombo, caravans rarely traveled more than six or seven days from home. In 1880, a Dutch coastal trader observed that among a group of caravan porters that had arrived in Cabeça da Cobra were men from the São Salvador district, whom he called "Masjikóngos" and identified by their crucifixes, their way of calling each other Dom, and their ability to write.[31] Besides their involvement in the long-distance trade as merchants and porters, some men from the Kongo heartland also accompanied caravans from regions further east as interpreters. In other words, the aristocratic tradition of learning Portuguese had placed these elites well to function as mediators in the export trade.[32]

Interlocking networks of kinship, either real or imagined, tied the different marketplaces together. Travelers from São Salvador could count on finding a relative—thus a home—in many of the places they visited. For example, the chief of Maquela do Zombo in 1886, who as a young man traded slaves in Ambriz, affirmed his kinship to Pedro V.[33] Closer to São Salvador, the chief of Kilembela, Count Dom Afonso, called himself a "brother" of Dom Pedro, while the head of the next village along the northern route also claimed to be related to the king.[34] Expressions of kinship such as "uncle," "father," or "son" did not necessarily signify a blood relationship—the king of Portugal was also a "brother" of Pedro V—but rather symbolized dependency or respect between persons of different or equal status. In conveying trust, familiarity, and friendship, declarations of kinship helped normalize relationships between political or trading partners who might otherwise remain strangers to one another.[35] In addition, the house of the Agua Rosada married its daughters to commercial partners elsewhere in Kongo to facilitate long-distance trade. For example, two Agua Rosada women were married to traders near Ambrizete, one a Kongo man named Dom Henrique Nequioa, the other a Portuguese agent of a factory in Mucula.[36] Because of these connections and partnerships, members of the Agua Rosada family became useful guides for European traders, as well as for explorers and missionaries traveling through Kongo in the late nineteenth century.

As many visitors to São Salvador found out, however, caravans organized in the capital seldom carried beyond the king's sphere of influence. The northern district of Makuta, providing access to Nsundi and Malebo Pool, was particularly hard to enter for carriers from São Salvador.[37] Padre Barroso had difficulties in assembling a caravan for an expedition to Bembe in 1883, as carriers were uneasy about traveling beyond the Mbrige River, which southbound travelers had to cross some thirty miles below São Salvador.[38] The German Kwango expedition of Willy Wolff and Richard Büttner experienced similar recruitment problems in 1885. With the help of Dom Pedro V and some European traders established in the kingdom, Büttner found sixty carriers and two foremen for an eleven-day journey to the Kwango River. The carriers, who were mostly from nearby Mbanza Mputu as the king could not find any volunteers in São Salvador, received their wages in goods worth 4,500 *reis* (about one pound sterling) in advance, but they still deserted Büttner halfway.[39] Wolff planned to get to the Kwango via Damba, in southeast Kongo, but could not find any carriers in the Kongo capital for the five-day journey to Damba and ultimately had to rely on the few men from Loango who had accompanied him so far. After finally reaching the Kwango, he commented that "in all the regions that I passed through the trade caravans only traverse short routes [and] normally only liaise the trades between two neighboring peoples."[40] The problem was not that porters were unwilling to carry for Europeans, but that in most Kongo districts one or two chiefdoms tended to monopolize transport services, so that foreign travelers constantly had to recruit new carriers to reach their inland destinations. Specialized trading groups like the Zombo, however, managed to obtain immunity through kinship alliances, participation in interregional cults, and the payment of tribute, which allowed them to trade high-value goods like ivory and rubber over longer distances.

Trade expeditions were often organized in the dry months after mid-September, when men had burned the grass and closed the hunting season and travel was relatively easy, with roads and rivers lying dry. Light rains returned in December, followed by heavy rains in March, by which time carriers were expected back home to help clear the land for the next agricultural cycle.[11] In the carrying season, a group of entrepreneurial "big men," owning stocks of trade goods and rubber, usually collaborated in recruiting carriers among their own followers and affiliated settlements. Caravans, or their composite parts, were thus a kind of family business in which the male members of a wealthy trader's household were employed according to rank and status as either head-men or carriers, while young adolescents often joined expeditions as servants carrying food and preparing meals. "When they are strong enough," the Baptist missionary George Cyril Claridge observed, "the boys go on the road with their fathers to carry their food and get a good training in the art of carrying a load, which will gain them cloth and meat in days to come."[42]

Some carriers were slaves. On his way to São Salvador in 1885, the German explorer Josef Chavanne encountered several groups of adult men, adolescents, and young boys bringing ivory, rubber, and groundnuts to Noqui, which he believed were composed of both slaves and freemen.[43] The participation of slaves in trade expeditions resulted from the fact that successful traders tended to invest their wealth in the acquisition of male and female dependents. Accord-ing to one observer, in villages on the caravan route along the Congo cataracts, which were all heavily involved in the carrying trade, only a third of the male population was free in 1887.[44] Another observer argued that these same villages were able to withstand the commercial encroachment of caravans commanded by Europeans because local chiefs could employ "their own subjects" for carry-ing.[45] It is hard to believe, however, that mainly slaves were used to man cara-vans. While porterage was hard work for everyone, it was not typically slave labor. Not only did carriers earn wages and prestige, but they also possessed a fair degree of autonomy. The hierarchy that existed within trade caravans reflected social relations at the village level, where chiefs were often big men, but rarely despots. Lieutenant Grandy became aware of the curbs on chiefly power when he tried to reach Makuta in 1873 with a group of carriers recruited with the help of Dom Pedro V, who had also placed two local headmen and his personal secretary in Grandy's service. Although they had received their full wages in advance, at Kilembela the carriers refused to go further; when one of the chiefs tried to convince his men to continue, Grandy said, "he was forcibly dragged away by his own people."[46]

It is worth emphasizing that the intricate network of trade routes branching out from São Salvador, whose basic grid was centuries old and had for much of that time supplied slaves to different Atlantic markets, was never seriously exploited for recruiting labor for cocoa plantations in São Tomé and Príncipe. Many of the contract workers for the Portuguese "chocolate islands" in the Gulf of Guinea were recruited, instead, through the Ovimbundu slaving net-works of central Angola.[47] As late as 1862, a Luanda merchant was caught shipping small numbers of slaves from the Congo River to a business partner in São Tomé, but this was probably an incidental offshoot from the illegal trade then carried on between Cuba and the Congo estuary.[48] The close collaboration between Portuguese and Kongo courts that developed in the decades after the closing of the slave trade never involved the provision of forced labor. Against this background, the attempted recruitment of 1,500 workers in São Salvador for the cocoa islands in 1913 was unexpected.

The absence of coerced migration from Kongo after the mid-1860s was not due to a lack of supply. Despite the closing of external outlets, slaving continued internally in Kongo into the early colonial period. Successful entrepreneurs invested part of their riches in the purchase of slave women and children, often imported from regions nearby, in order to enlarge the productive base of their households and increase their social power. Pawning of children, along with other possessions, was also widespread.[19] Local European traders as well as missionaries tapped into this domestic slave trade to fill their own labor needs. Trade factories depended on African labor for a variety of tasks, not all of which local freemen were willing to carry out. Sons or nephews of coastal rulers were often hired as brokers (*linguisteres*) following commercial agreements that regulated the exchange of rents for protection. Local freemen accepted different jobs at factories as a kind of apprenticeship to learn foreign languages and commercial skills, as long as the work was not considered degrading. In Banana, a business complex on the north side of the Congo estuary where many European houses kept their main stores, freemen from Cabinda were recruited as canoe men, cooks, carpenters, and domestic servants. But for tasks that freemen found too onerous, such as cleaning, loading goods, or cultivating factory gardens, slaves were bought or hired from local chiefs, or they were purchased from further afield. Along the coast north of Portuguese Angola, these factory slaves were often called *krumanos*, misleadingly close to, but different from, the free West African employees known as Kru-men or Kru-boys.[50]

European traders used local supply networks to obtain slave workers. Ivory and rubber caravans from the interior often brought small numbers of slaves to the coast, where African brokers sold them to different buyers, including Europeans. During a famine in the 1870s, coastal factories also took in refugees who sought protection after their own families could no longer feed them. For their work at the factories, slaves earned a monthly salary of two to three longs, which was not insignificant compared to other salaries. For example, canoe men generally earned three longs per month, a *linguister* between eight and ten longs, and female servants between four and six longs.[51] About the Afrikaanse Handelsvereniging, the largest European firm on the coast north of the river Dande, it was reported in 1877 that "they hold about 150 slaves, but these people are so well treated that, to all intents and purpose, they are free, and they are never sold or exchanged; in fact, it is their boast that they are the children of the Dutch house."[52] When overt trafficking became more difficult in the 1880s, traders began to fill their labor shortages by using official Portuguese supply channels.[53] Isaac Zagury, for example, attempted to recruit sixty male and female *serviçaes* (officially contract workers, but de facto slaves) from central Angola for his Congo factories.[54] In 1886, the Companhia Portugueza do Zaire (CPZ) imported sixteen adult men in their prime from central Angola, while the house of Daumas, Béraud & Compagnie obtained forty young adults, half of them women, through colonial channels.[55] The European reliance on African servile labor became visible in São Salvador, too, after factories moved there in the early 1880s.

A Time of Plenty

In the early 1880s, shortly after a significant chunk of the Kongo ivory and rubber trade had been diverted from the Atlantic coast to the lower Congo River, several European trade houses opened factories in São Salvador. Pedro V, the king of Kongo, was instrumental in shifting these regional trade patterns, although such changes required an understanding between all players involved, from coastal rulers, brokers, and interpreters to caravan leaders and European merchants. The initiative apparently came from Alexandre Delcommune, a young Belgian who traveled to Angola at the age of nineteen and there became an agent for the house of Daumas, Béraud & Compagnie. In 1877, he set out to diversify the business of the factory he was managing in the riverside town of Boma, which until then had specialized in the export of low-value palm produce, peanuts, and sesame seeds. Knowing that São Salvador was a hub for caravans of ivory and rubber, so-called rich produce, he proposed a plan to Pedro V for diverting coast-bound trade to the Congo River. For his collaboration, the king would receive a silex gun, a keg of gunpowder, or anything of equivalent value for every tusk or every twenty kilos of rubber arriving in Boma. Within a month, the first caravan from São Salvador crossed the Congo River in dugout canoes carrying twenty-one tusks and two tons of rubber. To facilitate trade between the Kongo capital and the lower river, Delcommune subsequently negotiated the construction of a factory on the river's south bank with the principal broker-chief (*mambouc*) of Noqui, Ne-Prato, who agreed to protect the factory and its personnel in return for the payment of several taxes. Following Delcommune's example, the Portuguese trader João Luís da Rosa also opened a factory in Noqui, while in 1880 the Nieuwe Afrikaanse Handelsvennootschap (NAHV) opened a store in nearby Ango-Ango to receive trade from São Salvador.[56]

The Agua Rosada sons of Pedro V were quick to capitalize on the development of Noqui as an export outlet. Dom Álvaro de Agua Rosada, educated in Luanda on a Portuguese stipend, became an agent for the house of Daumas, helping the French factory in their everyday dealings with local Kongo traders and chiefs, which included the recruitment of carriers. When Álvaro decided to become a teacher at a Portuguese mission school in Madimba, in 1883, his brother, Dom Manuel de Agua Rosada, took over his factory job in Noqui. Using the savings from his salaried positions with Daumas and the Catholic mission, Álvaro was able to purchase a title in the Order of Christ, cementing his place among the Kongo establishment. His death of sleeping sickness around 1890 cut short an honorable career in Angola's burgeoning colonial society.[57]

The rush for rubber soon pushed European businesses inland. To attract caravans to their coastal factories, traders in Noqui and nearby Ango-Ango and Mussuco initially entrusted merchandise to Kongo brokers (*curadores*) based along the road to São Salvador.[58] But in 1882, another agent of Daumas, Protche, set up shop in the Kongo capital in order to capture the rubber trade higher up the supply chain.[59] João Luís da Rosa (whose business was merged into the CPZ in 1885) and the NAHV followed Daumas in 1883 and 1885, respectively.[60] The land concessions that each of the houses negotiated with Pedro V followed "coast custom," which included the payment of goods for provided services. For example, Rosa paid the king annually twenty trade guns valued at forty thousand *reis* for his concession; in return, the king supplied Rosa with workers to build his factory and, in exchange for another two guns, carriers for transportation if requested. In addition, Dom Pedro demanded a fixed quantity of cloth for every box of rubber and every ivory tusk the factories collected. These customs, paid out in various goods, had an alleged value of 360 *milreis* (about eighty pounds sterling) by 1885, and that was before the NAHV added their factory to the two already established in São Salvador.[61]

Factories and mission stations drastically altered the landscape of the Kongo capital. In 1883, the king began to regulate the construction of foreign trade and mission posts in São Salvador through formal land grants registered with the Portuguese government in Luanda. The first concession was issued to the Baptist Missionary Society (BMS), who were building west of the town center toward the quarter of Prince Dom Manuel, himself a member of the Baptist Church. The so-called Boma road and the ruins of the old Cathedral demarcated the north side of the terrain of the English missionaries; to their south lay a town section known as Kivampa and the chapel of the new Catholic mission. João Luís da Rosa built his store north of the town center, along the road to Maquela do Zombo, while the NAHV constructed their factory on a plot between Rosa's concession and the king's village in the heart of town. Meanwhile, French traders developed between the exit roads to Damba and Kanda on the south side of town, close to the Kicolo quarter.[62] Within just a couple of years, therefore, the modern constructions of European traders and missionaries had encircled the royal enclosure in the center of São Salvador.

There was also a dramatic change in the movement of people along the old Boma road, which connected São Salvador to the lower Congo River. Throughout the nineteenth century, São Salvador had supplied middlemen traders at Boma with slaves and foodstuffs, to which peanuts and palm produce were added as export commodities in the late 1860s.[63] But the newly developed ivory and rubber trades to Noqui and adjacent outlets affected roadside communities more profoundly than the old slave trade. The Baptist missionary John Weeks observed "an increase of traffic on the road" from São Salvador in the 1880s.[64] For the transport of trade goods and other supplies, the factories and missions in São Salvador relied on a constant supply of carriers from the capital and its surrounding districts. When Josef Chavanne traveled the seventy miles separating Noqui from São Salvador in August 1885, he encountered caravans of up to two hundred men on a daily basis. Most of these carriers traveled in an environment that seemed familiar and safe to them. In contrast to previous times, when long-distance caravans were equipped with guns to protect themselves against roadside robbers, the only weapons these men carried were knives.[65] The increase in commercial traffic also stimulated the growth of a service sector along the trade routes. European houses paid village chiefs for the construction and maintenance of bridges over half a dozen impassable rivers between São Salvador and the lower Congo. Along the road women sold *luku* balls made of manioc flour, served in a palm oil or peanut sauce, with and without hot pepper (*gindungo*), which hungry travelers washed down with palm wine or millet beer. A hundred blue beads would buy carriers three *luku* balls and two spoons of soup; smoked fish could be added for a little extra. Although not an entirely novel phenomenon in the context of African long-distance trading, the business of these women struck Anton Greshoff, the head manager of the Dutch house in the lower Congo, as extraordinary.[66]

The arrival of trade factories in São Salvador transformed the Kongo capital from an important crossroads of caravan routes into a selling place for rubber and a distribution center for imported prestige goods. Pedro V was evidently pleased with this development, commenting in 1884 that "commercial [i.e., export] goods increase considerably, and would pour in even more if people were certain that they would find here all the necessary trade ware for their transactions."[67] The capital district witnessed a growing influx of foreign merchandise, not only because rubber traders came to barter goods at the factories but also because many residents found employment as carriers with the European traders, who paid out in textiles and other commodities. In 1889, traders exported more than 250 tons of rubber from the south bank of the Congo River, necessitating at least seven thousand journeys from São Salvador by porters carrying thirty-five kilos a time.[68] Eyewitness accounts reveal the impact of this burgeoning rubber economy on local labor supplies. Chavanne observed

in 1885 that during the carrying season, the adult male population of São
Salvador of about two hundred tended to be absent. Some of the men would
be out collecting rubber on their own account, while others carried for the
factories. Padre Barroso complained that it was hard to compete for labor with
European traders, who employed a lot of the locally available workforce by
paying high wages, thus making recruitment expensive for everybody.[69]

The writing of the Baptist missionaries, who had arrived in São Salvador
shortly before the trade factories, bringing their own economy of construction
works and transport requirements, best captured the kingdom's new economic
climate. In accordance with coast custom, the missionaries paid each helping
hand four yards of cloth per week, to which another twelve to twenty-four
yards were added if a worker stayed for the month. In addition, workers received
daily rations for subsistence, paid alternatively in food and beads, the local
currency. Among other things, widespread participation in the colonial economy
facilitated access to coveted textiles for many ordinary Kongo. William Holman
Bentley observed that when he first arrived in São Salvador, in 1879, only a
handful of men were dressed in European cloth, while the rest still wore locally
produced textiles (*mbadi*). A decade later, however, "cloth was to be earned by
any one who went to fetch our stores up from Musuku, or went as carriers in
the expeditions into the interior, or worked at the building of our house."[70]
Others saw that local blacksmiths smelted increasing quantities of imported
brass wire into ankle and arm rings, which elite women typically wore to symbolize their status.[71] European traders as well as missionaries were important
distributors of prestige items, especially clothing, which was one of the reasons
why their Kongo workers used to call them *mfumu*, "big men."[72]

Economic change around the trade and mission stations stimulated both
free and unfree migration to São Salvador. Visiting the town in 1888 after an
absence of seven years, during which at least three European factories were
established there, Bentley observed that the Kongo were engaging more in
trade than before. The population was increasing as the riches that townsmen
made by working as interpreters, caravan managers, and carriers and by trading
products were invested in women and slaves. Wage labor at the factories also
drew interested workers from neighboring districts to São Salvador. In addition,
the missions were turning the city into a safe haven for outcasts and refugee
slaves seeking shelter from persecution elsewhere. In the early 1880s, São Salvador counted some six hundred inhabitants living in approximately two hundred
homes, which were set in quarters demarcated by two main streets and several
side streets. In addition to its permanent residents, the town was home to another
three hundred people when markets were held nearby. In the second half of the
decade, São Salvador was expanding rapidly. In 1886, Padre Barroso claimed

that the population was three times larger than five years earlier; in 1889, he even estimated the number at 3,500 inhabitants. That was probably an exaggeration, as two other longtime residents, the administrator José Heliodoro de Faria Leal and the missionary Thomas Lewis, suggested a population smaller than 1,500 by the turn of the century.[73] Although their estimates varied, these different eyewitnesses were in agreement that São Salvador's population was growing during the rubber boom.

To accommodate São Salvador's growing population, several new villages and quarters emerged around the king's part of town, each of them headed by semi-independent big men. This particular settlement pattern was, in fact, a regional phenomenon, which had accelerated in the 1860s with the rise of the produce trade in areas closer to the coast.[74] Throughout the lower Congo, towns were simultaneously expanding and splintering through the influx of new dependents. Many young men turned wealthy in the export trade set up their own villages with acquired wives and slaves to mark their independence from their hometowns. These villages were often not more than hamlets, but a cluster of homes was enough to obtain jurisdictional rights. Thus along the caravan routes a regular pattern emerged, with large towns breaking up in distinct parts, creating a line of little hamlets. From Tungwa, a town in the wealthy Makuta district north of São Salvador, whose population of about 1,600 inhabitants in 1873 doubled in the next ten years, originated seven new villages in the 1880s.[75] In other words, the commodity trade encouraged a decentralization of social and political power in Kongo, as it enabled young adventurers to circumvent elderly control over access to women and build their own settlements.

Affluent members of the São Salvador community bought slaves mainly from ivory and rubber caravans coming from the eastern Zombo lands.[76] In fact, around 1880, slaves were traded in different directions across the wider Kongo region, following pockets of wealth accumulated in the growing commodity trade. For example, Malebo Pool, itself an important hub in the slave trade to the lower Congo, was partly inhabited by Kongo, Zombo, and Makuta slaves who had been exchanged along with imported textiles, rifles, and gunpowder for ivory from the upper river.[77] Contemporary observations tell us that in Kongo, as in other lineage societies, bought persons were incorporated in their host communities through structures of kinship.[78] Thus, according to Padre Barroso and other European eyewitnesses, masters tended to treat their slaves as if they were their children. Normally slave members of Kongo households were only sold under special circumstances, for example to pay unexpected fines or debts, a vulnerability that distinguished them from free kin. But a master bore full responsibility for his slave's affairs, including the arrangement of a spouse when the slave attained marital age. Elders employed male slaves as messengers, representatives, servants to trade or buy food at local markets, and as carriers in the long-distance caravan trade; female slaves were specifically acquired to help their free sisters in farming.[79] Many slaves had their own income and thus enjoyed some degree of autonomy. "For every third, sixth, ninth, and so on, journey a slave makes to the 'coast' for trading purposes with his master, he receives pay, and these sums thus earned are absolutely his own. He saves the money, trades with it, and thus lays the foundation of that personal wealth by means of which he is able to redeem himself. As a married slave, he receives extra pay for the above journeys."[80] In short, the commodity trade sustained the expansion of slavery in the post-abolition era but also created opportunities for slaves to move upward in society.

European trade houses became directly involved in local slaving practices through their purchases of *krumanos*. In addition, they accepted slaves and pawns to settle disputes with African rulers. Alexandre Delcommune, for instance, described how at the end of a conflict with the *mambouc* of Noqui, in 1879, he received two enslaved boys as compensation for the kidnapping of his factory agent.[81] Something similar happened during a conflict involving Guilherme Pereira, the Portuguese manager of the Dutch factory in São Salvador. Documentation on this case shows not only how European traders immersed themselves in African ways of conflict resolution, but also how they were assimilated by various practices.[82] The case began in 1892, when lingering hostilities between rubber carriers and village heads along the road to Noqui culminated in the pillaging of a small caravan carrying goods belonging to Pereira. In retaliation, Pereira abducted two caravan leaders (*capatas*) from Ondo, one of the villages implicated in the assault, thus forcing the Ondo chief to recover the stolen goods. It is unclear if the goods were ever returned, but to compensate Pereira for his loss and redeem the hostages, the chief offered him one male and three female slaves. Contrary to the chief's expectations, however, the *capatas* were not released but sent to the government in Cabinda to be tried for theft. Meanwhile, the four slaves stayed in São Salvador. Pereira handed the male slave over to a local chief who had mediated in his conflict with Ondo. Sometime in 1893, before Pereira passed the management of the Dutch factory on to another Portuguese trader (David Martins Jacinto de Medina), he gave two female slaves to his African factory broker, Malanda, in exchange for two small boys. Under Malanda's supervision, the women fetched water, cleared the bush, and cleaned the grounds around the factory. Pereira's fourth slave, a woman named Diancuaco, became the property of his African mistress, if only for a short time.

Like most European traders and administrators in early colonial Africa, Guilherme Pereira, who had lived as a bachelor in São Salvador since 1885, had a mistress (*amásia*), and her name was Filipa António da Silva.[83] Filipa seems to have purchased Diancuaco from Pereira with her own means. Diancuaco was a difficult slave to handle, however, and after several attempted escapes, Filipa decided to trade her. With the help of the king of Kongo, Dom Álvaro de Agua Rosada, Diancuaco was sold to the chief of Mbanza Songola, a town in the Madimba district south of São Salvador. At that point Diancuaco was separated from her baby daughter, whom Filipa took with her to Ambriz after she and Guilherme Pereira left the Dutch factory in São Salvador.

It is not unusual to find Africans with full Portuguese names in Angolan colonial records, but elites carried such names more frequently than did commoners. The last name of Pereira's mistress might indicate descent from one of Kongo's old ruling families, the House of da Silva, which was historically based in the western province of Soyo.[84] More likely, however, Filipa's origins lay in Ambriz, where she traveled in 1893 and where in 1857 the Portuguese priest José Tavares da Costa Moura had bestowed the Silva patronym on all baptized residents who already carried a Christian surname.[85] In any event, an intimate relationship with a woman of high social standing would have given Pereira inside information on local trade networks and close contacts with caravan leaders. For Filipa the benefits would not have been less significant, as Pereira's factory gave her direct access to the realm of European prestige goods.

Pereira's involvement in the exchange of slaves, which the government in Luanda examined in the context of a larger investigation into the conduct of Portuguese officials in São Salvador (see chapter 4), provides a glimpse of the intimate connections between European residents and the local population in the early colonial period. Because of their material affluence, European traders wielded power in society; but to be successful in business, they conformed to local customs and relied on local intermediaries, in particular the sons and daughters of elite families such as the Agua Rosada. Colonial processes of accommodation therefore moved in two directions, with Europeans adjusting as much to African economies and cultures as African middlemen did to imperialism.[86]

Endings

One visitor to the Congo in 1882 dubiously described the former slaving port of Noqui as "a place without importance." It was certainly this no more in the 1890s, when large, ocean-going steamers from Liverpool and Hamburg began to navigate the Congo up to Noqui, which fast became northern Angola's main export outlet.[87] Noqui's advantage over the slightly older ports on the Atlantic coast, such as Ambriz and Ambrizete, lay in its relative proximity to the main rubber-producing areas beyond the river Kwango. This chapter has shown how in the 1880s, a few European factories moved from Noqui to São Salvador to seize the rubber flowing through the Kongo capital closer to its source. In 1895, David Medina, a former agent of the Dutch house in São Salvador, pioneered a further movement inland to Maquela do Zombo, a central rubber market in eastern Kongo. Many traders were quick to follow Medina's example, and by 1910, eighteen different firms had opened stores in the Zombo district. From there a few adventurous traders moved even further east, until they reached the Kwango, but in such remote parts of Kongo, traders were constantly hampered by a lack of carriers. European commercial ventures thrived especially in places offering sufficient labor supplies to meet the rubber trade's heavy transport requirements.[88]

European merchants encountered little opposition to their settlement in Maquela, although they posed a serious threat to the business of independent caravan traders. Often under pressure from the colonial government, which set up a military post in Maquela in 1896, ever larger numbers of Zombo men were recruited to carry for the local factories. In the early 1900s, every year the Maquela factories sent around ten thousand loads of rubber to Noqui on the backs of Zombo carriers.[89] The caravans arriving in Noqui in this period were usually small. In the dry season, every day up to ten caravans of ten to twenty carriers trod the road from São Salvador, most of them loaded with rubber and some with ivory. When the seasonal rains started in December, their number decreased, while equally small caravans with coffee and palm kernels arrived from areas not so deep inland.[90] In this period, factories began to hire carriers individually, making carriers responsible for the safe delivery of their own cargos, even if they traveled in a group. At the same time, the Portuguese government introduced wage scales to regulate payment, which replaced the custom of wage bartering between caravan leaders and European merchants. These wages were partly paid in goods and partly in money.[91] Contemporary registers of imports through Noqui indicate which barter goods rubber producers, traders, and carriers received in return for their labor. Cotton textiles—red, striped, or blank, many of them produced in Great Britain—were the most valuable import overall. Other recurring commodities of significant value were dyed and printed cloths, army uniforms and second-hand suits, gunpowder, German schnapps and comparable spirits, as well as flintlock, percussion, and breech-loading rifles.[92] Carrying for Europeans thus gave many Kongo workers direct access to imported luxury items, especially foreign textiles, which had long been important markers of social distinction in Central African culture.[93]

While the center of European commerce had moved further east, São Salvador remained an important link in the transportation of goods between the Zombo district and the lower Congo River. All rubber dispatched by the Maquela factories was first carried to São Salvador, where loads passed through customs before being carried on to Noqui, 150 miles down the road from Zombo.[94] Except in the eastern Kongo region, where collecting and trading rubber were important sources of income, for most Kongo men carrying was the primary form of employment in the colonial economy. In 1903, the Portuguese administrator in São Salvador reported positively on the transport services supplied by the male population in his district, a kind of labor, he said, "to which they do not have to be forced."[95] Alongside the trade houses and the missionaries, the colonial government had become a significant employer of carriers, generally paying five hundred *reis* per day for porter services.[96]

Throughout Angola, favorable times for the carrying trade came to an end in 1913, as prices for wild rubber tumbled globally after the introduction of cheaper, high-quality plantation rubber from Southeast Asia. The economic climate in São Salvador had already been changing for some years, however. First, a colonial hut tax, officially introduced in Kongo in 1901, increased steeply after 1906. As long as there was a strong demand for carriers on the part of European traders, many households earned enough income to pay the tax and avoid the labor penalties for defaulting. But when two major employers, the NAHV and the CPZ, shut down their factories in São Salvador around 1910, local opportunities for gainful labor quickly vanished.[97] Colonial attempts to introduce alternative forms of wage labor would come at a great cost.

3

Christian Revival
in São Salvador

Supported by the Royal Geographical Society and the British investor and philanthropist Robert Arthington, in 1879 the Baptist Missionary Society (BMS) set up a mission post in São Salvador that became the first in a long string of stations throughout the Congo Basin.[1] A year later, Portugal funded the establishment of a secular Catholic mission in São Salvador, staffed by priests from the seminary of Cernache, which was meant to ward off a potential British threat to Portuguese interests in Kongo. Dom Pedro V could not have been more pleased about this sudden interest of white missionaries in his kingdom.[2] Despite occasional visits of priests from Luanda, Kongo had been denied permanent clergy since Capuchin friars were officially banned from the Diocese of Angola and Congo in 1834. Consecutive kings corresponded with Portugal about a missionary presence in São Salvador, which was considered vital for the health of the kingdom and the well-being of its subjects. Priests not only administered the sacraments but also ritually sanctioned the investiture of kings and chiefs and blessed the marriages and burials of the Kongo nobility. Their absence thus seriously undermined the status and legitimacy of Kongo's ruling class. But with the European scramble for Africa gaining pace, two contrasting sets of missionaries decided to settle permanently in the royal capital.

Judging by the number of outstations, students, and converts, the Baptists were more successful at missionizing than their Portuguese rivals in the early colonial period. More than they were willing to acknowledge, however, they built on a deep Roman Catholic legacy. In his seminal study of the history of Christianity in Africa, Adrian Hastings argues that the development of the Baptist Church in the lower Congo region needs to be placed "within the longer history of Kongo Christianity." He correctly points out that the first converts in

São Salvador were drawn from the local elite, which had continued to cultivate its Christian identity. Also the expansion of the church outside São Salvador through the use of African teachers was reminiscent of the way Kongo catechists had converted the country to Catholicism centuries earlier. Indeed, "the ease with which the school at São Salvador was got going, the zeal with which male members of the congregation were soon visiting neighbouring villages on evangelistic tours, even the courtesy and basically Christian attitudes of Pedro V . . . were all evidence of a genuine continuity." In Hasting's view, Kongo was unique in the African context for its almost immediate and "quite extensive popular enthusiasm for Christianity," which he explains by the fact that the new Christian expansion "was carried from and by a group already Christianized."[3]

Neither Hastings nor anyone else has yet looked at the development of the modern Catholic mission in São Salvador, but there was the same continuity between the old and the new, even if the head of the mission, Padre António Barroso, did much to distance his own work from that of his predecessors. But the reception of the new missionaries was not everywhere the same in Kongo. This chapter proposes that the continuity thesis offered by Hastings is essentially correct for São Salvador, but that a similar continuity did not exist outside the royal capital. Correspondence from the BMS and the Catholic mission demonstrates, first, that although the new missionaries were well received in São Salvador, elsewhere they were often suspected of practicing witchcraft. Second, both missions only expanded in Kongo after they had trained sufficient numbers of Kongo teachers who were able to breach this barrier of suspicion and connect different communities to the home churches in São Salvador. Third, expansion occurred most rapidly within the royal district, while outside this realm the missions struggled against opposition from local cults and a general lack of interest in the new Christian teaching. Finally, this chapter argues that while the new Christian churches relied on existing networks of kinship and patronage to expand outside São Salvador, in the process they reshaped Kongo's political landscape. For these growing church communities, often dominated by young members of established families, the Protestant and Catholic denominations became political identities more than doctrines of faith. Using their influence to connect the mission churches with elites outside the capital, consecutive Kongo kings played a critical role in this religious transformation. As the number of Christian outstations multiplied, moreover, they also managed to enhance their own prestige in the countryside.

White Missionaries

When BMS missionaries first came to São Salvador in the late 1870s, they saw the old Kongo capital as a provisional stage in a grander project of building a civilizing mission up the Congo River. But as the early visitors found a hostile reception in some Kongo districts north of the kingdom, they decided to set up the mission's headquarters in the royal city. This was the only place, Comber said, where they had "a cordial invitation to settle."[1] Aware that England and Portugal had different agendas in Central Africa, Pedro V did not wish to alienate any potential European partner. In 1878, he let the Baptist missionaries know that although he was "a Catholic King [with a] Portuguese crown . . . I am a friend of Portuguese and English whites."[5] Moreover, since all white men proclaiming the word of Christ seemed to offer the same spiritual benefits, Pedro had little reason to turn down the request of the Baptist missionaries to settle in his kingdom. Only later he would realize that they, in fact, did not always perform the same Christian rituals as Catholic priests had previously.

The way the Kongo perceived the missionaries, especially in regions outside the royal district, often varied quite a bit from how the missionaries viewed themselves. At first, missionaries were frequently compared to the kind of white man that many Kongo men had grown familiar with in the late nineteenth century: the European coastal trader. Away from the coast, white men, always traveling in the company of dozens of carriers, were commonly seen as either commercial intruders or potential trading partners.[6] But when missionaries made clear they were not interested in buying ivory or rubber, the question arose for what reason, if not for trade, a white man would want to settle among Africans. The Kongo often sought the answer in witchcraft, or soul-trading. In 1900, for example, Thomas Lewis reported on his first year among the Zombo in eastern Kongo: "They understand the business of a Government official or of a trader; but they cannot account for the purpose of a missionary in coming to them and not buying either rubber or ivory. . . . The general opinion among these people is that we come to take their souls away, and especially those of children, to be made into white men in the white man's country. They believe that it is our subtle way of carrying on the slave-trade."[7] Around the same time, his wife, Gwen Elen, wrote: "We have only been here six months, and the people, although they begin to know us a little, still cannot understand what we have come for. They say, 'These white men do not buy rubber or cows . . .' Some time ago there was heard a peculiar rumbling sound, like a very slight shock of earthquake. When they heard it they said, 'That is Lewis's train, taking the spirits away.' Some of the men had been to Tumba and seen the train there."[8] For many Kongo who had seen or heard about it, the new railway between Matadi and Léopoldville, finished in 1898, was an astonishing creation of the white man for which, presumably, local spirits had been transferred as payment.

The perception of missionaries as mediators of other-worldly powers was long-lasting and deeply rooted in Kongo understandings of how the worlds of the living and the dead were connected.[9] In this worldview, the dead control the fortunes of the living and, therefore, success or prosperity in this world is dependent on access to powers in the land of the dead. Only a select group of people have access to occult power (*kindoki*), which can be used constructively or destructively for public or private purposes. Priests (*nganga*) are expected to use their spiritual powers for the good of the community, whereas witches (*ndoki*) are those who abuse their powers trying to bring evil to particular individuals or the community at large. Indeed, social catastrophes, like epidemic diseases or economic hardship, are believed to be the result of witchcraft. The Kongo furthermore explain the extraordinary accomplishments of one person or one group of people by the suffering of another; hence someone can only be rich or powerful by "eating the souls" of others.[10]

Missionaries originated from Mputu, the land across the sea where all white-skinned people came from and where dead people traveled. Mputu was mentally associated with Atlantic commerce: light-skinned traders emerged from overseas with an impressive repertoire of commodities produced with the labor of dead African souls. Textiles, for instance, were believed to be woven by the spirits of the sea. The white man, having access to the sea, obtained the cloth by paying for it with the souls of those he collected as slaves, or those he otherwise bewitched to become slaves of the water spirits.[11] The mythology of Mputu also affected the ivory trade, which was for a long time carried out simultaneously with the historical slave trade. Caravans of ivory were often suspected to carry dead souls to the coast in elephant tusks.[12] Decades after their first arrival in Kongo, missionaries were still associated with the historical slave trade. "We are still—after ten years among them—believed to 'sumb'o mafwa,' *i.e.*, 'to buy the dead,' and to bewitch the people by our presence and teaching," wrote Lewis from Kibokolo in 1908.[13] On one occasion, a group of Zombo traders came into the house of John Weeks in São Salvador to look "for the shelves where you store the dead bodies until you have an opportunity of sending them for shipment at the coast."[14] Likewise, George Cyril Claridge remembered that many Kongo believed that he and his colleagues had come to Africa to buy up the souls of the dead; that they used cameras to catch their spirits, water tanks to store them, and trunks to pack and carry them away. Young Kongo students traveling overseas alongside their white teachers also aroused suspicion, and sometimes curiosity. When one of the mission's medical trainees returned from a visit to England (i.e., Mputu) some people wanted to know if he had seen two lost relatives of theirs.[15]

The idea that missionaries were witches causing death and misfortune explains why many Kongo communities received them with suspicion if not direct hostility. In 1878, Comber and Grenfell visited Tungwa, the largest town in the Makuta district north of São Salvador, intending to open a corridor for themselves between the lower Congo River and Stanley Pool. The local chief, Sengele, initially thought the white men had come from Ambriz in search of ivory, and the prospect of trade did not seem unappealing to him. But it was the visitors' suggestion to settle in Tungwa that upset the local community. People still had fresh memories of Grandy's earlier visit to Makuta and the smallpox epidemic then ravaging the country. According to Comber, "the people were afraid to allow us to live amongst them. . . . Drought, famine, pestilence, or death [was] feared, as the consequence of a white man's residence in the country."[16] Such fears were not unjustified for outbreaks of smallpox in Angola were especially related to European expeditions into the interior.[17] When Comber returned in 1880, determined to reach Stanley Pool via Makuta, armed men chased him out at gunpoint. The BMS made considerable progress in the Makuta region afterward, as villagers believed their attack on the white man was related to the subsequent death of their paramount chief, Bwakamatu, and a reoccurrence of smallpox. Even so, the mission remained prone to accusations of sorcery. In 1896, for instance, a recently invested Makuta chief prohibited all Christian teaching in his town because a local evangelist had presumably killed his predecessor by magic.[18]

Suspicions of witchcraft plagued the English missionaries and their African associates especially in the southern part of Kongo. In 1906, Robert Henderson Kirkland reported from the new BMS station in Mabaya, near Bembe, that the people of a town he had recently visited "had driven away their chief and all his relations on the charge of witchcraft. The witch doctor consulted had declared him guilty of bewitching and causing the death of his uncle, and goats, pigs and fowls in the town, and as this had occurred immediately after a visit of ours, the people had said at the witch-trying, 'We believe he is the witch, for the white man talked to him and drew (photographed) his house.'"[19] In the same region, a year earlier a man was killed because of alleged soul-trade. The responsible party, George Cameron explained, "believed that wicked man sold their fellows to me, and that I, in some mysterious way, sent their spirits to be slaves in Europe."[20] The BMS was forced to close the Mabaya station in 1915, when it had only two African church members. The fact that the white men, despite their magical powers, were unable to combat a devastating outbreak of trypanosomiasis had only aggravated their plight.[21]

In São Salvador the response to the new missionaries was different. There people immediately identified them as healers, like the Capuchin priests of old. As noted in chapter 1, the Kongo had originally welcomed Catholicism as an alternative religious cult, complementing and sometimes competing with other cults. The principal tasks of the priests—baptism, confession, marriage, crowning, and rainmaking—were substitutes for the traditional activities of local magicians and prophets.[22] This was still the case in the nineteenth century. Padre Boaventura dos Santos reflected on his visit to São Salvador in 1876 that the Kongo viewed a priest as someone "who handles the fetishes of God. . . . They believe that through the work of the priest they can obtain something and they hold him responsible for anything bad that happens." Some considered him an effective rainmaker, but others thought he was *ndoki*. Nowhere except in São Salvador and a few villages in the adjacent Madimba district was he allowed to baptize, for people feared he would bewitch them.[23] Similarly, when Thomas and Gwen Lewis first journeyed through Kongo in 1887, "a number of people came and knelt down before our tent desiring to know why rain had not come."[24] In São Salvador itself, the fathers of the new Catholic mission became known as "white magicians" (*mindele mia nganga*), or alternatively "white men of the Gods of wood" (*mindele mia Nzambi za nti*), a name that reflected their use of crucifixes. The Protestant missionaries, meanwhile, were generally referred to as "God's white men" (*mindele mia Nzambi*).[25]

Like elsewhere in the lower Congo, the success of missionaries in São Salvador became dependent on their ability to manipulate mysterious powers that African healers were unable to control. The nineteenth-century European expansion in Africa ushered in a period of turbulent change, as the Kongo witnessed not only the growth of mass trade, technological innovations, and a concomitant rise of young men to positions of wealth and power but also recurrent outbreaks of famine and disease. In these circumstances, accusations of witchcraft flourished and people began to look to the missionaries for clues to handle the obscure forces behind these different but related developments.[26]

As Kongo villagers judged priests especially on their powers to secure health, it was not surprising that the Protestant missionaries gained their earliest victories on the medical front. The Baptists quickly won a reputation in the region for their capacity to heal sick people, including chiefs. William Holman Bentley, for instance, became first known as the white man who had successfully treated Dom Daniel, the chief of Tungwa.[27] Medicine was, in fact, a tool that could turn any white man into a magician. Lau, one of Pedro V's wives and an early convert in the Baptist church, still remembered in 1899 how Lieutenant Grandy had cured her husband from smallpox almost three decades earlier.[28] Significantly, in the early decades, the Kongo showed greater interest in the missionaries' medical skills than in their evangelism. Statistical evidence shows that African membership of the Baptist Church in São Salvador had slowly grown since the arrival of the first missionaries in 1879 to reach 227 in 1903. Only in the following decade would the church population increase more rapidly, reaching 1,058 members in 1912. By contrast, the mission's medical work proved an immediate success. From 1895 to 1908, the BMS dispensary received about ten thousand visits per year, a number that would rise to a spectacular fifty thousand in 1912.[29] In other words, while the Baptist missionaries were initially seen as a potential cause of epidemic disease, by the mid-1890s they had started to convince people of the power of their medicine. On a single day in 1894, for instance, the BMS vaccinated 402 individuals against smallpox. "The people come from towns far and near, for they are terribly afraid of smallpox, and vaccination is something tangible which they can understand," one missionary commented.[30] With the arrival in 1907 of the first "medical missionary," Dr. Mercier Gamble, the BMS pioneered the systematic treatment of sleeping sickness patients in São Salvador, which, according to one scholar, became "the core of the station's medical work."[31] Success in alleviating physical suffering opened the way for attracting hearers to religious services. As the pioneer Kongo evangelist Mantantu Dundulu Nlemvo put it, "every mission station which has a doctor draws men into the road of faith. Many who do not want religion come to the hospital and change their thoughts when they hear the true gospel of Christ."[32] Selling the gospel was difficult, indeed, without proof of its benefits in real life.

Through their midwife practice, the Baptist mission reached out especially to women. It seems the practice was mainly created in response to the manifest concerns of Kongo women. Gwen Lewis, who started the practice in 1892, explained that "it came without seeking."[33] Faith in the life-saving capacities of female missionaries like Lewis explains to some extent the remarkable popularity of the BMS among Kongo women. If the missionaries could protect life, moreover, then their arguments about how to live it also gained some credibility. Although polygyny was a recurring issue in the Baptist community, the missionaries believed that the first couples who married in the Church convinced others of the benefits of a Christian lifestyle. As Thomas Lewis explained, "when the babies arrived the most scrupulous care was taken of them . . . for some years the loss of a baby was unknown among these Christians. They were the envy of the heathen, and the polygamists realised that the one wife fashion was good for securing a strong and large family."[34] This was probably too optimistic an assessment of the missionary challenge to a fundamental cultural institution. Medical work attracted followers to the mission mainly because Kongo men and women saw in the white man's medical prowess evidence of an effective healing cult.[35]

Chiefs, too, eventually became eager to convert and receive baptism, in hopes it would give them renewed access to the supernatural powers governing community life. Once converted, they often destroyed the charms of existing cults. On a visit to Tungwa, Bentley recorded that his Sunday dinner was "cooked with the wood of a fetish image four feet high, which was publicly hacked to pieces . . . by one of our new church members to whom it had belonged." Not surprisingly, perhaps, this was a charm against sickness, named *Kinene*, the Great One.[36] The community of Mbanza Mputu dropped its "fetishes" after chief Mbumba converted in the Baptist Church. Convinced that the new Christian cult helped Mbanza Mputu prosper, the chief of neighboring Kimpeche advised his followers to give up their charms, too.[37] Neither of these towns was unfamiliar with Christianity, however, and both had welcomed Padre Boaventura dos Santos to administer the sacrament of baptism in the 1870s. But the English missionaries appeared to carry new weapons that proved extremely powerful in these and other towns' battles with endemic diseases. In a region struck by a fatal mumps epidemic in 1897, a group of women brought a bundle of charms before two Baptist missionaries, saying "here are the things that tempt us."[38] Many missionaries viewed this kind of fetish destruction as a first step out of superstition. But at least one of them had enough historical awareness to realize that they were merely contributing to a long Kongo tradition of iconoclasm and religious renewal, the purpose of which was always to end suffering (witchcraft) and promote welfare.[39]

Missionaries performed a range of protective duties. Like European traders, they often earned the title *mfumu*, meaning "big man" or chief. They were rich, powerful, and great distributors of wealth, and therefore able to attract followers.[40] The Kongo usually saw white priests as protectors of social order and expected them to stimulate rainfall and secure peace. In response to their plan to move further north, one royal counselor warned the Baptists about the disastrous consequences this could have for São Salvador. "If you leave us and we go wrong, it is your fault," he argued.[41] Over time, many communities came to call on missionaries to adjudicate disputes.[42] Pedro V also used missionary excursions to establish political connections and solve conflicts between chiefdoms in his kingdom.[43] East of Kongo, Zombo elders invited Thomas Lewis to settle in their lands not because they wanted Christian teachers for their children but to protect their communities from the violence of local recruitment agents. The English missionaries would, indeed, become increasingly important as protectors of equity and justice when colonial exploitation intensified in northern Angola after 1900.[44]

Kongo Evangelists

"At its exceptional best," the historian Roland Oliver once wrote, "the process of Christianization was a genuinely religious phenomenon," by which he meant that missionaries and their schools were serving secular ends more than they originally intended.[45] Indeed, in the early colonial period, Christianity was especially popular among young African men and boys who tried adapt to the modern changes affecting their societies by learning foreign skills and techniques, including literacy. But just as missionaries saw Bible-reading as ancillary to the object of Christian evangelism, for students, too, visiting the mission school was never an entirely worldly affair. Missionary teaching was an "instruction in the new magic," an introduction to the skills of the white man who seemed to hold the key to a new era. [16] Also in Kongo, where people had been exposed to European cultural influences for almost four hundred years, the nineteenth-century industrial revolution influenced people's view on the colonial-era missionaries. Young Kongo men came to the mission schools mainly for vocational training, in hopes this would help them succeed in life and allow them entry into a world of extraordinary material splendor.

Even if the white man held the key, however, the spread of Christianity throughout Kongo in the early colonial period was mainly the work of African teachers, as it had been in previous centuries. [17] By themselves white missionaries were rather ineffective, partly because of the limitations caused by their small numbers, but also because of their skin color, which continued to arouse suspicion in many black Africans. The adoption of Christianity by a great number of young Africans, according to Richard Gray, "succeeded in reducing the personal influence and impact of the Whites to an acceptable minimum." Many of the missionaries' young apprentices became societal role-models and some went on to become the instructors of a wider population of believers. They "became respected as the intrepid pioneers and interpreters of a new age. This was the golden era of the catechist, the bush-school teacher, the clerk and literate boss-boy." [18]

For the BMS, which aimed to establish free churches in Angola and Congo like most Protestant missions at the time, missionizing through African catechists was a matter of policy. "Africa must be evangelised by her own people," Gwen Lewis wrote in 1894. [19] But even in São Salvador, the BMS initially struggled to attract large crowds to their church and school. Interest was limited to the elite, including King Pedro, who frequented Sunday Mass and sent some of his sons and nephews to the mission to study Portuguese; but "the desire for education," as the missionaries put it, was generally small. [50] The arrival of European trade factories in the 1880s stimulated a wider interest in the white man's craft, and in the next decade many African traders began to send young dependents, including slaves, to work or study at the central mission or one of its outstations. [51] As some of these students became catechists themselves, they facilitated the further expansion of the mission outside São Salvador. Indeed, as the table indicates, the increasing use of Kongo personnel was crucial to the Baptist mission's success. Only after 1900, as the BMS significantly increased the number of outstations, staffed by Kongo teachers and evangelists, was the

BMS church statistics, São Salvador, 1885–1910

	Stations	Evangelists	Day-school teachers	Students	Church members
1885	1	—	—	50	—
1890	2	1	—	108	33
1895	6	2	4	324	101
1900	9	4	18	738	151
1905	72	10	78	2052	465
1910	206	80	140	3577	882

Source: BMS Annual Reports, 1885–1910.

mission able to attract a growing number of students from the country around the capital.

The Baptist Church strongly depended for its growth on the influence that consecutive Kongo kings wielded outside São Salvador. Outstations were built first of all in villages that maintained close political, economic, or kinship ties with the Kongo capital. In areas that were only weakly affiliated with São Salvador, the church was far less successful in finding adherents and its work was continuously hampered by witchcraft accusations. The BMS had to close its Mabaya station near Bembe in 1915, as the local missionaries were seen as a cause rather than a solution to sleeping sickness and famine. In the Zombo district around Kibokolo, where Lewis had established the Comber Memorial Station in 1899, the church only created two substations and baptized five Africans in the first decade. The missionaries frequently collided with chiefs, elders, and priests, especially over the poison ordeal that was part of traditional justice. They earned some success through the young men they had managed to recruit as workmen and porters, but these little gains were lost again in 1910, when a local purification movement promising everlasting life on earth pulled followers away from the missionaries.[52]

While the station in Kibokolo struggled, the church in São Salvador flourished. In studying the pioneer generation of African school teachers in the São Salvador district, a picture emerges that contradicts the assumption that in Kongo, "slaves, persons accused of witchcraft, marginal villages, and other socially insecure elements were the first to convert and important men the last."[53] Elsewhere this was often the case, but it was not so in the kingdom. Here the first converts were largely drawn from political and economic elites, including the king's household. Furthermore, the São Salvador mission was remarkably successful in attracting women to its school. In the beginning, women attended Mass, but used to sit at the back, considering it "a man's palaver."[54] But once the BMS opened a special school for girls in 1888, female students quickly outnumbered their male colleagues at the station. In fact, only after 1896 were there again more boys than girls in day school. The British missionaries owed their popularity among Kongo women to a large degree to some of Pedro V's wives, whose decisions to join the church convinced others to do the same.

The process of conversion started in familiar fashion, with missionaries importing prestige goods and pieces of currency to hand out as presents, to pay workmen, carriers, and road tolls, and to purchase food and other supplies. This material splendor made a strong impression on the Kongo population, especially the young men who were recruited to help build the station or to accompany the missionaries on their excursions outside the capital. Thus the first students were often drawn to the faith for material gain, or because, as some of them put it, they wanted to become like the white man. Vita, one of São Salvador's pioneer school teachers, recalled the moment when the missionary Herbert Dixon came to his village asking the chief for schoolboys. Many local youths feared enslavement, but Vita viewed the white man differently, and his thoughts reflected the ambitions of the first generation of mission students. "If I go with the white man I shall learn how to get rich like him."[55] Like Vita, other early school dwellers grew attached to the church and would eventually enable its expansion outside São Salvador. The radicalism of these first converts should not be underestimated, even in a place like Kongo, where people had been familiar with Christianity and other aspects of European culture for centuries. The colonial missions were different from their predecessors in the sense that they operated in, and symbolized, a new imperial environment, the transformative impact of which was felt through mass trade, technological change, and growing European power. As James Pritchett has argued, conversion symbolized a readiness to become part of a new public: "It announces one's new vision of the world, one's willingness to engage rather than retreat from modernity . . . one's desire for experimentation with new social forms and productive processes."[56]

Many of the pioneer evangelists had started their path to conversion as interpreters for the first group of missionaries arriving in Kongo, with whom they usually forged close personal bonds. Some traveled to Europe with their tutors to improve their knowledge of Western culture and their language skills, which they required to become intercultural mediators. The first African convert of the Baptist Church was William Mantu Parkinson, a student from São Salvador who helped Thomas Comber in setting up the Wathen station near Ngombe Lutete in the Congo Free State. He was baptized in 1886 and married

Group of men in São Salvador, ca. 1912 (Arquivo Histórico Militar, Veloso e Castro collection, PT/AHM/FE/CAVE/VC/A10/Álbum A10/2302; © AHM)

to a freed slave from the upper Congo, Aku. Parkinson became a figurehead in Kongo politics after 1910, but relatively little is known about his background. Very likely, he had been on the road before joining the BMS, using the experience thus gained in his function of caravan headman for the mission in the early 1880s. At the opening of the Baptist Church's new chapel in São Salvador in 1899, he told a large audience about the buzz going around town two decades earlier, when Comber asked the king for permission to settle and people wondered if these Englishmen had come to buy rubber or slaves. Not long after Comber's death in 1887, Parkinson left the mission to become transport manager at the Lukungu station along the road between Matadi and Léopoldville.[57] He thereby set a pattern for the next generation of mission-educated men, many of whom were able to capitalize on the growing economic opportunities in Belgian Congo. As John Weeks noted in 1913, "hundreds of our native Christians work on the railway as stokers, guards, brakesmen, storekeepers, and stationmasters."[58]

More details are available for Nlemvo, who helped Bentley write the *Dictionary and Grammar of the Kongo Language* and translate the New Testament.[59] Nlemvo was born around 1871 as Donzwau (Dom João) Mantantu Dundulu into an established Kongo family. His father died on the day of his birth, and Mantantu spent his early years at the house of his paternal uncle, occasionally helping his mother carry produce to market. But at the age of six his maternal "uncle," Dompetelo Bidi (Dom Pedro Bidi, in fact a cousin of his mother), claimed authority over him and took him to Lemvo in the Madimba district south of São Salvador. Pedro Bidi was a Catholic ivory trader of Zombo origin who had settled in Madimba, where he became the elected chief of Lemvo. He had bought the title of *tulante* from the king of Kongo for five thousand strings of blue glass beads and a slave, and to symbolize his Christian identity he used to wear a copper cross. Bidi had planned a career in trade for Mantantu, and he once took his young nephew with him on a journey to the coast. But in 1880 the boy's life took an unexpected turn when, through Pedro V's intervention, Mantantu was put under the care of Bentley, who named him Nlemvo. Later in life Nlemvo confessed how much he had initially feared the evil disposition of *Mfumu Bentele* with his mysterious medical powers. Nlemvo's transfer to the white man invoked images of cannibalism and slavery, not only in the young man himself but also among his relatives. When Bentley took Nlemvo on the first of his three visits to England, rumors spread that the king had sold the boy for cloth to the white man; afterward, his mother dared not touch him. But Nlemvo was never fully detached from his Kongo community. In 1887, Tulante Bidi died and his nephew, now a young evangelist at Wathen station, was chosen to succeed his uncle, inheriting his title and his seven wives. Nlemvo accepted the title against the payment of a fee in textiles to the king, but he refused to marry the women. As a further sign of the changing times, within a year of his election he returned to his office in Wathen, favoring his evangelical position above that of a Kongo nobleman, although he still often donned a civet skin to symbolize his chiefly status.[60]

In 1888, Nlemvo married Kalombo Kavwazwila, a freed slave from the upper Congo, who had been sold in Léopoldville in 1883 by Arab travel companions of Henry Morton Stanley, but was then ransomed by Thomas Comber. Kalombo had made her long journey from enslavement to freedom alongside Aku, who was married to Mantu Parkinson. Unlike their Catholic counterparts, Protestant missionaries in the lower Congo had no official policy of ransoming slaves, but in the early years they often took in slaves and refugees. Thus the Livingstone Inland Mission, which built its first station in Palabala in 1878 and expanded northward from there, purchased slave children to fill their schools as free children were difficult to recruit. Parents were either suspicious of the missionaries or expected their sons to be paid for their training, as was usual at European trade factories.[61] Ransomed slaves were also the first inhabitants of the village built around Nlemvo's house next to the Wathen station, reflecting the poor integration of the mission in the Ngombe Lutete community in the late 1880s. "If any man wore a shirt or trousers he was not allowed to enter the village," Nlemvo later recalled, "for he was the friend of the White Man, that is, a witch."[62] Although a free man himself, Nlemvo had no qualms about entering a monogamous relationship with a slave woman. In 1901, after his first wife died, he married another freed slave, Masengo Nsenga Madia. She had been abducted from her home near Dilolo in the eastern hinterland of Angola and ended up a slave in Luanda. There she was adopted by a Dutch trading family, who around 1895 transferred her to the Baptist missionary John Bell and his wife to become their domestic helper at the Wathen station.

The first African teachers to make an impact on the diffusion of Protestantism in northern Angola were António Nlekai and Kivitidi. Both originated from the eastern Kibangu district, an erstwhile Catholic stronghold and home of the legendary Beatriz Kimpa Vita.[63] They were educated at the mission in São Salvador and, in 1887, were part of the first group of converts baptized in the local church—the others being Matoko and Ndelengani, both royal counselors, and Luzemba, another elite recruit who would later head the church's Underhill station.[64] Kivitidi started out, in 1879, as John Hartland's interpreter and apprentice and later became the assistant of Thomas Lewis. Still a bachelor, he built a stone house for himself next to one of the missionary homes, symbolizing his rising status in São Salvador and causing the envy of the king and, undoubtedly, other local notables too. In 1888, Kivitidi got married and was appointed as evangelist at the church's first substation in Etoto, a town of about four hundred people in the Madimba district. In Etoto, his job was to spread the missionary teaching to regions south and east of São Salvador. Three days of the week were dedicated to evangelical duties; the rest of his time Kivitidi devoted to carpentry. After two years, he resigned from his religious office to concentrate on trading and tailoring, although he continued "to live the life of a Christian man."[65]

Like Nlemvo and Kivitidi before him, Nlekai moved to São Salvador because of an agreement between the missionaries and the chiefs. In 1899, he still remembered the day that Comber and Hartland visited Kibangu and took a number of young men with them to the Kongo capital for schooling, including Kivitidi. Nlekai himself came to São Salvador with Herbert Dixon a few years later, and after Dixon left in 1884, he became the assistant of John Weeks. He started working as a teacher in 1889 in Mbanza Mputu, where his most important achievement was the conversion of the powerful Garcia Mbumba, a contestant for the royal throne who controlled one of the exit roads to eastern Kongo, thus providing the church with an entry into the populous Zombo district. The BMS soon appointed Nlekai as chief evangelist for the districts east of São Salvador, but like Kivitidi, he occupied himself with more than just religious activities. In 1892, he opened a school in the village of Mawunze, suggesting to his English patrons that he could live there off an income made in trade. But they did not agree and put him on a monthly salary of eight guns.[66] As the Baptist Church was meant to be self-governing and self-supporting, Kongo teachers were not paid with European funds but received a salary collected among local followers. For many that may not have been enough, though, and some teachers developed a few sidelines to add some currency to their basic income.[67] Vita, another Kibangu native, eventually took over Mawunze from Nlekai. He ran the station together with his wife Ndungani, a daughter of the king, until it was closed in 1896 for lack of students; the couple then moved on to teach in Mwingu, Madimba.[68]

A different story is that of the slave Miguel Nekaka, grandfather of the later political leader Holden Roberto. Nekaka was the son of a wealthy Zombo chief but was cast out by his family on suspicions of witchcraft. Eventually his family sold him to a local rubber and ivory trader, who on a journey to São Salvador in the early 1880s passed him on to Dom Pedro Mpembele, a trade broker in the capital. In his autobiography, Nekaka remembered his first impressions of São Salvador, a town where mysterious white men had erected large homes to conduct their affairs. Still a slave, Nekaka became an apprentice at the Portuguese factory, where one day he saw Padre Barroso reading a set of papers, which aroused his curiosity about the world of letters. He wanted to learn Portuguese so that he could become a trade broker himself, but when Barroso showed little interest in him, he found the Baptist missionaries more welcoming and began attending classes at the English mission. When his master died, his adoptive uncle, Thomas Lewis, claimed him for the Baptist mission before Pedro V could assert his authority over the kinless Nekaka. He was baptized in 1889, married to Diwambaka, and appointed preacher in 1898, in which capacity he worked for many years in communities near the Congo border. In 1912, Nekaka became the official spokesman of the Baptist Church in Angola and as such returned to São Salvador in December 1913, at the time of the great Kongo uprising. In the years after the revolt he owned a trade factory in São Salvador, another reflection of the never waning material concerns of the Kongo preacher class.[69]

The first female students at the mission were several wives of Dom Pedro V, starting with Wavatidi, a slave woman. Wavatidi had been married to the king in return for the protection he gave her mother in a legal dispute. Defying the will of her husband, she converted in the Baptist Church, and when the king died in 1891, she was set free, remarried, and became an evangelist. In addition to Wavatidi, in 1888 the Baptist missionaries baptized another five of Pedro V's wives.[70] As these women often resided in villages outside São Salvador, they were instrumental in the expansion of the Church outside the capital. When Thomas and Gwen Lewis first visited Madimba, they found in the village of Etoto "a wife of the King of San Salvador . . . one of my schoolgirls, and two schoolboys, who afforded us something of an introduction." Local women interrupted their farm work to hear Mrs. Lewis speak outside the king's wife's house.[71] Months later, Etoto became home to the mission's first outstation.

In 1899, Lau, then senior woman deacon, recalled how the example of Wavatidi and other wives of the king had encouraged her to join the church. She was not the only one: some sixty young women attended the school for girls in 1888, many of them coming from outside São Salvador; by comparison, only about forty to fifty boys were enrolled in school that year. A third of the female student body was married, and many seemed to act against their husbands' wishes.[72] One of the early students was Bwingidi, a girl of about eleven in 1889, who had escaped to the BMS from her marriage to a local big man. The missionaries compensated the man for the bride price he had paid and took her in. She remained under their protection until she married Nlekai and settled as a school teacher in a village outside São Salvador. The missionaries later found out, to their regret, that Bwingidi had not married Nlekai "freely" but had instead been "betrothed" to him by her elders.[73] Misinterpreting bride-wealth arrangements as purchases or slavery, missionaries often complicated their own attempts to attract women to the mission.[74]

The early enrollment numbers of the mission's school for girls are impressive, but they conceal the conflicts behind female participation in church life. While many male youths came to the mission in hopes of finding material rewards, some of the girls were drawn in because they had relationships with men enrolled in school. "It is important to let the girls understand," Gwen Lewis commented, "that we take them and teach them for their own sakes, and not simply because they are engaged to certain boys." Others were taken out of the mission by their elders as soon as they were married. Despite their numerical dominance, therefore, many female students did not stay at the mission very long. "Unfortunately we can never keep them as long as we keep the boys, because they get married too soon," Lewis lamented.[75] Conflicting ideas about women's functions in society often caused friction between the missionaries and the Kongo communities they worked in.

The Baptist mission could be a threatening force to men, as it offered women an unprecedented opportunity to escape social control. Female members of the royal family often ignored orders from the king to stop visiting the Baptist church.[76] Apart from slaves, many women accused of witchcraft, women escaping from involuntary marriages, and women running from cruel husbands found a safe haven with the British missionaries, who often found support in their attacks on "tribal customs" from the long-time Portuguese administrator, José Heliodoro de Faria Leal.[77] Not surprisingly, elders and chiefs usually offered

Group of women in São Salvador, ca. 1912 (Arquivo Histórico Militar, Veloso e Castro collection, PT/AHM/FE/CAVE/VC/A10/Álbum A10/2301; © AHM)

the strongest opposition to the work of the Baptist missionaries. For instance, shortly after Thomas and Gwen Lewis started teaching in São Salvador, a man approached Mr. Lewis with the question of whether his wife could not be taught to obey her husband. The man was especially unhappy with Mrs. Lewis's lessons about individual salvation and threatened to send his wife to the Catholic school instead.[78]

While the number of women attending day and evening classes increased over the years, so apparently did male discomfort about this situation. Missionaries usually interpreted attempts by lineage heads to control the labor and sexuality of their female dependents in terms of slavery. "There is a great deal of opposition now to girls coming into the station," Gwen Lewis explained, "because the men find that they will not be slaves afterwards."[79] Kings and chiefs frequently collided with the missionaries on account of their "definite stand against slavery and oppression," as Robert H. C. Graham put it, and sometimes violently resisted the conversion of their wives and daughters.[80] Missionaries confused social control with slavery; yet their observations reflected a change in gender relations under early colonial rule. In the wake of the 1913 uprising, Kongo chiefs demanded an official prohibition for women to settle marital disputes in São Salvador, a clear sign that the erosion of male authority was a lingering concern for Kongo chiefs, as it was elsewhere in Central Africa.[81]

Male opposition to female school attendance was most tenacious outside the royal district. While elders understood the benefits of a European education for their sons, they saw no use in it for their female dependents, whose economic lives were mainly defined by domestic work. Among the Zombo, Gwen Lewis found great difficulty in getting hold of women. In 1902 she reported that "as yet I cannot get any girls to school. Some want to come very much, and one little thing came several afternoons running; but she has been stopped by her master, and it is the same with the others . . . it is so different from where we have been before. There the difficulty was to find time to talk to all the people who wanted to be taught; here the trouble is to get the people to listen. . . . The chief of Nzamba has promised to bring me some girls, and I believe he is trying to get them; but he owns a number of little girls and does not like to give them up, and the other people are just the same." At the same time, not all women were interested in missionary teaching. "One of the women who lives close by has just been here to sell plantain. I asked her why she did not come to service; she said, 'What will you give me for coming?' and that is the answer one usually gets." Social norms, along with opposition from traditional priests and the labor demands of local rubber traders, depressed early enrollment numbers at the church school in Kibokolo. In striking contrast with São Salvador, therefore, the first Zombo students were all young children, often motherless and neglected.[82]

Catholic Revival

Pedro V was evidently pleased with the arrival of the English missionaries in São Salvador. Before long, however, he realized that they were different from the white priests who had previously visited the kingdom. Specifically, they did not invest chiefs in the Order of Christ or baptize the masses, which were the two main tasks earlier performed by Catholic priests. The king was furthermore aware of Portuguese misgivings about British intrusions in the kingdom. In 1879, therefore, he assured the governor of Angola that the plans of the Englishmen "to make houses of stone, and to teach the boys and girls" would not damage Kongo's relationship with Portugal.[83] When he later reiterated that the Englishmen had not come for political motives but for the teaching of God only, he added that the kingdom was still in need of Catholic clergy. "The said missionaries told me they did not come to take the crown from the king of Kongo, that they only hold firm to the faith in God. Therefore I respectfully ask your Excellency to send some priests here. I return the Kongo to how it was in previous times and the times of my ancestors, I will not give up my friendship."[84]

Portugal responded to the British missionary presence in Kongo by sending a mission of its own to São Salvador in 1881, whose aims were "religious as well

as patriotic."[85] While the state-sponsored Catholic mission was a clear precursor
to effective colonial government in Kongo (see chapter 4), this chapter is primarily concerned with its impact on African social and religious life. The arrival
of the padres caused some worry on the part of the Baptist missionaries. For
instance, John Hartland believed that the Portuguese priests would unfairly
benefit from the kingdom's Catholic heritage and its traditional alliance with
Portugal, which gave the priests "a power and standing that no [Kongo] would
dare to question."[86] But his suspicion proved unfounded. The fact that some of
the most powerful political figures in São Salvador—including Dom Álvaro
Matoko (counselor), Dom Miguel Ndelengani (blacksmith), and Dom Manuel
Matengo (secretary and son of Pedro V)—became affiliated with the Baptist
missionaries indicates that Kongo's Catholic tradition was not an obstacle to a
religious changeover. The difference between both religions was only slight
from an African perspective to begin with. In principle, the Kongo perceived
all white clergy in the same way, that is, as magicians or healers, independent of
their religious denomination. As soon as the priests had arrived in São Salvador,
therefore, some townsmen began to shop around at both churches, trying to
figure out which god was more powerful, the one of Portugal or the one of the
English.[87] Among these customers was the king himself, who alternated his
church visits with such regularity that Padre Barroso wondered whether he was
truly Catholic.[88]

Contrary to Hartland's predictions, the Catholic mission struggled to get
a foothold in São Salvador, in part due to a problem of its own making. The
bishop of Angola, who oversaw the Kongo mission, was officially instructed
that the new missionaries did not have to work as "fast" as their predecessors,
who baptized people by the hundreds but let them linger in "superstition."[89]
This new religious policy upset Pedro V, who urged Barroso to baptize and
take confession from all people young and old, no matter if they were unaware
of Church doctrine. "If you continue like this, my people will not come anymore
because they are used to having people come over from elsewhere to baptize."[90]
Yet Barroso replied that he had nothing to do with the customs of his Catholic
predecessors and was only willing to baptize adults who knew the principles
of the faith, apart from children and the dying.[91] The same rigid standards
were applied to the other sacraments. Thus the "unconverted"—in Barroso's
definition—could not be married nor be granted a Christian burial except by
clemency of an episcopal authority, which was now also required to consecrate
kings.[92] This uncompromising attitude estranged many inhabitants of São
Salvador from the Catholic missionaries. The dying, for instance, no longer
called on the priests to commend their souls to God, as they had in the past, but
rather asked the English missionaries for assistance in their final moments.

Although Barroso and his colleagues administered about a thousand baptisms during their first three years in Kongo, they were mainly conducted among children on journeys away from the capital.[93] Christian burials were only reintroduced in 1890, while the sacraments of the Eucharist and Extreme Unction were only administered again from 1895 and 1903, respectively. The basic sacrament of the Lord's Supper was distributed more frequently after a new church building opened in São Salvador in 1904, while the arrival of the Franciscan Sisters of Maria in 1907 and the Society of the Sacred Heart of Jesus in 1909 (both set up for the education of Kongo women) further helped to widen reception of Holy Communion.[94] By this time, however, the Catholic Church already lagged far behind the Baptist mission in popularity and adherence.

Enthusiasm to join and work at the Catholic mission was initially so low that the Portuguese priests depended on coerced labor for its sheer survival. In August 1882, five male convicts from Portugal arrived in Kongo with their wives, some with children, to establish a small farming community around the station. These immigrants were supposed to grow food for the mission and serve as a model of civilization for the local Kongo population. But the project was an immediate failure as these families, poorly fed and neglected by the missionaries, barely survived their first weeks in Kongo and did not get along with their patrons.[95] Instead of developing wage labor, like the BMS at their station, the padres found a solution to their labor and subsistence needs in the redemption of slave children. A proposal was designed to recruit children in southern Angola, although there is no evidence suggesting this plan was actually carried out.[96] The Portuguese priests seem to have taken the same path as their Spiritan brothers in Soyo, which was to purchase slave children from trade caravans coming from the northeast.[97] According to the German explorer Josef Chavanne, who visited São Salvador in 1885, the majority of the fifty-eight students then enrolled at the Catholic mission were slaves from the Makuta and Zombo regions.[98] After the establishment of formal colonial rule, moreover, the mission began to use official recruitment channels, which local trade factories also exploited to fill their labor needs. In 1886, for instance, the mission contracted twenty *serviçaes* (contract workers) for a sum of 500 *milreis* (110 pounds sterling); these apprentices were very likely shipped in from central Angola.[99] Even in 1896, the mission contracted twenty *serviçaes* through the house of Lemos & Irmão, underlining the priests' longstanding difficulty in finding or paying local workers to sustain the mission.[100]

Other slaves came to the mission in more haphazard ways. In 1892, the priests intervened in a legal dispute between one of the royal counselors, Sábado, alias Capitão Ginginha, and the elders of Kimalu. After King Álvaro XIV had decided the case in the counselor's favor, Ginginha was arrested by the colonial administration for incarcerating at his home three individuals from Kimalu. They had probably been enslaved as a result of court proceedings, but Ginginha protested that they were his "children." While the administration was forced to act against slavery to some degree, it lacked incentive to undermine the legality of royal jurisprudence. After deliberating with his Portuguese patrons, the administrator and the priests, the king declared that the slaves would neither remain with Ginginha nor be returned to Kimalu, but were to become "slaves of the Church," adding to the growing servile community of the mission. Like their Baptist colleagues, the Catholic missionaries also offered shelter to women who escaped from bondage. The result was that, against official policy, quite a few adult females were living at the mission station, a "morally untenable" situation in the eyes of some local Portuguese observers.[101]

The mission naturally attracted a number of local enthusiasts as well, whose eagerness to learn and carry the Catholic tradition forward was stronger than the deterrents put in place by the new padres. Some of these devotees came from São Salvador, while others had been recruited by Barroso on his travels outside the capital.[102] The Catholic mission would, in the end, owe its success to the initiative of this core group of Kongo converts and their parents, which zealously appropriated the rituals of the Church, starting with baptism. Baptismal records from 1876 and 1877 suggest that the recipients of Catholic baptism were normally infants and young children belonging to elite families, which carried aristocratic names like Dias de Estrada or Afonso Noronha de Menezes. Significantly, these records reflect the ascendancy of a few noble families within the Kongo community. Besides the Agua Rosada, there was at least one other prominent family in São Salvador, which was named dos Santos. Baptismal records show that both families were connected through marriage. For instance, the parents of one-year-old Pedro, baptized on 28 November 1876, were Pedro de Agua Rosada, a royal secretary, and Maria José dos Santos.[103]

Besides baptism, the Kongo also embraced the possibility of canon-law marriage that the new missionaries would offer them. The priests were initially reluctant to assist church members in marrying because they questioned the moral credentials of the potential brides. "I have boys in the mission with European habits and a certain degree of civilization," commented a disparaging Barroso in 1887. "The families want to marry them. They like to build their homes within eyesight of the mission. The boys want to marry legitimately, but women here know little more than to dig up soil and in general live a degraded life, being unfaithful to their husbands. Moreover, those from São Salvador have been more or less infected by Protestantism and those purchased in Zombo are true savages."[104] Responding to the popularity the BMS enjoyed among Kongo women, in 1888 the Catholic mission opened a school for the religious instruction of girls, which immediately attracted some fifty students.[105] Two years later, some of them were considered sufficiently acquainted with the principles of Catholicism to be married in the Church.

Between 1890 and 1909, the Catholic Church consecrated sixty-four marriages in São Salvador.[106] Many of the newly wedded Kongo were of noble descent and came from different towns and villages in the kingdom. For example, in 1893, Pedro de Agua Rosada, a twenty-two-year-old police officer in São Salvador, married Maria Carolina Gimbo, a twenty-one-year-old woman from Kimiala, a royal stronghold in the Madimba district. In 1909, after Pedro had passed away, she was remarried to Bernardo Monomundele Kimo, a young carpenter from Pangala and protégé of the royal counselor Manuel Lopes de Almeida. Also in 1893, Álvaro de Agua Rosada, a twenty-eight-year-old trader from São Salvador, married Ponciana Diaunino from Casanje, a marriage that seemed to strengthen bonds between families living in different centers along the northern Angolan caravan routes. It is important to remember, however, that not all royalty married in the Catholic Church. In 1896, for example, two daughters of King Álvaro were married in the Baptist Church, a clear signal that the Kongo ruling class was split between both churches.[107]

While Kongo elites reappropriated the institution of canon-law marriage to sanctify their marital unions, the Church also brought in and wedded strangers, some of whom were slaves. For example, in 1894, the twenty-five-year-old Afonso Kassoka, a Zombo slave who had been purchased by the missionaries, was married to twenty-one-year-old Ana Bonga from Kimalu. In 1929, their daughter Luzia married a local stonemason, which suggests that despite their low origins, the Kassoka family became full members of the Catholic community.[108] In 1895, the twenty-six-year-old stonemason João Corvo Secca married a woman from Tuku, Maria Cameza, who at twenty-five was approaching the higher end of the age spectrum (she died in 1903). A Zombo husband was also found for twenty-six-year-old Maria Luiza dos Martyres, who was widowed in 1896 from Joaquim Delgado Pembele, a former day laborer in São Salvador; her new spouse was a young man named António Kaila. School registers suggest that since the mid-1880s, when the padres first incorporated a group of enslaved Zombo children, few other Zombo men entered the Catholic mission.[109] In other words, many of the Zombo men who married in the Church a decade later were probably redeemed slaves, and they often married Kongo women who, in terms of age, were somewhat past their prime.

Kongo initiative gave rise to the first extension of the Church outside São Salvador. In 1883, chiefs in the Madimba district requested a school to instruct their sons and nephews in matters of religion and the Portuguese language.[110] Barroso immediately appointed Dom Álvaro de Agua Rosada, Pedro V's eldest son, as a teacher for a monthly wage of twenty thousand *reis*, which was enticing enough for him to resign from his position as interpreter at the factory of Daumas.[111] Two years later, the mission decided to construct a school and a home for a resident priest in Kinganga, a former Capuchin hospice about thirty miles south of São Salvador, which became the seat of the São José de Belém parish.[112] While the school boarded students from outside the region, prominent members of the local Madimba community took control of the mission's religious affairs. Between 1907 and 1909, six couples were married in the Church and settled as Christian families in nearby Nazaré. The husbands were all young men from established Madimba families, and had attended the mission school for several years before marrying. The general description of the brides in the matrimonial records as workers (*trabalhadoras*) should not distract us from the fact that they, too, were mainly of noble descent.[113]

By the end of 1907, the core of Kongo's Catholic community was formed by thirty-five married couples, most of them living in São Salvador. Model Christian villages, idealized nuclei of Western civilization, did not exist in Kongo, with the possible exception of Nazaré. The Portuguese mission had established fifteen village schools within a radius of three days from São Salvador—mainly northeast and northwest of the capital—where Kongo catechists taught Christian doctrine, Portuguese language, and technical skills to over six hundred students. While the schools aimed to instill a love in young Kongo students for Portugal and Our Lady, their main attraction was material. "Previously nobody cared about schools," wrote the catechist Pedro Lukanga de Agua Rosada in 1905, "but today many districts ask our missionaries to open schools. They understand that every man needs to be civilized."[111] Throughout the kingdom, village schools produced stonemasons, carpenters, tailors, and typographers, convincing many skeptical chiefs of the benefits that a school would bring to their own communities.[115]

The establishment of Catholic village schools, the choice of their location, and the relaxation of standards for the preparation of catechists ("some useful advice as deemed necessary") all happened after 1900 in response to the rapid expansion of the Baptist Church in northern Angola.[116] This was a battle that the Catholic Church was not going to win quickly, if at all. In 1908, the BMS had 187 outstations in the São Salvador district, providing education to more than three thousand students, while there were only twenty-eight Catholic village schools, serving the needs of about a thousand Kongo enthusiasts. The only place where the priests were able to compete with the English missionaries was São Salvador, where separate Catholic schools provided education to local men and women as well as to male boarders brought in from other places, possibly as redeemed slaves.[117] Clearly, both mission churches built on Kongo's long

Catholic heritage. But the new missionary expansion in the kingdom did more than refashion the old Christian tradition. As young Kongo teachers spread the Gospel in the countryside, teaching students new skills and exposing them to modern Western culture, they constructed new religious bonds between communities. These bonds often connected villages to one of the two churches in São Salvador, creating a religious division within Kongo society that soon also had political implications.

Religion and Politics

The political impact of the Baptist and Catholic missions was twofold. On the one hand, the new churches underlined the position of São Salvador as a spiritual center in northern Angola, strengthening the reputation of the Kongo kings in the region. On the other hand, denominational rivalry promoted the formation of "politico-religious" factions once Kongo converts began to identify themselves and others according to their respective church affiliations. While there was distrust between the Protestant and Catholic missionaries from the start, this did not necessarily prevent cooperation between them or create sectional rivalry within the Christian community.[118] Initially, most Kongo did not differentiate between the two churches on the basis of doctrine but rather because of practical matters such as the provision of health care and other material benefits. In the 1890s, however, some converts began to formulate new group identities based on their religious affiliation. The Catholic superior, Pinto de Albuquerque, complained that BMS students "pass every Sunday during the Holy Sacrifice . . . by the church door with their hats on, saying afterwards to our pupils and people that they did so because our religion is not real."[119] The priests themselves certainly contributed to the growing antagonism between both church communities. For example, they published a propaganda booklet in Kikongo on the "words of the Protestants," feeding an anxiety among their followers about the visible affluence of the Baptist community.[120] Celebrating the first anniversary of the new church building in 1905, Catholic stonemason Affonso Fernandes Nimi wrote: "Earlier we had a small chapel and not everyone fit. . . . Many complained because they could not hear and did not know which the true religion was. Some only wanted to hear the false religion of the Protestants because they showed their church to everyone and invited everyone to hear their religion. After we had our church they made fun of us saying that we did not have trained stonemasons."[121]

In São Salvador, only a wall separated the grounds on which the two missions had built their churches. But in the countryside most villages that had welcomed a mission school became either Catholic or Protestant, while only a few accepted the protection of both religions. Under these circumstances, local conflicts quickly turned into religious battles. For example, a dispute between two neighboring villages in the Ntanda district northeast of São Salvador, one of which hosted a Catholic teacher and the other a Protestant one, ended in the burning of the Baptist school chapel.[122] Irrespective of the intentions of the Baptist missionaries, this religious segregation also gained an international dimension, as both communities associated themselves with different foreign patrons. "In São Salvador religious and political principles are connected," a local administrator wrote in 1900; "to be Catholic is to be Portuguese, to be Protestant is to be English."[123] These political divisions would play an important role in the election of Manuel Martins Kiditu in 1911 and the revolt two years later.

While the re-evangelization of Kongo intersected with divergent political loyalties in the kingdom, the new missionary presence also increased the general allure of the Kongo capital. On festive occasions, both the Baptist and the Catholic Church drew large crowds to São Salvador, where visitors were reminded of the close connections between the king and the missionaries. When the Baptist Church opened its new chapel in 1899, about a thousand men and women attended service. Many had come from the villages in the countryside around São Salvador and stayed with family or friends in the capital. Before the service started, honor was paid to King Henrique Nteyekenge (1896–1901), who was Catholic in name only. "The King was present," recorded Gwen Lewis, "and when his photo was put on the sheet we allowed the audience to clap."[124] The churches, in turn, benefited from the visits of traders, embassies, and other strangers to São Salvador, who would spread news about the missionaries among the relatives and friends they saw on their way home.[125]

As in previous centuries, local elites appropriated the Catholic calendar to sustain the prestige of the Kongo polity. On these religious holidays, however, the kingdom's allegiance to Portugal was now also played up. Thus on Halloween, 31 October, 1885, Pedro V celebrated the anniversary of Luís I of Portugal during the inauguration of his new stone house. Pictures of Portuguese royalty that decorated the interior walls of the king's new residence were shown to the public. "That day São Salvador was full of people," Pedro later told the governor of Angola, "as from all around people came to attend our party, which was very much national, and show their respect and admiration for the majestic characters about whom they had already heard so much."[126] Another important holiday was the Feast of the Immaculate Conception, on 8 December, chosen by the Portuguese mission to officially inaugurate its new church building in 1904. That day some three hundred students from Catholic schools in São Salvador and villages nearby were joined by more than a hundred chiefs from different regions, not only to praise the Holy Virgin but also to celebrate the religious and brotherly bonds between Portugal and Kongo. This event was sure to enhance the reputation of Portugal outside São Salvador, "thus facilitating our entry into less hospitable regions," as one priest put it. The annual celebration, he added, created "sympathy for all that is Portuguese."[127]

But the most important holiday of the year was the Assumption of Mary on 15 August, celebrated since 1904 at the new church of São Salvador. In 1912, almost two hundred chiefs from the wider Kongo region assembled in the capital, surrounded by catechists and about three thousand relatives and other followers, to attend the annual festival.[128] The scale of this official celebration was later trimmed down because the anti-clerical Republican government of Portugal (1910–26) reduced the funding of Catholic missions. In 1924, therefore, the Kongo community turned to the Feast of the Sacred Heart to celebrate the king and bless the lands of the kingdom.[129] These celebrations indicate that deep into the early twentieth century—longer than often assumed—the king remained a central figure in Kongo's Catholic cult, which chiefs and peasants kept up to address common worries about public health, fertility, and peace in general.

4

Portugal and
the Agua Rosada

In 1888, Portugal formally occupied São Salvador, a possession handed them at the Congo Conference in Berlin three years earlier, adding an administrative residence to the European trade and mission stations already established there.[1] Initially Portuguese ambitions in this part of Angola were limited to staking out sovereignty—especially in relation to the adjacent Congo Free State—and protecting local business interests, but after 1900 the colonial government's functions were extended to direct taxation and labor recruitment. For these and other tasks, the Portuguese relied on local intermediaries, which the kingdom provided. Members of the Agua Rosada and Kivuzi nobility, who had maintained close connections with Portugal since at least the mid-nineteenth century, often played the role of power brokers on behalf of their foreign patrons.[2]

In a famous essay, Terence Ranger argued that to co-opt local rulers many colonial regimes developed a concept of "Imperial Monarchy," emphasizing African assertions of kingliness and decorating chiefs and headmen "with some of the stage props of nineteenth-century European ceremonial drama."[3] In the kingdom of Kongo, nearly the opposite happened, as Africans themselves sustained an old monarchical tradition despite Portuguese efforts to curb royal power. Initially, Portugal invested substantial resources to enhance the prestige of Dom Pedro V (1860–91), whom they lavished with gifts from their own king and rewarded financially for his loyalty. In collaboration with the ruling Agua Rosada and Kivuzi houses, the colonial government also cultivated the principle of matrilineal descent as an established custom to determine royal successions (against an older tradition of throne rotation between competing factions) in order to create a dependable relationship between Portugal and Kongo's ruling families. From the beginning of his reign, Pedro V expertly negotiated state incomes and educational opportunities for his closest associates and relatives. With the arrival of traders and missionaries in São Salvador in the 1880s, economic and educational possibilities for Kongo elites increased even further. Yet the Agua Rosada family was able to exploit its clientship to Portugal in still another way, as the nascent colonial administration needed local agents to extend its influence in northern Angola, impose order along the trade routes, collect the hut tax, and mobilize labor for local factories. Both parties seemed to benefit from this relationship, as it strengthened the positions of the royal court and its European patron at the same time.

The extent to which the official Portuguese approach to the kingdom after 1900 was removed from established practice was therefore significant. In hopes of strengthening its grip on local power structures, the colonial government repeatedly proposed the abolition of Kongo's royal title and its supplementary privileges and the demotion of the king to the more humble and controllable position of *juiz popular* ("native judge"). Kongo's ruling elites observed these Portuguese initiatives critically. Not only did they understand that within the colonial system a *juiz popular* weighed less than a king, but more importantly, the official denial of kingship to the chief of São Salvador threatened to weaken the function of the *ntotela*, the ritually sanctioned ruler of the kingdom. Ultimately, however, Kongo's political tradition prevailed over imperial design, as the colonial government failed to undermine the allure of the royal office. Despite changes in the king's official title, the Kongo continued to believe in his power to provide peace, fertility, and protection from drought and epidemics, a power still celebrated in the 1920s, as noted in chapter 3. Significantly, because the rulers of São Salvador whom the Portuguese had formally appointed as "chiefs" or "judges" were still widely respected as *ntotela*, they were even granted the regalia that Portugal initially wanted to do away with.[4]

To analyze these and other complexities in the construction of colonial hegemony in northern Angola, this chapter first describes how Portugal re-occupied São Salvador in the wake of earlier attempts to intervene in Kongo politics through a state-funded Catholic mission. It then examines two case studies showing how members of the Agua Rosada house, sons of Pedro V, were able to gain influence as colonial intermediaries by dominating the coercive elements of state power. The third section analyzes the election of the first three Kongo kings succeeding Pedro V, who died in 1891, showing not only how Portuguese involvement in local succession disputes increased over time but also how under the impact of colonial rule Kongo elites changed their existing notions of honor. While the title of *ntotela* survived colonial attempts to abolish

it, investitures in the Order of Christ and other traditional titles lost part of
their glamour as local notables found new ways of manifesting power and
prestige. Individuals close to the center of imperial rule began to use ranks in
the colonial army as marks of honor, while for mission-educated young men
respectable lifestyles were mainly obtained by becoming a teacher, office clerk,
or trader in colonial society.[5]

The final section examines the complicated and drawn-out election of
Manuel Martins Kiditu in 1911. The political struggles preceding his election
pitted the Catholic and Baptist communities against one another. But they also
revealed popular discontent about recent kings who, under colonial tutelage,
had extended their political power at the expense of the people. Kiditu's election
can be read as an attempt on the part of both old and young elites, Catholic as
well as Protestant, to defend Kongo's tradition of kingship against an increasingly
interventionist colonial government.

Padre Barroso's Political Mission

While it is debatable to what extent missionaries in Africa represented the
economic agendas of imperial governments and businessmen back home, there
can be little doubt that, in the 1880s, priests were the main agents defending
Portuguese colonial interests in the lower Congo region.[6] Adopting a new policy
of territorial contraction in Angola, in 1870 the Portuguese government ended
its decade-long military presence in São Salvador, leaving Dom Pedro V without
colonial troops to back up his fragile authority. Governor-General Francisco
Cardoso argued at the time that there were few benefits to staying in the kingdom, as "the Kongo has not the least importance, politically or economically,"
for Portugal.[7] When industrially powerful nations from northern Europe began
to assert their presence in the lower Congo, however, an influential lobby of
Lisbon traders and industrialists forced their government to articulate Portugal's
ancient connections to the Kongo kingdom and protect their economic interests
in the region.[8] The establishment, in 1880, of a Catholic mission in São Salvador
was a political response to the previous arrival of British missionaries of the
BMS, who were seen as a direct threat to Portugal's "historical" claims to
Kongo lands. As the Angolan governor argued, the Baptist mission was there
"to prepare [Africans] for an English occupation."[9] In fact, during the European
scramble for Africa, the main task of Padre António Barroso, the head of the
Portuguese mission, was to monitor the movement of foreign explorers and
missionaries in the African interior and see what influence their local protégé,
Dom Pedro V, could exert on chiefs on the lower Congo River, the focal point
of international competition.[10]

Pedro V was therefore critical to Portuguese efforts to shape political developments north of Angola. Although the king's authority in the region was limited, his loyalty was Portugal's main trump card in the European race for the Congo. At the same time, Pedro hoped to extend his own influence in Kongo by allying himself to Portugal. Thus, in 1884, shortly before the Berlin Conference, the Portuguese employed the king in their effort to stop the flurry of treaties Henry Morton Stanley was signing with Kongo chiefs on behalf of the International African Association. Dom Álvaro, Pedro's son and secretary, protested in writing against the cession of land rights to the Association by Palabala, whose rulers received their chiefly powers from the king of Kongo but were otherwise independent of São Salvador.[11] In early 1885, furthermore, Pedro sent embassies to his alleged "vassals" on the Atlantic coast and the banks of the lower Congo, offering them the protection and prestige of an alliance with Portugal. These rulers had found more attractive patrons, however, in the foreign trade houses established there.[12]

The king's devotion to promoting Portugal's imperial agenda came with a price tag. For instance, the presents Pedro V received in 1883 from the Catholic mission alone were valued at a hundred *milreis* (about twenty-two pounds sterling) per month.[13] When the king ordered luxury items for himself, he usually asked his Portuguese benefactors to include presents for other Kongo notables, too.[14] Pedro would then make sure his clients knew where these lavish gifts came from. On the birthday of Luís I of Portugal in 1884, for example, he treated his followers to "an abundant dinner" in his *lumbu* (royal enclosure), where traditional foods were mixed with imported cans of fruit and fish, so that they, too, "celebrated this day with great enthusiasm and happiness."[15] In other words, the king stood at the center of a distribution network that provided Portugal the loyalty of a small segment of the Kongo nobility in exchange for prestige goods.

But Pedro V wanted military support more than he craved fine goods. On several occasions before the colonial partition of Africa, Pedro asked Portugal to bring back their troops to São Salvador. In 1883, he explained in a letter to the governor of Angola, Francisco Ferreira do Amaral, that "for sustaining my influence among the peoples inland and for the peace among my subjects it would be convenient to have a permanent military force close to me, so that I will not lose my authority over some people who, seeing me without the powerful support of the Portuguese, have not always submitted quietly to my orders."[16] Amaral was unable to answer Pedro's request favorably, as Portugal was not in a position to force their will in the ongoing European negotiations over the Congo. Shortly after the Congo Conference ended in 1885, the governor was more receptive to Pedro's continuing pleas, although he was in no hurry to occupy São Salvador now that Europe's major powers had deferred to Portugal's "rightful" claims to land in northern Angola. The new governor-general of Angola, Guilherme Augusto de Brito Capelo, likewise opined that the king was only interested in colonial troops for his own safety, while a de facto submission of the Kongo kingdom to Portugal would never happen "except through force."[17] In a sense, the wars that ravaged Kongo in 1914–15 would prove the governor right.

Despite these outward signs of dependency, it would be incongruous to describe Dom Pedro V as a puppet of the Portuguese regime in Angola. In 1885, the German traveler Chavanne observed that the king manipulated the British missionary presence to wring favors from the Catholic missionaries. "The king is no fool as a politician, [and] with an African-born shrewdness he sees right through the . . . outside appearance of harmony between both missions and gains profusely from that."[18] Padre Barroso, who was among Pedro's foremost advisors and edited many of his letters, grew increasingly frustrated with the limited influence he was able to exert on the king.[19] Although revered among Christians throughout Kongo, Barroso was unable to earn Pedro's undivided loyalty, to fit him in a modern Catholic straitjacket, or to stop the rising influence of the BMS in São Salvador.

By 1887, the Angolan bishop, António, realized that Portugal's mission to the Kongo kingdom was not delivering the desired results. The padres were neither able to compete with the BMS, which gained increasing popularity through their medical dispensary and employment of female missionaries, nor control the social habits of the Kongo elite. As the bishop explained:

> On the religious side, the king who was already Catholic long before the establishment of the mission there . . . now wants to marry and [our] superior [Barroso] is not sure whether to receive him, because he does not know if he is Catholic or not. The rest of the old Christian community is in the same state or worse. Nobody is admitted to Holy Communion, including the king. On the political side, padre Barroso declares that his continuation in S Salvador does not serve [our] political interests and that his influence there would even be damaging to those interests.[20]

Two years later, a disappointed Barroso left Angola to embark on a more glorious career elsewhere in the Portuguese empire.

In August 1888, just before Barroso's departure from Kongo, the colonial government stationed fifty soldiers in São Salvador, responding to rumors that a political faction led by Dom Rafael of Kunga was planning a coup to regain the throne it had lost to Pedro V in 1860. It thus seemed that Pedro had it his way after all. However, because the colonial government was now sovereign in São Salvador, the king lost the authority to levy tribute from passing rubber caravans and extract rents from local trade factories. In compensation, Portugal awarded him a monthly stipend of thirty thousand *reis* (about seven pounds sterling), a small sum compared to his earlier revenues.[21] From that point on, the colonial administration, instead of the priests, would be in charge of sustaining São Salvador's network of patronage, although the government in Luanda continued to dispense goods to Kongo's ruling class through the Catholic mission for at least another decade.[22] Members of the king's household would play important roles in the extension of state power in northern Angola. Especially the Agua Rosada sons of Pedro V were able to advance their careers by occupying key positions in the nascent colonial government, as two cases discussed below demonstrate.

Colonial Intermediaries

In November 1894, the colonial government started an inquiry into the conduct of three Portuguese employees in the administration of São Salvador.[23] Headquarters in Luanda had been alarmed by rumors that these officials had engaged in homosexual acts and human trafficking, and that they were responsible for the misconduct of locally stationed African troops. Investigators also queried witnesses about stories that adult women were living at the Catholic mission and that priests had bought slaves pledged in a royal palaver. The witnesses— fourteen Africans and six Portuguese missionaries and traders—gave different and sometimes conflicting accounts of the events they were asked about, and in the end the inquiry produced little conclusive evidence for or against the Portuguese officials. Together, however, these testimonies convey an intimate view of the social landscape of São Salvador in the first decade of colonial rule. Previous chapters have already mentioned the case of Diancuaco, the female slave of a Portuguese trader and his Kongo mistress, and the recruitment of slaves by the Catholic mission. The focus here is on the main event discussed in the inquiry, the theft and recovery of European mailbags, which illustrates the important role of the Agua Rosada in the exercise of state-sponsored violence in northern Angola.

The event took place in 1892, when the administration of São Salvador organized a police campaign to recover a number of stolen mailbags from villages along the road to Noqui. There were strong suspicions that Africans had been enslaved during the police raid and that local administrators had been complicit in the seizure of slaves. As discussed in chapter 2, the 1880s were tumultuous times for communities along the caravan road between São Salvador and Noqui. Located on the south bank of the lower Congo River, some seventy miles from its estuary, Noqui was fast becoming the main outlet for northern Angola's export trade. On a daily basis, groups of carriers brought rubber, ivory, coffee, peanuts, and palm produce to factories in Noqui, where these products were loaded on ships destined to Liverpool, Rotterdam, and other ports in Europe. It seems the carriers' desire for female companionship along the road caused friction with some of the village elders, who occasionally arrested passing trade caravans. In February 1892, the newly appointed administrator of São Salvador, Francisco João de França, paid these villages a visit with a small military detachment warning them to keep the roads open.[21] But hostilities between the local chiefs and the trading community of São Salvador continued.

In June, conflict erupted again as a group of carriers transporting mailbags from Noqui to São Salvador was taken hostage in the town of Congo dia Ntino. Only a few years earlier, a military expedition from the Kongo capital had punished the chiefs of Congo dia Ntino for obstructing transit to the lower river. This time, the administration of São Salvador dispatched a force of seventy-six soldiers, many armed with Snider-Enfield rifles, to recover the stolen mailbags and liberate the hostages. As the soldiers carried out their mission, they burned a number of hamlets, arrested five chiefs, confiscated valuable trade goods, and killed some of the alleged "rebels" (*salteadores*). Manpower for this rescue mission was mainly supplied by the incumbent king, Dom Álvaro de Agua Rosada (1891–96), and Dom Henrique de Agua Rosada, son of the late Pedro V.[25] This was not the first time that the royal family had participated in a conflict between their European patrons and independent Kongo authorities. In March 1884, for instance, Pedro V united several chiefs from his district to build a militia of a thousand men to descend on Noqui, whose rulers had blocked the exit roads to São Salvador because of an ongoing dispute with the local merchant community.[26] For the Agua Rosada and their followers, the connection with gun-supplying factories provided opportunities to assert power in ways unimaginable a decade earlier.

The key figure in the police raid on Congo dia Ntino in 1892 was Dom Henrique de Agua Rosada, an elder son of Pedro V. About forty years old, Henrique had ably profited from the professional opportunities the new European presence in São Salvador afforded the descendants of Kongo's ruling families. Henrique began his colonial career around 1880 as an interpreter for the BMS but later became a Catholic school teacher in the parish of Encoge on the southern fringes of Kongo. Upon his return to São Salvador, he first worked as caravan headman (*capata*) on the Noqui line alongside his relative, Dom António de Agua Rosada, and then as police officer (*oficial de diligências*) for the colonial administration, a position previously held by another one of his relatives, Pedro de Agua Rosada Júnior. Henrique was a respected man in town, going

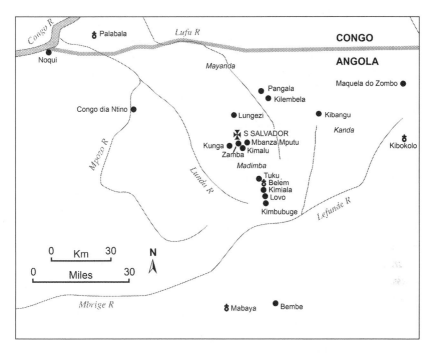

São Salvador district, ca. 1900

by the name of Cavalheiro (nobleman), and had accrued a number of followers.[27] He not only provided men for the expedition to Congo dia Ntino, like king Álvaro, but also joined the mission in person. Rumor had it that the resident, França, had given volunteers the promise of booty, including slaves. This was denied by Henrique himself, but according to another witness in the inquiry, Padre Luís António Pequito, captives were taken and brought to São Salvador.

The investigators wanted to know whether the now ex-resident of São Salvador, Francisco João de França, had taken any action against this and other cases of human trafficking in his district. Pequito claimed that França had released some of the captives taken during the raid but otherwise showed little interest in "native questions," including those involving slaves. Other witnesses were of the opinion that França's attitude to slavery was inconsistent, and that he did little to stop slave transactions when the royal family was involved. For instance, he confiscated a woman seized by a local headman, Dom André, during the raid on Congo dia Ntino. When the same Dom André purchased an insubordinate pupil from the Catholic mission, França ordered the boy's immediate release from bondage. But when a court servant, named Cabinda, complained at the Portuguese residence that a younger son of Pedro V,

Dom Henrique Malevo, had captured two of his children, França decreed that only one was to be returned to Cabinda. As for rumors that França sexually abused his African employees and other young townsmen, Pedro de Agua Rosada Júnior claimed that he was dismissed from his function as police officer because he rejected the advances of his superior. Many witnesses confirmed this and other stories about Franca's sexual behavior, with the most interesting opinion coming from Dom Henrique Cavalheiro, who stated that if França had intimate encounters with other men, it would have been "with people of his house, but never with people from Kongo." The questioning of witnesses on França's homosexual encounters led to unexpected findings regarding the issue of slavery. According to a former scribe of the administration, França once sent Henrique Cavalheiro and his brother António de Agua Rosada to Diadia, a market on the road to Noqui, to purchase two boys for his household. The boys later ran away from the residence but were recaptured with the help of the king of Kongo. This example shows that not only European traders but also colonial administrators relied on local slave markets to recruit domestic servants.

While the inquiry was primarily concerned with the conduct of Portuguese administrators, by investigating slave transactions it incidentally conveyed the central position of the Agua Rosada family in the everyday affairs of the São Salvador community. As the colonial momentum gained pace in the late 1870s, opportunities for members of Kongo's ruling family to enlarge their wealth and power increased. Agua Rosada men were among the first to serve as interpreters and caravan leaders for missions and trade factories, receive missionary education, and occupy jobs in the nascent colonial administration. These government posts were particularly related to the coercive elements of state power: the police and the army.

One of the most notable mediators in the employ of the European community in the kingdom was Dom Álvaro de Agua Rosada, alias Tangi. Like the aforementioned Malevo, Tangi was a younger son of Pedro V. Baptist missionaries saw them both around 1880, then still young lads, sitting with their father as he received clients in need of a favor or wanting to discuss business with him. Henrique Malevo, the elder of the two, was soon hired by the BMS as an interpreter on their caravan journeys; he would later become a government employee, tasked, among other things, with compiling population registers for the hut tax.[28] Tangi, by contrast, went to study at the Catholic mission under Padre Barroso, who took him to Lisbon in 1888 to develop his language skills and knowledge of Portuguese culture. Shortly afterward, he was appointed lieutenant in the so-called *segunda linha*, the auxiliary troops of the colonial army. In this role, he negotiated the establishment of trade factories and a government post with the rubber-trading chiefs of Maquela do Zombo in the mid-1890s, and then helped the Portuguese administration expand further east toward the Kwango. Later he settled as chief in Kaio, a township along the Maquela road, close to the border with the Congo Free State. In these eastern parts, he was known as a *mundele andombe*, a black white man, the name people gave to Africans who dressed and behaved like their colonial patrons.[29]

Tangi became a formidable power broker for Portugal in the contested frontier zone between Angola and the Congo Free State. Since the Berlin Conference, these two colonial regimes had been competing for control over local supplies of labor and wild rubber.[30] While the Congo Free State mainly depended on the might of its colonial army, the Force Publique, to exact loyalties from local chiefs, Portugal relied more on the network of patronage radiating out from São Salvador to gain hegemony. Because the border between Angola and the Free State was not clearly demarcated until at least 1913, soldiers of the Force Publique easily walked into Angolan territory to recruit carriers, whereas Portuguese factories in São Salvador and Maquela do Zombo often sent their recruitment agents to villages in the Free State. In 1907, the governor of the Free State complained that near the border post of Tumba-Mani "black agents travel up and down between the villages, probably sent by Portuguese traders, searching for carriers for the Noqui-Maquela line, and even use threats to put the natives at their service."[31] Village elders were often forced to supply carriers in order to pay for prestige goods that factory agents had offered them on credit. Some of the "black agents" in European employ were chiefs themselves, like Dom Mateso, who around 1901 had moved his village from the Free State to Angola and regularly supplied carriers to a Portuguese trade house in Maquela do Zombo.[32] Others were African employees in the Angolan colonial army, like Tangi, who placed themselves in the service of factories in Maquela.[33]

For settlements in this frontier zone, these were stressful times, as armed groups raided villages on both sides of the border to steal people and property—especially rubber—and assert claims of authority. Tangi established his reputation as a *mundele andombe* in this environment. In 1895, he offered his protection to Zombo chiefs trying to shield their people from abduction by agents from the Free State. Three years later, soldiers of the Force Publique captured Tangi near Ngombe, in the Free State, while he was instigating local chiefs to resist State demands for carriers. According to one witness, Tangi told village elders to ignore "the white man of Bula Matari" (the Kongo name for the Congo Free State) because they were the "children" of the Portuguese resident in São Salvador.[34] Tangi thus enunciated new bonds of patronage between Kongo chiefs and the colonial authorities in São Salvador, based on older liaisons between these same chiefs and the Kongo kingdom. His tactics were not

Chief Mazamba, 1906 (Biblioteca Nacional de Portugal, A. Matta, "Álbum sobre o Congo português e belga")

everywhere effective, as some chiefs saw him as a troublemaker. In 1899, for instance, Tangi visited Luvaka, a border town twice invaded by the Force Publique, where he drafted two children for the Catholic school in São Salvador but failed to open the area to the Portuguese mission.[35] Chiefs also rejected Tangi's claims to paramountcy based on his descent from Pedro V, the late king of Kongo.[36] Nevertheless, most chiefs in this borderland seemed to prefer the patronage of São Salvador to the violence of the Force Publique. For some of them the shock was great when officials in charge of demarcating the colonial border told them their villages fell under Free State authority. These chiefs claimed kinship ties to a current or former king of Kongo, identified as Christians, and had long since supplied carriers to São Salvador. They hoisted Portuguese flags—obtained from people like Tangi—to symbolize their loyalty and keep the slavery associated with the Free State at bay.[37]

Three Kongo Kings

In extending their own lines of patronage and power, the Agua Rosada family also advanced Portugal's influence in northern Angola. It therefore became increasingly important for the colonial government to control royal successions in São Salvador, in order to make sure their allies stayed in power. To keep rival factions from making legitimate claims to the throne, the united Agua

Rosada and Kivuzi clans, which were both based in the Madimba district south of the capital, pretended that succession was in principle hereditary, invoking notions of matrilineality that regulated family affairs throughout West Central Africa.[38] While this proved an effective strategy overall, it created problems of its own. Candidates favored by either Portugal or the Kongo electorate often lacked the ideal prerequisites for kingship, because they had mixed religious backgrounds or did not fully conform to the principle of matrilineal descent. Once in power, moreover, kings often advanced their own political agendas, provoking unrest among the kingdom's constituency, whereas Portugal wanted reliable rulers who would not upset the political status quo. In short, colonial hegemony in Kongo had to be continuously improvised, as Portugal and the Agua Rosada depended on one another and neither party was able to control events completely.

Within weeks after Pedro V's passing in February 1891, a committee of royal counselors and chiefs from around São Salvador elected Pedro's nephew, Mfutila Dom Álvaro de Agua Rosada Nginga Nkanga, as the new king. Before his election, Álvaro was a paramount chief in Madimba, co-ruling about sixty townships with two social partners, one of whom was an elder son of Pedro V.[39] His election was quick but not undisputed. At first, the authorities in São Salvador feared protests from Dom Rafael, based nearby in Kunga, but his clan decided to keep quiet. The group behind another old foe, Dom Garcia Mbumba of Mbanza Mputu, did put in a claim for the throne. For the Portuguese, however, Mbumba was unelectable: not only did he represent a different clan, he had also converted to the Baptist Church, and so his loyalties seemed to spread in dangerous directions. Coached by the Protestant evangelist Nlekai, who was himself a scion of the Kongo aristocracy, Mbumba withdrew his candidacy to avoid a war of succession. In compensation, he received the title of *noso mpidisipi*, granting him a privileged position at the royal court, though it appears he had little respect for the kings succeeding Pedro V.[40]

The Portuguese authorities supported the election of Álvaro XIV, but their relationship with the new king soon proved as ambivalent as it had been with his predecessor. They occasionally relied on the king for military support (Álvaro supported police campaigns to Congo dia Ntino in 1892 and Mbanza Mateca and Conco in 1896) and in return awarded him an honorary rank in the colonial army.[41] But the government was unable to fit the king into a Luso-colonial straitjacket. Álvaro was nominally Catholic and let his sons study at the mission, but his ties to the Church proved very loose; by the time of his death in 1896, he had not received any of the sacraments. More troublesome than his lack of faith in the work of the Catholic priests, however, were his efforts to exploit his rivals through the kingdom's judicial system. Toward the end of Álvaro's reign, a new Portuguese resident, José Heliodoro de Faria Leal, lamented the government's inability to end the custom of royal palavers (*fundações*) by which kings administered justice and amassed wealth. Given that Portugal supported their reign, the Agua Rosada were supposed to rule as "modern" chiefs and not as "absolutist" despots, as he put it. The Baptist missionaries saw the king as a "hard, disagreeable man." In fact, according to one eyewitness, Álvaro resented any kind of outside interference in his business and near the end of his life was prepared to purge all Europeans from the kingdom.[12]

Álvaro was the only colonial king whose election went according to "custom." When he died in 1896, at age forty-five, there was no candidate fulfilling the ideal prerequisites of matrilineal descent. Dom Pedro de Agua Rosada Lelo, a seven-year-old boy from Madimba, came closest to being the king's "natural" heir. Lelo was a nephew of Álvaro XIV through his father and a grandson of Pedro V through his mother. Through his father, Dom Nicolau of Lendi, Lelo was also affiliated with the Baptist Church, although the counselors did not consider this a problem. His age was, however, and it was decided to postpone Lelo's installation and appoint a regent in his stead. The colonial government arranged a Catholic education for Lelo with the Holy Ghost Fathers in Huila, in southern Angola, to wean him from the Baptist missionaries. While his return to São Salvador was often considered, it never happened. After Lelo had finished his studies at the Huila seminary, in 1905, the government decided to keep him in southern Angola to prevent him from occupying the Kongo throne. Especially Resident Faria Leal doubted the dependability of a young educated nobleman who had already seen too much of the world to accept the role of client king quietly. After leaving the seminary, Lelo became a police officer in Mossâmedes and later postmaster in Lubango, a function he abandoned in 1911 amid rumors of anti-colonial agitation.[13]

At first, Faria Leal had one of his own protégés in mind for the position of regent, namely Pedro Kavungu Kalandenda, who was Lelo's uncle. A São Salvador native, educated at the Baptist mission and now in his mid-twenties, Kalandenda worked as a translator for the colonial government. Although drink and polygyny had cost him his church membership, Kalandenda refused to convert to Catholicism, a necessary requirement for kingship. This cleared the way for Dom Henrique Nteyekenge Kondwa, a twenty-three-year-old Kivuzi born in Madimba, second cousin of the late Álvaro XIV, and nominally Catholic.[14]

Nteyekenge did not hold any political title before his appointment as regent, but the carrying trade had turned him into a man of considerable standing in São Salvador. Indeed, his work as a commodity and palanquin porter had earned him enough wealth to create a household like that of any well-respected

Kongo elder. Once in office, he used the emerging structures of colonial rule to increase his social and political power. In 1898, for instance, Faria Leal gave the king permission to conscript criminals and other outcasts for military service outside the Kongo kingdom. With the help of his associates in Madimba, Nteyekenge went beyond his mandate and began to recruit people at random in the name of the government. This provoked a revolt among a number of Kongo chiefs, in particular the ruler of Mateca, who had earlier collided with Álvaro XIV and whose men were now deported as forced laborers to Cabinda.[45] The colonial government generally abstained from intervening in the political affairs of the king, especially when its own interests were not directly affected. Records of the BMS suggest, nonetheless, that under British pressure the administration often forced Nteyekenge to release women and slaves he collected from trade caravans and neighboring villages.[46]

After Nteyekenge's passing, in 1901, the colonial administration asked the royal council to recommend another interim ruler, while Lelo was still in Huila. The council was unable to reach an agreement about two early contenders, Dom Álvaro de Agua Rosada Tangi and Mfutila Dom Garcia Kibelongo, the chief of Kimiala in Madimba, who, like his brother, the late Álvaro XIV, demonstrated some unease about Portuguese rule in Kongo.[47] The administration therefore backed the candidacy of a third contender, Pedro de Agua Rosada Mbemba, the *nenkondo* (count) of Tuku in Madimba. The Portuguese perceived Mbemba as "an ordinary heathen and nominal Roman Catholic," ignoring the fact that he had been baptized in the Baptist Church in 1888. But Mbemba had since "backslidden through polygamy" and lost his church membership, which facilitated his formal conversion to Catholicism upon his installation in May 1901.[48]

Mbemba maintained his relations with the Baptist missionaries and often sought their advice, until he aligned his interests more closely with those of his Portuguese benefactors.[49] Using missionary channels to extend his influence in the region, in 1905 he endorsed the creation of twenty Catholic schools in the countryside around São Salvador. Conflicts with other chiefs now began to unfold along religious lines. In 1907, for instance, Mbemba warned the chief of Lungezi, an ally of the Baptist Church, that to retain his title he should convert to Catholicism.[50] Threats like these stemmed from old political oppositions within the kingdom but also reflected a growing religious division in Kongo society in the early 1900s. Significantly, Mbemba also oversaw the introduction of the hut tax, which further tightened his bonds with the colonial government and weakened his allegiance to the kingdom's constituency.

None of the successors of Álvaro XIV was officially recognized as king. In fact, the colonial administration saw in the absence of Dom Pedro Lelo an opportunity to eliminate the royal office. Administrators were convinced the kingdom was already a fading institution, which could be eradicated by withholding the royal title from candidates who were not more than substitutes for the "legitimate" heir to the throne, who was biding his time in southern Angola. As Governor-General Brito Capelo explained to his superiors in 1896, Nteyekenge was merely appointed as chief of São Salvador, "without the treatment of king, in order to slowly put an end to these old customs."[51] As chief, his official function was to take care of "native questions of little importance" until Lelo reached adulthood.[52] His successor, Pedro Mbemba, was appointed as *juiz popular*, a new title for African chiefs, which included a monthly salary of ten thousand *reis*, a third of the stipend previously dished out to kings.[53] While the colonial government thus tried to devalue the position of highest chief in the capital, the Kongo populace nonetheless saw Nteyekenge and Mbemba as traditional kings, *ntotela*, because they were installed as rulers of São Salvador and also behaved as such. The colonial government realized, in fact, how difficult it was to convert its official abolitionist doctrine into practice. Even in official correspondence, administrators referred to both rulers as "kings," while Mbemba was eventually awarded a royal stipend in accordance with the respect he received from his constituency. Ultimately, the two kings were buried at the royal cemetery as Henrique III and Pedro VI, with their coffins traditionally wrapped in velvet cloth offered by the king of Portugal.[54]

At the same time, kings and other men of power found new ways of expressing their status under colonial rule. While the old Order of Christ still carried prestige among many Kongo chiefs, elites who had been co-opted by the colonial state started looking for new titles of distinction to demonstrate authority. During the reign of Álvaro XIV (1891–96), a remarkable fashion for colonial military titles took hold of the Kongo ruling class. Álvaro himself obtained the honorary rank of colonel in the colonial army, and his successor, Henrique Nteyekenge, was awarded a similar title. In 1903, Mbemba received the title of major and an army uniform to affirm his status, while two years later he was promoted to lieutenant colonel. As he himself explained, he wanted a military rank to "earn the respect of my subjects."[55] For other notables, like Álvaro Tangi or Dom André de Souza Soqui, the rank of lieutenant involved the performance of actual military duties, which were especially related to maintaining order and the recruitment of labor.[56] The distribution of such titles can be explained as an attempt by the government to socialize an African ruling class through the colonial army, as Terence Ranger has suggested.[57] Significantly, however, the initiative for these decorations often came from the recipients themselves. The fact that Mbemba also lobbied for military titles on behalf of his followers indicates that for the Agua Rosada and Kivuzi families

Funeral of Dom Pedro Mbemba, 1910 (photo by unknown author, private collection, reproduced with permission of José Carlos de Oliveira)

these titles carried importance.[58] Acutely aware of the colonial transformation of the kingdom and the future role of the Portuguese government in shaping society, they coveted imperial honors to affirm their authority in a changing political environment.

The Election of Manuel Martins Kiditu

The election of a new king upon the death of Mbemba in June 1910 was for the first time disputed along church lines. There was a growing division within the kingdom between Baptist and Catholic communities, as local elites had begun to use ecclesiastical channels to articulate their agendas. "All native questions in São Salvador are influenced by the missions," commented José dos Santos, interim administrator at the time.[59] Early in July, the administrator invited two parties to his residency to discuss potential candidates for the throne. One group, rooted in the Baptist Church, still considered Pedro Lelo the legitimate king of Kongo. The other faction, based in the Catholic Church, thought Lelo's long absence from São Salvador had made him a stranger to the community and recommended Manuel Martins Kiditu, a Kivuzi from Madimba and a distant relative of the late Mbemba.[60] As the conference reached an impasse, a committee of royal counselors argued that, in matrilineal terms, the most legitimate successor of Mbemba would in fact be his nephew, a twenty-one-year-old trader named Manuel Fernandes Komba. Some of the Catholics but none of the Baptists agreed; after all, Mbemba himself had only been king in Lelo's absence. The resident believed the Protestants were under the sway of Lelo's uncle, Pedro Kalandenda, a prominent figure in the community who stood to gain politically if his nephew were elected king. Dos Santos warned his superiors about the risks of appointing a candidate supported by the Baptist community. "It is known that there is an almost complete separation between the natives affiliated with the two missions and . . . that for the natives being Protestant is being English . . . In São Salvador the disputes between the missions are not religious questions, but real political struggles."[61] His advice was therefore to appoint Komba and prevent Lelo from returning to the kingdom.

Political turmoil in Europe added fuel to the fire, as the Republican revolution in Portugal in October 1910 strengthened the anti-monarchical tendencies of colonial administrators in Angola. District Governor José Cardoso, for instance, believed Portugal's generous treatment of Mbemba had inflated the importance of the chief of São Salvador; he suggested the government appoint Komba as *juiz popular* with a monthly salary of fifteen thousand reis.[62] In Kongo, the establishment of the Portuguese Republic appeared to have little effect "on the position and dignity of the King," as one missionary put it.[63] But the anti-clerical and anti-royalist tendencies of the revolution in Portugal were bound to influence the rivalry between Protestant and Catholic groups.[64] The Republican movement specifically threatened to undermine the old triangular bond between Kongo, Portugal, and the Catholic Church, giving members of the Baptist Church a chance to use their association with the United Kingdom to lay an exclusive claim on Kongo's monarchical tradition.

The force of this ideological battle was revealed at the funeral of a Catholic woman in Conco in December 1910. When a young catechist from São Salvador, Nensala, urged a BMS evangelist from Lungezi, Sebastião Kapela, to take off his hat out of respect for the deceased, Kapela retorted that he did not take orders from a junior and had lost all respect for crucifixes and other Catholic symbols. In his opinion, the Catholics were a kingless lot; without their king, the priests would soon be leaving and the country would remain in English hands.[65] The larger issue at stake in this altercation, which itself never became more than a fistfight, was not the survival of the kingdom but rather the definition of Christianity within it. For centuries, Catholic symbols had been central to Kongo political culture, with kings and other noblemen invoking Catholic priests, Portuguese monarchs, and the cross to legitimize their rule. Now several influential chiefs, including Garcia Mbumba of Mbanza Mputu and Rafael Badi of Lungezi, had joined another Christian tradition that rejected the special status of the clergy and the power of the cross. This religious bifurcation did not undermine the status of the king or his Christian identity in Kongo, but it challenged the dominance of the Catholic cult in Kongo politics.

Precipitation by Komba ultimately pulled the two opposing camps out of their stalemate. The counselors of the late Pedro VI urged the colonial authorities to settle the matter swiftly, for the lack of a king was creating unrest among chiefs in the Kongo realm. The government itself also wanted the election resolved, because it needed a supreme ruler to mediate with a growing number of chiefs who had risen against the hut tax.[66] The election finally moved forward when Komba made the mistake, in early 1911, of occupying the royal enclosure and proclaiming himself king. This caused a stir among both Catholics and Protestants, as neither group had unanimously accepted his candidacy, which was now seen as an imposition from outside. In April, counselors and representatives from both parties came to inform Resident Faria Leal, who had returned from leave in Portugal, that they all wanted Komba out of the *lumbu* and accepted Manuel Martins Kiditu as the best available candidate.[67]

Kiditu was in many ways a product of Portuguese colonialism. Born around 1872 in the village of Lunda to Isabel Diaquenza, a peasant woman of significant standing, Kiditu entered the Catholic mission as a young boy and became one of the priests' favorite protégés. In 1893, he traveled to Luanda in the company of Padre Albuquerque and King Álvaro XIV, who considered him still a *moleque*, a young lad.[68] The following year, at the age of twenty-two, he married in the Church to Maria Tombe from Tuku, a royal stronghold in Madimba. After completing his Catholic education, he began working as a stonemason and interpreter for David de Medina, a Portuguese businessman in Maquela do Zombo; by 1909, back in São Salvador and already widowed, he was trading on his own account.[69] Faria Leal probably knew Kiditu personally and did not object to his candidacy, but in the Republican spirit he could not appoint him as *ntotela*. Despite local protestations that "all people have a chief who represents them," that is, a ruler traditionally invested with the powers to protect his people, Kiditu's function would be that of *juiz popular* without the stipend of a king.[70]

According to a Kongo manuscript from the 1920s, Kiditu was generally respected for being "wise in the ways and customs of the white men."[71] Local elites had nonetheless grown wary of the corrupting influence of colonial power on the royal office. In a meeting with the resident, two spokesmen for the Baptist community, Pedro Nefwane Talanga and William Mantu Parkinson (the BMS's first convert, recently returned from Belgian Congo, at that point a trader in

Manuel Martins Kiditu and entourage, ca. 1912 (Arquivo Histórico Militar, Veloso e Castro collection, PT/AHM/FE/CAVE/VC/A10/Álbum A10/2306; © AHM)

São Salvador), revealed the dissatisfaction of the Kongo populace with previous titleholders, whose reputations were tainted by the royal court's extortion of fines, taxes, and labor for military recruitment. Like other traditional rulers in colonial Africa, the Kongo kings had lost their sovereignty under European domination, but they had gained power at the expense of their own people. The Baptist community demanded an assurance in writing from the new king that he would not exploit his powers in the vein of his immediate predecessors, and also insisted on the appointment of several new counselors to keep the king in check. Before his installation, therefore, Kiditu had to sign a declaration in Portuguese, written in short and simple sentences, which imposed six conditions on his reign.[72]

The first rule imposed on Kiditu stated that the king was not allowed to fine anyone without the consent of his counselors. Secondly, he must not oppose any religion, for religious practice was free. This condition was a direct reference to the agreements of the Berlin Conference, which protected the freedom of religion in the Congo Basin, including northern Angola; it was probably inserted at the request of the BMS, whose followers had suffered the intimidations of Pedro Mbemba, a Catholic. Third, the king had to announce his policies officially, so that he could not send out his tax collectors at random, for example.

The fourth condition stated that Kiditu had to love and be good to all people. While this might sound like a nebulous description of the king's basic duty to protect his subjects, the ideal of love and peace was, in fact, a recurring theme in the coronation oaths of Kongo kings since the seventeenth century. For example, Pedro II had to swear before his installation in 1622 that he would treat his subjects like a father, while in 1764, Álvaro XI was told not to misuse his powers and to rectify the abuses then current in the kingdom.[73] In a similar vein, the fifth condition imposed on Kiditu read that he must stop the ongoing exploitation of the Kongo people. Finally, the king acknowledged that disobedience of these rules would lead to his expulsion.

By putting his signature under these conditions, Kiditu accepted the rules of conduct imposed on him. While these rules were based on notions of proper political behavior that were deeply embedded in Kongo political culture, the elites articulating them were products of the modern colonial missions.[74] The newly elected royal council consisted of an equal mixture of Catholic and Baptist church members. The Catholic community was represented by two sons of the late king Álvaro—Henrique Lunga, a tailor, and Feliciano dos Santos Rosa Nembamba, stonemason—and by Manuel Lopes de Almeida, a former counselor under Pedro Mbemba.[75] While the brothers' inclusion signaled the arrival of a new generation in Kongo politics, through them, the Madimba aristocracy was still able to hold a firm grip on the royal court. Feliciano Rosa's biography conveys how narrow the bonds between the ruling clans of the Madimba district were. Born in Kimiala in the early 1880s, Feliciano entered the Catholic mission school in São Salvador in 1890; in 1906, he married a distant cousin, Isabel Diamuene, the daughter of Pedro de Agua Rosada, son of Pedro V.[76] Significantly, the presence at the royal court of three new Protestant counselors—Pedro Talanga, José David Nlandu, and William Parkinson—ensured that other outlying districts of the kingdom, where the Baptist Church was more firmly established, also had a voice in Kongo politics.

On 1 July 1911 Kiditu was invested as chief of São Salvador, initially without the crown, scepter, and ermine mantle that his predecessors had still been allowed to use, but which the Republican government had confiscated along with the other regalia, as Kiditu was officially appointed as *juiz popular*. His installation developed into a remarkable spectacle, which reflected a meeting of different political ideologies and cultural fashions. Kiditu, dressed in a jacket with a hat and cane, resembling a modern Kongo gentleman, was seconded by two senior relatives from Madimba, Tulante Buta of Lovo and Mfutila of Zamba, who carried old Kongo swords of status.[77] In a published photograph of the event, these two prominent chiefs can be seen wearing a combination of European dress and wrappers made of local cloth. A group of mission-educated

Ceremony at the installation of Kiditu, 1911: Mfutila of Zamba (*left*) and Tulante Álvaro Buta (*right*) (Leo Bittremieux, "Overblijfselen van den katholieken Godsdienst in Lager Kongoland," *Anthropos* 21 [1926]: 804 5)

men in European outfits, probably including some of the new royal counselors, and three white men representing Portuguese rule in Kongo surrounded the two chiefs as they carried out a *sangamento*, a ritual performance that sanctioned the rule of kings.[78] Kiditu's election, as depicted in this image, symbolized the convergence of old and new customs, as traditional chiefs and young modernized elites both tried to keep the kingdom from falling under the pressure of European colonial rule. Unfortunately, some of the same elites would be liable to the further corruption of the royal office in subsequent years.

Conclusion

The installation of Manuel Martins Kiditu in 1911 affirmed the arrival of a new, mission-educated political class in São Salvador. Whereas in the 1880s royal counselors had been among the first to convert in the new Christian missions, the counselors surrounding Kiditu were actual products of missionary education, as was the king himself. This new elite represented a generation that had embraced the cultural changes of the early colonial period. By 1910, young men in suits and women wearing aprons, or skirts and blouses, were a common sight in

São Salvador. On special occasions, men added polished shoes, hats, and ties to their outfits. When they married, they did so in the church and that entailed a commitment to monogamy. But outside the increasingly cosmopolitan capital, many villages were open to change, too. Some chiefs had allowed the establishment of mission schools in their communities, and many used newly imported garments as markers of distinction, as they had done in the past. "The proud chiefs of old times, dragging their rich cloths [*panos de benza*] behind them, with an air of disdain, wearing caps embroidered with gold or silver, umbrellas, silk, and thick ivory bracelets, have almost all become despicable blacks wearing imported jackets, chintz, and felt [*alpaca*] hats."[79] The author of these words, the longtime resident Faria Leal, ignored the fact that these "despicable" chiefs were keeping up a fashion for foreign luxury items established at least four centuries earlier.

There was little the chiefs could do against the loss of wealth and power they suffered under colonial rule. The hut tax, in effect since 1908, cut into the riches they gathered through participation in the rubber trade. Scrutinized by missionaries and the colonial government, it became harder for them to convert their remaining wealth into slaves, a traditional way of projecting social power. Documentary and photographic evidence suggests that, by the time of Kiditu's election, a younger, mission-educated generation had moved up in Kongo society at the expense of the old slave-holding elite. At the same time, the size of São Salvador's population was decreasing. In 1896, the town had roughly one thousand inhabitants, but by 1912 there were only about seven hundred. One explanation offered for this population decline was that recent kings had fewer followers than their nineteenth-century predecessors had. Only Mbemba had been in a position to build up a social base, having been a prominent chief in Madimba, whereas neither Nteyekenge nor Kiditu had carried out political functions before becoming king. Another explanation was that many of the old royal counselors, who used to invest their wealth in women and slaves, had passed away and been replaced by mission-educated politicians who represented different mores. While these new elites still carried the old political tradition forward, in their modern lifestyles there was less room for slavery and polygyny. Finally, many of the catechists who were trained and married in São Salvador departed with their families to set up schools in the countryside.[80] Thus the capital had shrunk in size, although through the work of these same evangelists the bonds between São Salvador and the surrounding towns were strengthened.

Old as well as new elites defended a political tradition that saw the king at São Salvador as a source and symbol of collective well-being. Soon after his official appointment as "native judge," Kiditu was popularly recognized as *ntotela* and even received the regalia by which the legitimacy of his rule was affirmed.[31] To underscore what the Kongo electorate expected from Kiditu as a king, the royal counselors installed him on a set of conditions that echoed the oaths sworn by his seventeenth-century predecessors. One condition not spelled out on paper, but which became apparent during Kiditu's downfall two years later, was that in order to protect his people the king had to be a good negotiator with Kongo's political overlord, Portugal. But when the Portuguese government opened Kongo to the recruitment of migrant labor and came to rely as never before on the mediation of the king, it were precisely Kiditu's negotiating skills that were called into question.

5

Forced Labor

Colonial efforts to coerce Kongo subjects into contract labor for plantations in Cabinda, the Angolan enclave north of the Congo River, were the underlying cause of the 1913 uprising in São Salvador. In the years preceding the revolt, soldiers and policemen from São Salvador targeted village heads throughout the Kongo realm with demands to round up workers for the enclave. The violence these colonial agents inflicted and the cash imperative created by the colonial hut tax compelled many young men to sign up for low-paid plantation labor, until the revolt interrupted the recent flow of migrant labor from the kingdom. This was not the first time Kongo villagers were confronted with the coercive power of the colonial state. Since colonial authorities started helping European rubber traders in Maquela do Zombo in the recruitment of carriers, around 1900, the government had demonstrated a readiness to use force in regulating African labor supplies. But the recruitment of migrant workers for Cabinda was the first manifestation of a formalized system of labor coercion in the kingdom itself. To understand the impact of colonial labor policies in Kongo, this chapter examines the concrete forms of coercion that Africans were exposed to when the Portuguese government tried to put abstract labor laws into practice.

Compulsory labor has been a central theme in the historiography of twentieth-century Portuguese colonialism. In the case of Angola, the extant literature has focused mainly on discursive strategies of rule and their impact on policy formation, while too little attention has been paid to the everyday lives of workers and the actual conditions of work under colonial rule.[1] To understand why coercion became a fundamental part of Portuguese labor policies in Africa, scholars often refer to the Law of 1899, which subjected all native inhabitants of the Portuguese empire to a "moral and legal" obligation to work.[2] More specifically, it has been argued that this decree was the product of a racial discourse developed in Portugal in the aftermath of the abolition of slavery, which emphasized the civilizational benefits of compulsory labor for Africans.[3] However, an approach that seeks elemental clues to the workings of empire in nationally specific political traditions makes Portuguese colonialism seem exceptional in the wider African context, while it does little to explain the variety of forced labor practices that Africans experienced in the colonies.

There was, of course, nothing distinctly Portuguese about the use of forced labor in colonial Africa. Many colonial regimes relied on coercive measures to extract labor cheaply from economies with poorly developed labor markets, and considered the use of violence legitimate if it helped Africans become more productive.[4] An examination of metropolitan views on African labor and their codification in law also cannot explain the actual coercion that Africans were exposed to, which was often inflicted by colonial agents operating beyond their mandate. In fact, the application of force during tax collection and labor recruitment was never prescribed by law. While twentieth-century Portuguese labor codes all stemmed from the fundamental premise of the Law of 1899—laying down the African duty to work—they also articulated a belief that labor contracts had to be engaged by consent. The importance of colonial labor legislation, as one scholar put it, "is not what it said but how it was actually put into practice."[5] The fundamental problem of the colonial state in Angola was that it lacked the infrastructural power to effectively implement and administer the laws and policies that officials in Lisbon and Luanda designed.[6] In São Salvador, specifically, the task of exercising colonial rule fell upon a few low-level officers, who received assistance from the king of Kongo and a small army of African soldiers and policemen.

Colonial control of African labor was severely restricted by the absence of free (i.e., wage) labor in northern Angola.[7] Kongo carriers had worked for European traders and travelers against payment for decades, but their employment was generally determined by the same customs that regulated the traditional caravan trade. Village chiefs and caravan leaders, acting on the carriers' behalf, controlled the hiring process. Wages were paid out in goods and had to be negotiated for every job, although they became more standardized as European factories gained control of the inland rubber trade after 1900. Kinship obligations thus created social constraints on one side of the struggle over labor in early twentieth-century Kongo, limiting European access to local labor supplies.[8] Colonial officials often legitimized compulsory labor as a necessary tool to "free" African workers from the reactionary influence of their elders.

Coercion was therefore an essential element of colonial attempts to transform Africans into wage laborers, although it had its limits. Colonial rulers were never fully comfortable with violence, which provoked resistance among Africans and elicited criticism from within their own ranks as well as from international observers, most notably the British.

To understand how forced labor policies were put into practice in northern Angola, this chapter analyzes the process of labor mobilization at the village level. It portrays colonial labor recruitment as a makeshift affair, in which low-level government functionaries relied on local aides to bargain with chiefs over labor supplies.[9] The coercive nature of colonial rule became visible in the soldiers who visited Kongo villages to collect taxes and labor and who routinely used violence to convince elders and their kinsmen that a Cabinda contract created the means to meet their fiscal obligations to the government in São Salvador. These contracts were comparatively unattractive and elders might have preferred to employ the labor power of their subjects elsewhere. While some young men signed up voluntarily, as they looked for money to pay the hut tax, earn purchasing power, or gain some economic leverage over their elders, others only went to Cabinda under the threat of force.

Because direct taxation was a central element in colonial strategies to transform African labor, this chapter first examines the imposition of the hut tax in the Congo District. Next, it discusses the use of government coercion in the mobilization of carriers for trade factories in eastern Kongo. Third and most importantly, it analyzes the conscription of Kongo workers for several agricultural firms in the Cabinda enclave, a process that was closely monitored by the British missionaries in São Salvador, whose protests forced the colonial government to scrutinize its own recruitment strategies. To understand why chiefs resisted further cooperation with the colonial administration toward the end of 1913, the chapter concludes with a reflection on the impact of colonial recruitment on existing labor relations at the village level.

The Hut Tax

Signaling their state-building intentions, colonial governments throughout sub-Saharan Africa began experimenting with different forms of direct taxation around 1900, including hut, head, and poll taxes. By taxing African incomes and property, governments hoped to reduce the reliance of colonial treasuries on tariffs and to stimulate the monetization of African economies. But for European rulers taxation was a moral issue, too, as it was meant to transform "the primitive and barbaric into good, industrious and governable colonial subjects."[10] The extent to which taxation was an effective tool for transforming colonial economies and subjects remains disputable, but its imposition fundamentally altered existing relationships and agreements between colonial rulers and the peoples they colonized. Especially in societies where regular payment of tribute did not previously exist, colonial taxation threatened to undermine African autonomy in the political and economic sphere. First, tax collection depended on the collaboration of chiefs and thus required their transformation into colonial intermediaries. Second, to earn the money to pay taxes, peasants were required to invest in cash crop production or seek wage employment in the colonial economy. Non-payment was often punished with compulsory labor. Not surprisingly, the introduction of direct taxes caused popular resentment and resistance throughout colonial Africa.[11]

When the colonial government in Luanda introduced a general hut tax in 1906, it effectively refashioned an existing model of tributary relations between Portuguese and African authorities, as payment of tribute in slaves or other goods had long been part of Angolan "vassal" treaties.[12] In the nineteenth century, Portugal tried on several occasions to formalize the imposition of direct taxation on African communities, beginning in 1848 with the introduction of the *dízimo* tax on property, income, and agricultural output. But since these efforts systematically failed, the colonial treasury remained into the early twentieth century largely dependent on revenue from import and export duties. Within Angola, the Congo District was a special case. A hut tax of 250 *reis* per dwelling was formally introduced upon the creation of the district in 1887, possibly to compensate for the prohibition of import duties in the Congo Free Trade Zone, of which the district was a part. In 1901, collection of the hut tax started in Cabinda as well as in the kingdom of Kongo, where Pedro VI (1901–10) may have presented the tax to loyal followers as a form of tribute. Thus some Kongo populations were already acquainted with colonial taxation before the introduction of the general hut tax in 1906.[13]

The legal framework of the hut tax, which made chiefs crucial to its administration, was meant to facilitate collection and minimize the chance of resistance. When the general hut tax was introduced in 1906, its rate was set at six hundred *reis* per home, payable in cash, cattle, or produce.[11] Chiefs were responsible for collecting payments in their villages, for which in theory they received a significant commission, as did the official compilers of tax lists and revenue collectors. In practice, however, taxation was an ad hoc affair that in lieu of a salary gave the officers in charge a chance to steal money, livestock, and even children.[15] In regions where tax registers were lacking, which in Angola were many, paramount chiefs were expected to collect a sum that putatively covered the population they represented. While failure to pay was punishable with imprisonment or compulsory labor, tax agents were prohibited from using violence unless they encountered opposition.[16]

Payment of the hut tax in goods, while discouraged, was inevitable, as a cash economy was only poorly developed in northern Angola in the early 1900s. On the coast, exports of high-value rubber kept a barter economy between Africans and Europeans in place. The value of large transactions was still measured in prestige goods, especially cotton textiles, although the sale of palm produce and peanuts stimulated the use of smaller currencies. In São Salvador, blue glass beads—called *nzimbu za ndombe* or *coral matadi*—were the main currency for small transactions until about 1910, when Belgian, French, and Portuguese coins gained primacy. East of the Kongo capital, however, the use of blue beads and other imported currencies, such as quilts and sea shells (*nzime-mbuli*), remained widespread for many years.[17] The colonial government officially prohibited tax payments in foreign currencies to stimulate the circulation of Portuguese silver coins. But around 1912 many households in northern Angola still used Congolese francs, obtained in markets near the Congo River, to pay the hut tax.[18] Meanwhile, Zombo merchants were allowed to use rubber to pay taxes, which the government exchanged for cash at factories in Maquela and Noqui.[19]

Shortly after its introduction, the hut tax was subject to steep increases. From six hundred *reis* per home in 1906, it was raised to a thousand *reis* in 1908 and 1,200 *reis* in 1909. These were large sums for many households, especially for ones that produced little surplus or did not participate in lucrative trades. Local administrators were, in fact, aware of the difficulties many families had in paying the required amounts. In 1910, the interim resident of São Salvador, José dos Santos, requested the tax be reduced to a thousand *reis*, as most people in his district lacked resources to pay more.[20] In Ambrizete, tax collection was initially suspended because several villages were struggling with food shortages. The coastal hinterland was especially vulnerable to crop failures because of the area's sandy earth and its irregular rainfall. Under these circumstances, the local administration demanded workers for road building as an alternative to monetary taxation. In 1911, the hut tax still due for 1909 was reduced to six hundred *reis* as several populations were again suffering from drought.[21] In short, while the weight of taxation increased over the years, forms of collecting were often improvised and adapted to local circumstances. Colonial exploitation, as Michael Watts points out, "had political-economic limits and the revenue system reflected this in its flexibility."[22]

Colonial suppleness also had its limits, however. Although the Portuguese government decided to impose the hut tax first of all on regions deemed submissive and sufficiently prosperous, presumably "docile" communities responded violently to the arrival of tax collecting agents from the start. Tax revolts had economic as well as political reasons. The hut tax not only created new and often intolerable financial burdens on African households, but many Kongo chiefs, not accustomed to paying regular tribute to any overlord, also considered colonial taxation illegitimate. In the five years prior to the great Kongo uprising of 1913, resistance flared up in almost every corner of the Congo District where colonial agents dared to set foot, and the effective colonial occupation of northern Angola was mainly the result of military campaigns to "pacify" populations resisting the hut tax.[23]

Direct taxation has often been considered a gauge for measuring state power. In Angola, like elsewhere, a skeletal colonial administration was forced to devolve tax collection to local officials and their African delegates, giving rise to corruption.[24] In Kongo, moreover, village heads did not see the tax collectors dispatched from São Salvador as agents of the colonial state—still an abstract entity—but rather as emissaries of the king and his Portuguese patrons. This is not immediately clear from documentary evidence found in colonial archives, but traditions collected in the Damba region of southeast Kongo indicate that colonial forces often legitimized their efforts to levy taxes with claims that the king of Kongo had authorized collection. These traditions not only depict the hut tax as a turning point in the relationship between colonizers and colonized but also tell us that both sides understood moments of conflict and the process of colonial submission very differently.[25]

Long independent from São Salvador politically, Damba was still connected to the kingdom economically, as Soso traders used to drive cattle through the Kongo heartland on their way to markets near the lower Congo.[26] The first campaign to subject Damba to colonial rule was, in effect, an attempt to bring southeast Kongo back within the political orbit of São Salvador. In October 1909, according to official Portuguese accounts, a military officer named Galhardo embarked on a five-day journey to Damba in order to collect the hut tax, taking with him about a dozen African troops. After they arrived in Damba and infuriated the local chiefs by calling them dogs and slaves, they were driven out by an army of three thousand men.[27] Significantly, in Damba, this encounter has been remembered as a betrayal on the part of the king of Kongo. Why, the elders of Damba asked, did Ntotela, who no longer distributed power everywhere, accept Portuguese rule without consulting them? The king might have his reasons for collaborating with Portugal—the visitors were told—but he had to leave Damba alone. And so, according to one oral account, the white man and his black soldiers returned to Mbanza Kongo (São Salvador), into the sea, and back to Europe.[28]

The imposition of the hut tax not only lowered the esteem Damba leaders still had for the king of Kongo but also changed their perception of Europeans. Damba ivory and rubber traders knew the white man from their caravan expeditions to the coast and they had recently allowed the settlement of some European factories in their community.[29] For them, this friendly relationship with Europe, in which they played the role of hosts, stood in stark contrast with the colonial demand for tribute. Memories of the wars that followed Damba's initial resistance to taxation are cast in the idiom of witchcraft, with shape-shifting chiefs fighting, beating, but ultimately fleeing from the magical powers of the white man.[30]

As caravan routes formed a basic grid for the flow of information between different Kongo regions, rebel communities otherwise independent from each other were encouraged by revolts taking place elsewhere. In the months following the expulsion of colonial soldiers from Damba in 1909, news about this event spread along the trade route to Ambrizete that passed through Kimbubuge, inspiring local chiefs to reject taxation. In August 1910, Chief Tulante of Kimbubuge came to São Salvador with four hundred armed men to demand an exemption from the hut tax, arguing that their Damba neighbors, about fifty miles to the east, were not paying either. The Portuguese administrator remained passive, acknowledging his own lack of military power, while explaining to his superiors in Cabinda that the Kimbubuge region "is one of the poorest in the district and . . . can hardly pay the tax now in force."[31] While the spirit of resistance was channeled through the caravan routes, the colonial government relied on the same communication lines to suppress revolts. As troops moved along these paths, news about the power of their weapons traveled ahead of them, convincing many village elders that to be subjugated was wiser than to resist. So Tulante of Kimbubuge gave up his resistance to taxation shortly after the township of Mateca, southwest of São Salvador, had been militarily subjected to Portuguese rule.

In Mateca, too, the hut tax was associated with expansionist forces emanating from São Salvador. This had long been a dissident community within the Kongo kingdom, whose leaders had criticized the Agua Rosada's subordination to Portugal since the late nineteenth century. Their first act of resistance was the expulsion of a priest who had come from Madimba to advise villages in the region to pay the hut tax. Next, they attacked their neighbors from Conco, who were affiliated with the Catholic mission and accused of siding with the authorities in São Salvador. In July 1911, government troops burned down Mateca and arrested paramount chief Fiakete. Shortly thereafter a military post was established in Kimbubuge to control the regions on the southern fringes of the kingdom. Military posts were simultaneously set up in Bembe and Kibokolo, an important rubber market south of Maquela do Zombo, giving the colonial government control of the main access routes to Damba. In October 1911, colonial forces occupied Damba without encountering great opposition and began to levy the hut tax there. After Damba, chiefs from the Mayanda and Kanda districts north and east of São Salvador also resigned themselves to colonial power. Officers from the Kongo capital immediately began collecting taxes in the Kanda highlands, where chiefs unable to pay in money or goods offered carriers instead.[32]

For relatively affluent communities, like those of the rubber trading Zombo, discontent about taxation was not so much caused by its financial burden as by the violence on which the government relied to levy taxes. In May 1911, a coalition of different Zombo chiefs closed the roads to Maquela and refused to supply carriers to the local European community, as colonial soldiers had murdered one of their peers. This incident signaled the birth of a new political environment in northern Angola, which was dominated by tax collectors whose arbitrary and violent behavior went generally unchecked. As one British missionary explained, "the system of sending armed black soldiers with a native chief was altogether a bad one. The fact was that these emissaries of the Government collected for themselves many times over the taxes due, and when Zombo eats Zombo there is trouble."[33]

The measures taken by the colonial administration in the wake of the Zombo revolt are an indication of the extent to which the imposition of the hut tax changed existing relations of power in Kongo. First, the administration arrested the rebel chiefs and removed them from office. The colonial government was not in the habit of electing or appointing village chiefs, but when the military campaigns to impose taxation started, it created sufficient military power to replace headmen opposing the colonial order. Second, after 1911, the government began to use a corps of locally recruited policemen for tax collection and labor recruitment. It was believed that these so-called *cipaios* were less abusive to the communities they worked in than the soldiers they replaced, who were usually outsiders from other parts of Angola. Because their function required basic literacy and skill in arithmetic, *cipaios* were commonly recruited among young men who had enjoyed a colonial education, as the case of Afonso Cupessa demonstrates. Cupessa frequented the Catholic mission school in Madimba from 1890, married in the Church in 1903, and after working as a teacher and carpenter for a while he was hired by the government as a policeman.[34] However, since *cipaios* were chronically underpaid—receiving one hundred *reis* per day, half the official wage of a contract worker (*serviçal*) in Angola—they often fell into the same pattern of exploitation and violence as the soldiers before them.[35] In fact, the *cipaio* system had the unwanted effect of detaching African recruits from their own communities, both socially and morally, by turning them into tools of colonial domination.

Despite official measures to strengthen the reach of the state in northern Angola and make its rule less arbitrary, colonial control remained brittle. The government's ability to levy taxes varied widely between regions, and violence continued to mar the collection process. In 1912, resistance against the hut tax flared up again in different parts of the Congo District, pulling the colonial government into a series of military campaigns that would not end for another three years. São Salvador was, at that moment, the only place where colonial demands for revenue were not yet violently contested.

Labor Recruitment

Under Portugal's First Republic (1910–26), colonial officials for the first time elaborated a legal framework to mobilize African labor in Angola's Congo District. Starting from the premise that Africans had a moral duty to work, the new regulations essentially aimed to restrict the choices Kongo peasants had for meeting their labor obligations. This provided low-level colonial administrators with a legal justification for coercing their African subjects into contract labor. For them violence became a "political strategy," although the higher-ranked officials in Luanda or Lisbon who designed the regulations often felt uneasy about the use of state-sanctioned violence in the labor market.[36]

But before colonial laws were introduced to organize labor recruitment in the Congo District, local officers had already found other ways to legitimize the imposition of forced labor on Kongo communities. The infamous Law of 1899, in particular, gave administrators in Angola a legal incentive to put different kinds of labor coercion into practice. In theory, Africans were free to choose how to fulfill their "moral" duty to work, and there was little in the law that prescribed or even allowed the use of violence in labor recruitment. But a clause that called for state coercion in case of non-compliance with the law seemingly authorized local governments to press Africans into public work projects or transport services for the government and private employers. In particular the growing number of trade factories established in Maquela do Zombo, in eastern Kongo, came to rely on government support to recruit carriers.

At first, carrier recruitment was an unregulated business that offered opportunities to local brokers who had connections with the Portuguese administration, often established through their earlier affiliation with the Catholic mission. In 1901, Baptist missionaries in São Salvador reported that "people of the outlying towns have been greatly oppressed by young men . . . who, on the plea of recruiting carriers for the resident and traders, demand food, fowls, and drink, and act most tyrannically in other ways."[37] Near the border with the Congo

Free State, villages were plagued not only by local recruitment agents but also by rubber stealers from across the border. "Men wearing European clothes are continually robbing these poor people near the border, some professing to have the authority of the Congo State Government, and others that of the Resident and King of Congo."[38] After complaints were lodged at the administration in São Salvador, the Portuguese resident tried to instill order by appointing a limited number of local brokers as official recruitment agents. Since there was such a great demand for carriers to work the transport route from Maquela to Noqui, however, in December 1902 the government stationed 150 soldiers in São Salvador specifically to help the factories in recruiting labor. Because of this measure, soon more Kongo men were carrying for European houses than for independent African traders.[39]

While the colonial government initially let European traders negotiate wages for transport services directly with chiefs, after 1900 it decided to regulate payment by introducing wage scales. Over time, official wages for carrying decreased significantly. In 1903, carriers were paid seven thousand *reis* for a return journey between Noqui and Maquela, which could effectively be made within a month. By 1909, this payment had been reduced to six thousand *reis*, while in 1911 it was officially set at five thousand *reis*.[40] The government claimed there was never a shortage of labor in the carrying trade, but it is clear from missionary reports that carriers were increasingly forced into service. "Under the present system," Thomas Lewis wrote in 1902, "the Government official at Makela is practically a recruiting agent, running all over the country and demanding under threats and penalties so many carriers from native chiefs for the various trading houses."[41] In 1906, the colonial authorities in Maquela do Zombo even imposed a system of compulsory carrying on villages. Chiefs were officially required to supply one carrier for every three homes in their area, although factories often bribed recruitment agents to collect more.[42]

From their station in Kibokolo, missionaries of the BMS were close observers of the colonial conscription of carriers and the conflicts it provoked between communities in eastern Kongo. Kibokolo was a densely populated district south of Maquela do Zombo. Its central town, Nzamba, was located along the trade route from Maquela to Damba and had about five thousand inhabitants when the British missionaries arrived there in 1899.[43] Some of the local Zombo chiefdoms were more interested than others in servicing the transport needs of the European community in Maquela. For example, Kimalomba, north of Kibokolo, was on good terms with the Portuguese authorities and a reliable supplier of labor to the local factories. But in Kibokolo, carrier recruitment proved more difficult, as many chiefs were rubber traders with labor needs of their own; some preferred to supply workers to the BMS, who paid better

Zombo carriers, 1906 (Biblioteca Nacional de Portugal, A. Matta, "Álbum sobre o Congo português e belga")

wages than the Europeans in Maquela. What complicated recruitment in Kibokolo most, however, was the abuse emanating from the government in Maquela.[44] Negotiations between traders and chiefs over labor, which often involved the advance payment of goods in return for manpower, tended to break down when soldiers appeared in the villages to collect contracted workers. "Cloth and spirits are given out to chiefs and headmen for rations for a certain number of carriers. Now, the people cannot resist the temptation of cloth and 'gin,' and they receive goods and consume the drink; but when the carriers are to be sent in it is not such an easy matter, and then the trouble comes."[45] Underpaid soldiers also fended for themselves, using their superior weaponry to loot the villages where they were supposed to pick up carriers. Such trouble came to Nzamba in October 1902, when a company of thirteen soldiers came to collect an agreed and paid for number of carriers. A dispute over pigs and goats led to a gunfight that killed two foremen, the heir-chief of Nzamba, and a government soldier. Colonial troops, supported by a thousand armed men from Maquela and Kimalomba, subsequently burned down eight Kibokolo towns. In the aftermath of this conflict, the colonial authorities made resettlement conditional on the provision of carriers.[46]

Episodes like this indicate that for low-level administrators the normative codes inscribed in colonial labor legislation legitimized whatever means deemed necessary, in their eyes, to push Africans into contract labor. In point of fact, the idea that Africans not only had a "moral" duty to work but could also be compelled to work for Europeans pervaded all government levels in the Congo District in the early twentieth century.

Cabinda

A colonial law regulating the recruitment of workers for private businesses in the Cabinda enclave, introduced in March 1911, sealed Kongo's fateful transformation from a thriving rubber hub into a potential reservoir of migrant labor. With cocoa, coffee, and palm tree plantations expanding in Cabinda in the early twentieth century, local planters became increasingly dependent on external supplies of manpower, especially since many Cabindan workers found more attractive employment opportunities in the growing urban economies of French and Belgian Congo and the ports of Luanda and São Tomé.[17] The government of the Congo District, located in the enclave, responded to the planters' needs by specifically designating the region south of the Congo River as a recruitment area for plantation labor. The new law stipulated that only men between the ages of fifteen and sixty and women older than sixteen could be contracted for Cabinda, and this only for a maximum of one year.[18] To press Africans into contract labor, the government published another decree in May, which forced peasants to either visibly occupy their land and develop it for cash-crop production or hire out their labor by signing up as contract workers.[19] Since commercial agriculture was still poorly developed in Kongo and land usage was governed by the principle of group tenure, instead of private ownership, this second regulation severely restricted the legal options for Kongo peasants to avoid compulsory labor.

While the government had thus created a legal framework to facilitate the mobilization of migrant workers in Kongo, it seemed hesitant to implement the laws. Significantly, a visit of the king of Kongo, Manuel Martins Kiditu, to the district governor in Cabinda set the recruitment process in motion. In the middle of 1912, Kiditu came to inform Governor Cardoso that his subjects had trouble paying the hut tax, which, after a series of military operations in 1911, had been imposed on them with greater force. The rubber economy was no longer providing Kongo families with sufficient income, and the production of cash crops was not a viable alternative in the interior. Although the rubber trade had not yet collapsed in northern Angola, its center had shifted eastward to Maquela do Zombo. The two most important employers in São Salvador, the Nieuwe Afrikaanse Handelsvennootschap (NAHV) and the Companhia Portugueza do Zaire, had recently closed their local factories, as a result of which labor opportunities in the carrying trade were shrinking. Several chiefs in the kingdom had raised funds so Kiditu could travel with two counselors to Cabinda and negotiate a solution to their fiscal problems with the Portuguese government. Cardoso suggested they take up contracts in the enclave, where plantation workers were in short supply. It is unclear how Kiditu felt about the governor's proposition, but in the absence of an alternative plan, he consented. In doing so, the king enabled the first official labor migration from São Salvador under colonial rule, which would be introduced with such violence that it ruined the country and caused his own demise.[50]

When recruitment started in the kingdom, the Kongo needed good governance more than ever, but instead, Republican reforms were undermining the efficacy of colonial rule in São Salvador. As part of a larger set of administrative changes in Angola, the Portuguese residency in Kongo was moved to Maquela do Zombo, economically a more important town than São Salvador. In addition, in 1912, the experienced and locally esteemed administrator José Heliodoro de Faria Leal was replaced by Abílio Augusto Pereira Pinto, who was new to Kongo.[51] When Pinto left São Salvador to direct the new residency in Maquela, in 1913, the local administration was left in the hands of the station chief (*chefe de posto*) Paulo Midosi Moreira, a man with little formal training who had started his career in the Kongo capital as a scribe in 1902.[52] By marrying a daughter of the Kongo aristocracy, Moreira became firmly rooted in the local community, where he was generally known as Senhor Paulo.[53] According to the Baptist missionary Thomas Lewis, Moreira knew his way around the country, but "was looked upon by the people as a very hard man."[54] As the second highest colonial official in the kingdom, he was usually in charge of tax collection and labor recruitment. In 1914, when Portuguese officials were busy apportioning blame for the atrocities that had been committed and for the political unrest in the kingdom, the interim governor of the Congo District, Jayme de Moraes, described Moreira as a violent and incompetent man of little intelligence.[55] In principle, the administrative reforms of the early Republican period were meant to make colonial rule more effective, but in São Salvador they gave rise to increased despotism, as the government delegated its affairs to an unskilled clerk and his local police force.[56]

It is important to emphasize that the Cabinda recruitment was not a single, large mobilization of workers. Instead, laborers were recruited in small groups following specific requests from plantations in Cabinda. Between August 1912 and September 1913, about six hundred recruits in total left Kongo to work in the enclave. Most of them ended up on the farms of Hatton and Cookson, a trade house from Liverpool whose presence on the Angolan coast dated back to the 1850s; the Companhia de Cabinda, a younger firm that specialized in the cultivation of cocoa and coffee; and Roça Lucola, a plantation owned by the Companhia Colonial e Agrícola do Congo Português, which produced cocoa, coffee, and palm fruits.[57] Wages were officially set at a hundred *reis* per day, to which employers added an equal amount in rations, paid either in money or in food. On Sundays the workers were free and received a gratuity of soap, tobacco, matches, and salt.[58]

The British consul in Luanda, Francis Drummond-Hay, thought the labor regulations were "quite satisfactory, and are equitable, and the pay is good."[59] But what did the migrants themselves think of these contracts? For them, the trade factories and mission stations back home offered the only comparable experience of wage labor. A salary of 2,600 *reis* per month (rations excluded) was significantly less than what many trade houses south of the Congo River paid to carriers and domestic servants. Carriers on the Maquela-Noqui line earned about five thousand *reis* per month, less, it should be noted, than what they had earned in previous years. Factories in Damba at the time hired servants for monthly wages of up to five thousand *reis*, while in Ambrizete carriers earned 7,200 *reis* and domestic servants 3,900 *reis*.[60] In fact, the hundred *reis* that workers earned in Cabinda equaled the daily wages paid to street cleaners in São Salvador in 1912.[61] Against this background, the men who signed up for Cabinda must have found the contracts generally unattractive. A local agent of Hatton and Cookson commented that the migrants working on his property tried to supplement their income by saving on food. "At the moment, the labourers engaged here, including those from San Salvador, are living on mangoes, of which there is an abundance here, and with their rations money they buy articles which take their fancy to take home with them at the expiration of their contract."[62] Only by saving on food were migrant workers able to amass wages comparable to those earned back home.

Unattractive wages, the long-term absence of male workers from home, and the prospect of plantation labor were all factors explaining the general lack of enthusiasm for the Cabinda migration scheme. As volunteers were in short supply, recruiters began to employ extra-legal means to contract workers. In August 1912, Governor Cardoso sent a request for fifty laborers to São Salvador on behalf of Hatton and Cookson. Within a month, fifty-one men were enlisted. Later in August, the Companhia de Cabinda asked the government to recruit twenty-five plantation workers. By early October, this request had also been satisfied.[63] While the official correspondence from São Salvador did not give any hint of troubles or irregularities, eyewitness accounts from the Baptist missionaries suggested force had played a significant role in the recruitment of these workers. Reverend Thomas, writing to the British consul, criticized the use of government troops for recruitment purposes and compared the ongoing process to "a kind of conscription."[64] Thomas had witnessed the arrival in São Salvador of the first recruits for Hatton and Cookson, some of whom he knew personally, as they were church members from the Lungezi region north of the

Kongo capital. He suspected that the Portuguese administrator in São Salvador, Resident Pinto, ordered chiefs to supply labor, as he understood from several men that they had been compelled to go. None of the recruits really knew by which company they had been contracted; it was rumored to be the "English house," indicating how little in accordance with official regulations this enrollment was. Pinto would later reveal that when the first fifty workers had been gathered in São Salvador, a Catholic missionary advised him not to mention that "they are going to Cabinda, because this could provoke a revolt."[65]

Very soon, Kongo villagers received discouraging news from their friends and relatives in Cabinda. In October 1912, a group of migrants from Lungezi, members of the Baptist Church now working for Hatton and Cookson, wrote home to inform both their chiefs and the Baptist community about their experience in the enclave. Two of their letters were forwarded to the British Foreign Office to spur a humanitarian campaign against labor exploitation in Portuguese Congo. One of the authors was António Zakwadia, who had been a school teacher for the BMS in the Lungezi region from 1907 to 1911.[66] In the first letter, addressed to the church in São Salvador, the men wrote that they had arrived safely in Cabinda and that their main task was to cut trees for firewood, which was not a cause for complaint. But they also claimed they had to work on Sundays, which would have been illegal, and that they were often whipped by their English boss, Mr. Royle, the factory manager.[67] The second letter was addressed to chiefs Garcia Noso of Lungezi, Álvaro Sengele of Kunku, and Afonso Mfutila Mebidikwa of Mwingu.[68] This letter raised three important points. First, it was a firm complaint about the cruel treatment the workers received at the hands of the "white man" (Royle) and his African overseer, and about the meager daily rates the workers received to purchase food. When confronted with these charges, Royle naturally dismissed them.[69] Second, the men pointed out that they were in Cabinda because their chiefs encouraged them to go, adding that they would not have gone if they had known the condition they now found themselves in. Third, the authors clearly believed that the king of Kongo had the capacity to do something about their plight, as they asked their chiefs to report back to the king and the Portuguese resident in São Salvador. From their titles—Noso, Sengele, and Mfutila—it is clear these chiefs were traditionally invested rulers whose spiritual authority stemmed from their connection to the Kongo capital. This letter therefore seems to suggest that the king himself had convinced the chiefs to round up volunteers for Cabinda.

While bad publicity from Cabinda was spreading in the kingdom, labor recruitment continued in Kongo under the watchful eyes of the Baptist missionaries. Paulo Moreira, at the time still secretary, usually took charge of escorting conscripts from their villages to São Salvador and then on to Noqui for further shipment to Cabinda.[70] Missionaries monitored his movements closely and reported their observations to the British consul in Luanda. According to them, several recruits had said they had been compelled into service, with some despairing they were "going to their death." The missionaries also claimed that planters in Cabinda paid Secretary Moreira and Resident Pinto a commission for every passport they issued. The BMS had furthermore received alarming information that government agents were committing atrocities, and that Moreira was possibly involved.[71] When Governor Cardoso received a copy of the BMS report, he responded with skepticism. In his view, it was unlikely that the resident and his secretary received special fees for their services. The Cabinda companies always sent their requests for workers to the district government and never dealt directly with the local administrators who provided them. According to Cardoso, the missionaries put too much faith in the words of their African informants, giving "the appearance of rigorous inquiry to an exchange of impressions for shabby cloth." Moreover, he thought of Moreira as a decent officer, "though capable of using violence when the circumstances demand it."[72]

Before long, however, official British protests forced the administration in São Salvador to explain its recruitment methods. The first government report emerged in the wake of a recruitment campaign in the Kanda highlands, east of São Salvador, where Moreira was sent in December 1912 to round up workers for Roça Lucola.[73] The Kanda region had long been difficult terrain for the colonial authorities. In 1905, local chiefs had confronted the military commander of Maquela do Zombo, who had planned to recruit carriers in their district with the assistance of the renowned agent Álvaro de Agua Rosada Tangi, son of the late Pedro V. At the time, the Maquela factories were drastically short of carriers to offload their rubber stocks to Noqui and promised to pay the commander a hefty fee for every single carrier he contracted. Unfortunately, the reckless harassment of one of the Kanda chiefs sparked a widespread rebellion, which closed the region to tax and labor collectors for the next five years.[74] Some chiefs had reluctantly begun to pay the hut tax in 1911, however, and now the government wanted more.[75] Because the Kanda region was dotted with BMS outstations, some evangelists could witness the ongoing recruitment for Cabinda from nearby. Using evidence from the BMS as well as information provided by Moreira, Resident Pinto drew up a report that eventually reached colonial headquarters in Luanda.[76]

Pinto documented the government's recruitment campaign in Kanda in astonishing detail, revealing how colonial agents routinely employed violence to extract resources and manpower. His report showed how labor recruitment was intricately tied to the collection of the hut tax. To stimulate enrollment, tax rates were ruthlessly increased in 1913 to levels above 1,500 *reis*, a clear departure from the government's earlier flexibility with regard to taxation.[77] Policemen operating as collectors generally gave chiefs two options: either they arranged for their subjects to pay taxes, or they could try to round up "volunteers" for migrant labor. Chiefs who decided to supply workers were usually able to recruit only one or two men from every village in their area. Government agents would visit as many villages as needed to raise the stipulated number of recruits, and violence played a critical part in their negotiations, especially when chiefs were reluctant to cooperate. Although some men went voluntarily to Cabinda, or were pressured by their elders to go, many were compelled to sign up as they witnessed recruitment agents violating their female kinfolk and assaulting their chiefs. African soldiers and policemen clearly committed most of the violence, but Paulo Moreira was usually around and it was rumored that he partook in the atrocities.

Resident Pinto frankly admitted that he used to take prisoners to make chiefs comply with what he called "the rules." At the same time, he acquitted Secretary Moreira of all criminal charges. But the governor-general of Angola, Norton de Matos, was not convinced by Pinto's moral defense of government coercion. He commented that the methods used by the administration in São Salvador were inconsistent with the Republican labor law of 1911 and his own circular of December 1912, which stated that government officials were not to act as recruitment agents. In his view, the law stressed clearly that the initiative for contract labor had to come from Angolans themselves. "It is not with violence of the worst kind but through persuasive rewarding and right working conditions that a stream of labor from the villages to industrial and agricultural centers will be established."[78] District Governor Cardoso, in turn, protected his subordinates. In his opinion "violent means [are] indispensable for the implementation of the labor regime in regions where until today people have lived languidly."[79] Such disparate views on the occurrences in Kongo point to a fundamental problem of the early colonial labor reforms in Angola: the Republican government wanted to promote a wage economy in a situation where the cost of free labor was relatively high; concretely, European employers would not offer wages high enough to attract workers voluntarily.[80] The use of coercion to reduce the cost of labor carried the risk of international condemnation and had, therefore, to be kept within bounds. Without proper supervision, however, local colonial agents resorted to violence in order to push Angolans into low-paid plantation labor, thus exposing the Portuguese government to accusations of slavery it so bitterly wanted to avoid.

Conclusion

By a set of laws issued in 1911, the colonial state defined most African subjects as legally underage and therefore ineligible to sign labor contracts without the consent of their chiefs, thus affirming its own dependency on chiefs when it needed access to African labor supplies.[81] In light of the foregoing discussion of colonial taxation and labor recruitment, such seemingly absurd laws bring the relation between young Kongo workers and their elders under scrutiny. To what extent did chiefs effectively control the labor power of their subjects? Who signed up for Cabinda? And if workers "volunteered," who or what stimulated them? These are hard questions to answer, because the Angolan colonial government never inquired into the African labor relations on which their own recruitment schemes had such a tremendous impact. Like most colonial administrators, the Portuguese "learned to profit from African systems of production and not ask too many questions about how they functioned."[82]

Splinters of information emerging from records on the Kongo revolt of December 1913 make it possible to understand the lines of authority between chiefs and their dependents. First, during negotiations over plantation labor for São Tomé and Príncipe in the months ahead of the revolt, Kongo chiefs told the Portuguese authorities they would "not let any man go" to the archipelago. While these words seem to convey dominance, the chiefs had not taken their decision autocratically. When Paulo Moreira, then head of the administration in São Salvador, asked the chiefs' spokesman, Tulante Buta, why he refused to supply workers, Buta replied, "I cannot, the people are not willing to go." Moreover, during the war palaver later in December, some recruits were still waiting in São Salvador to depart for Cabinda, and the question arose whether they should be allowed to leave. A few chiefs made clear that these men themselves wished to go, after which Buta declared, "Well, if they wish to go they may go. We cannot say anything against it."[83] These examples suggest that while chiefs controlled access to the labor of their followers, they did not have complete authority to decide over its use.

From the moment European traders and missionaries arrived in São Salvador, around 1880, chiefs were no longer the sole employers of their sons and nephews. Chiefs still mediated in the recruitment of carriers, and many continued to organize their own trade expeditions, but European competition for labor increased the bargaining power of young men in relation to their elders.[84] In fact, the influence elders wielded over their male dependents had been decreasing since the 1860s, as widespread participation in the rising commodity trade reduced existing inequalities in power between generations. At the same time, it is important to look beyond the structure of generational conflict.

Conflicts and disagreements existed, but fathers and sons, or uncles and nephews, did not necessarily frame their relationship in terms of rivalry. As Frederick Cooper explains, both chiefs and subjects had an interest in the opportunities opening up with the European demand for plantation labor in colonial Africa. With their wages young workers gained a level of independence, while household heads "often tried to insure that young men would leave and return, bringing back the fruits of their labor."[85]

About six hundred men were recruited in the São Salvador district in 1912–13 to work in Cabinda. Among them were members of the Baptist Church; at least one of them had been a village school teacher in the years before his migration. In Kongo, as previously noted, Christian education was enjoyed especially by members of elite families, even if missions also reached out to the socially marginal. In short, it is very likely that recruits were drawn from the same class of young men that previously sought employment in the carrying trade or at one of the mission stations. The wages were comparatively unattractive. But with the rubber economy plummeting and teacher salaries remaining low, there existed few alternatives for ambitious young men to find the resources they needed to pay the hut tax, assemble bridewealth, or buy luxury items.

Apart from the Cabinda contracts and the (still mainly hypothetical) option of occupying their own lands as commercial farmers, the Kongo found two ways to respond to Portuguese tax and labor demands. The first was to migrate to Belgian Congo. By 1912, a growing number of Kongo men and women were seeking jobs across the border in the nascent urban areas along the Matadi-Léopoldville railway, initiating what would become a long migratory movement of Kongo people from northern Angola to Congo.[86] As young workers moved to Congo in order to escape the hut tax and its forced labor penalties, or earn the money their families back home needed to meet their fiscal obligations, taxation in Angola effectively promoted the wage economy of a neighboring colony. While some used migration as an "avoidance" strategy, for others the response to colonial exploitation lay in overt resistance. Discontent about the government's new labor regime grew within Kongo as complaints about working conditions in Cabinda were spreading, migrant workers were not returning on time, and salary payments were often also coming late. Meanwhile, the recruitment process itself was marred by violence and abuse. Both chiefs and subjects could have benefited from the labor opportunities in the colonial economy, but in 1913, a sense of exploitation overwhelmed all.

6

Political Breakdown

Colonial policies designed in Lisbon and Luanda came down hard on the African populations who lived in the orbit of agents representing state power in Angola. As previously noted, the coercive element of these policies became decreasingly abstract as they trickled down the colonial ranks into the hands of low-level administrators and their local African aides. The present chapter looks at the influence of colonial rule from another angle, surveying recorded statements by chiefs who were confronted with the demands of tax collectors and labor recruiters. Even more than the official reports on tax and labor exaction, these testimonies underscore the central role of African intermediaries in the daily exercise of colonial rule. Moreover, since the chiefs articulated not just their own afflictions but also, more fundamentally, the suffering of the wider Kongo populace at the hands of state agents, their statements provide a unique window on the Kongo experience of colonial exploitation.

The fact that government violence was not imposed by external agents — from Portugal or other parts of Angola — but was enacted by individuals from within the Kongo community itself constitutes the underlying drama in the history of colonial exploitation in early twentieth-century Kongo. The political context of colonial oppression remained narrowly defined in the eyes of chiefs, elders, and followers alike. In December 1913, Kongo chiefs responded to the abrupt hostility of the colonial regime in São Salvador by staging a rebellion aimed at cleansing the community of evildoers, including King Manuel Kiditu, the one held most accountable for the sudden loss of peace in the kingdom. The revolt against São Salvador was primarily an attempt to remove the king and some of his closest associates, while rebel chiefs dismissed the idea that the few white officials stationed in the capital were relevant targets for them. Significantly, the uprising displayed some of the fundamental qualities of a typical Kongo renewal movement: the chiefs explained disorder and injustice as the result of greed, envy, and maliciousness within their own group.[1] Explicit accusations of "witchcraft" (*kindoki*) were absent from the recorded discourse of the insurgents, but there is every indication that they saw the social destruction wrought by taxation and labor recruitment as the work of witches, people who used occult power for selfish ends. Indeed, to most chiefs it was clear that the violence of colonialism was brought on by the selfishness of local government agents, which is why their spokesman, Tulante Álvaro Buta, framed the question of political change in terms of moral regeneration. His palaver after the assault on São Salvador showed a striking resemblance to a seventeenth-century collective healing ritual known as *mbumba kindonga*, in which, says John Thornton, "old jealousies were aired and unspoken anger released" before existing dissensions were buried and the community could start anew.[2] But on this occasion, Kongo rebels did more than just clear the air. Purification also consisted of the expulsion of wrongdoers from the kingdom, so that justice and harmony could be restored.

From his election in 1911, Manuel Martins Kiditu's reign was conditioned by a set of rules that combined a traditional focus on the king's protective duties toward his subjects with a modern recognition that he needed to be an effective negotiator with Kongo's colonial overlord. One could argue that Kiditu's mandate was doomed from the start, as he was expected to shield the Kongo community from political forces far beyond his control. But such an argument ignores the significance of African agency in the colonial system. First, the Kongo case substantiates Achille Mbembe's claim that the emerging structures of the colonial state enabled some Africans with power to enact their "obscure drives" to humiliate and exploit the powerless.[3] The level of Kiditu's involvement in state-sponsored violence can be a matter of contention, but from a contemporary Kongo perspective this question was irrelevant. Kiditu was put on the throne to cushion the impact of colonial taxation by promoting economic welfare and halting the corruption that tainted the rule of his predecessors, but he failed miserably on both accounts. Under his reign, São Salvador went through a period of economic decline, and colonial rule became more abusive as tax collection was linked to the recruitment of migrant labor. Moreover, Kiditu appears to have been just as fraudulent as previous kings.

At his installation in 1911, the king was seconded by Tulante Álvaro Buta, who alongside Mfutila of Zamba ritually sanctioned the legitimacy of his rule. Two years later, however, Álvaro Buta headed the rebellion that deposed Kiditu and hurled the Kongo into a long guerrilla war with the colonial government. Buta's explanation of his attack on São Salvador, delivered in a speech and recorded on paper in the days after the revolt, captures the motivations of the rebels better than any other surviving document. It is an insider's account of Kongo's early colonial history, relating in gripping detail how excessive demands for tribute and manpower and the arbitrary violence of local government agents gave rise to feelings of humiliation, betrayal, and deception. To redress these wrongs, Buta and his allies sought to expel the king, who had broken the social pact with his constituents, and renegotiate the terms of colonial rule. Before analyzing Buta's chronicle of events, however, this chapter first examines the failed negotiations between the government, the king, and an assembly of chiefs over the provision of contract workers for São Tomé and Príncipe, a crucial episode in the history of the revolt.

Rebellion

The great revolt of 1913 came on the heels of an official Portuguese attempt to make the Kongo kingdom an important supplier of labor to São Tomé and Príncipe again, four centuries after Kongo slaves first populated the sugar producing archipelago in the Gulf of Guinea. Kongo generally fell outside the Central African slaving networks that since the 1870s had provided these small but fertile islands with most of the workers for their growing cocoa plantations.[1] In 1913, however, the Portuguese government officially extended recruitment for the islands to Angola's Congo District in hopes of diminishing its reliance on the slave trade channels that supported labor exports elsewhere in Angola. While this planned recruitment never materialized, the failed negotiations between the colonial administration, the king, and about fifty Kongo chiefs over migrant workers in October 1913 constituted a crucial phase in the build-up to the revolt in December.

Only four years earlier, in 1909, a British anti-slavery campaign had forced the Portuguese government to suspend the export of labor from Angola. To British humanitarian activists it was clear that the conditions under which contract workers—alternately called *colonos* or *serviçaes*—were recruited in Angola and labored on São Tomé were closer to slavery than to free labor. In several ways, Angolan migration to São Tomé was a continuation of the historic slave trade to Brazil: the supply channels were almost the same and the chances of plantation workers returning home were extremely small. Contracts were officially for five years, but automatic recontracting on the islands was a common method to keep workers in bondage. During 1908 and 1909, for instance, only thirty-eight workers from Angola were repatriated from the islands, out of the many thousands whose contracts had expired.[5] In response to international scrutiny, the Portuguese government not only closed the export trade but also published a law to regulate the future migration of Angolan *serviçaes* to São Tomé, indicating where in Angola labor recruiters were allowed to operate and how they should conduct their business. The installation of Portugal's First Republic in 1910 gave rise to a flurry of labor regulations that, among other things, limited contracts for São Tomé to a maximum of three years, put recruitment in the hands of officially appointed agents, and allowed Angolan migration to restart in 1913.[6] In September of that year, Portugal for the first time designated the Congo District as a recruitment area where agents were authorized to collect up to 1,500 workers for plantations in Príncipe until the end of the year—a large number, considering that during 1913 in total about one thousand *serviçaes* were shipped from Angola to São Tomé and Príncipe.[7] The district was singled out to supply the minor island of Príncipe because officials considered the Kongo region a low-risk area for the spread of sleeping sickness, which migrants from other parts of Angola had already carried to Príncipe.[8] But the fact that the king had earlier been responsive to labor demands from Cabinda undoubtedly influenced the government's decision to seek plantation workers in Kongo, too.

In the middle of October 1913, a Portuguese agent known as Godinho arrived in São Salvador with a plan to conscript as many workers as the law permitted. On behalf of the *chefe de posto*, Paulo Midosi Moreira, Manuel Kiditu summoned from around the kingdom about fifty headmen whom the government the year before had officially recognized as paramount chiefs (*mfumu antete*, "first chief"), whose function was to assist the government in tax collection and the mobilization of labor. Notes of this meeting were taken by a Kongo interpreter at the request of the British missionary Sidney Bowskill, who relayed his report to the Baptist Missionary Society back in England.[9] Moreira began by explaining the reason for the white man's visit to São Salvador, which was to enlist 1,500 men and women to work for one year in São Tomé and Príncipe. Then, in accordance with new government standards, the terms of the contract were laid out: part of the workers' salaries would be paid in advance, another part on the islands, and a final part upon their return home. The chiefs were also informed about daily rations, housing, hospital arrangements, and the nature of the work on the cocoa farms. But when all was said and done, they refused to cooperate. Through their spokesmen, Afonso Kalanfwa and Tulante Álvaro Buta—one a Protestant from the Nkanda region, the other a Catholic from Madimba—the chiefs made clear that their refusal had nothing to do with the terms of the contract. Nor, it should be added, were they influenced by the humanitarian campaign waged against the Portuguese labor regime in São Tomé and Príncipe. As the missionary George Cyril Claridge later explained, "the request for workmen for [São Tomé] did not in itself fill the people with that dread which we have . . . come to associate with it. They did not know the meaning of [São Tomé] labour as we know it. When they said no, they did so in the light of their immediate experience, especially that part connected with Cabinda."[10]

The chiefs' refusal was born out of local struggles over labor and a strong conviction that the government's demands had reached their legitimate bounds. "We paid your hut tax. When asked for carriers we gave them. When labourers were asked for plantations at Cabinda we gave them. Now we have only men like ourselves—old men." That is how the Earl of Mayo repeated the words of the Kongo chiefs in the British House of Lords in the summer of 1914, after the BMS had brought the labor conflicts in São Salvador to international attention.[11] Governor-general Norton de Matos, a Republican modernizer who strongly believed in the superiority of free labor, explained the chiefs' resistance to contract labor differently. He found the escalating political conflict in Kongo hugely embarrassing, not least because the outside world was watching, but he could not share the humanitarian concerns of British activists. While Norton de Matos tended to abhor the use of violence in the exercise of colonial rule, he had little patience for traditional chiefs who, in his view, impeded the formation of a modern wage economy in Angola. "What rights do the chiefs . . . have to oppose the wish of the natives of São Salvador to go and gain a remunerative salary from their labor?" In his opinion, "these chiefs fear exactly what I most desire: that the native gains in civilization through temporary emigration, that he returns with eyes more open, better informed about what his labor is worth, more man and less slave of the land, or less humble subordinate of the chief."[12] For Norton de Matos, the chiefs represented backwardness. Seeing them indiscriminately as self-seeking autocrats, he overestimated the authority the chiefs wielded over the labor of their subjects and failed to recognize their legitimate concerns about the implementation of colonial tax and labor laws.

In the span of a few years, the colonial government had pushed Kongo chiefs and their communities to the limits of their endurance. Villagers were at a point where they had to sell their basic possessions to be able to pay the hut tax, and to escape such deprivation many families either defied their fiscal duties or decided to move to Belgian Congo.[13] In contrast to central Angola, where Ovimbundu chiefs were able to satisfy Portuguese labor demands by sacrificing part of their slave population to the government, in Kongo people of slave status did not form a discernible economic class and the colonial system of compulsory labor affected slave and free alike.[14] Under these circumstances, the chiefs almost unanimously decided to oppose further labor demands from the government. With the help of Manuel Kiditu and the ever loyal Álvaro

Tangi, the administration managed to draft about thirty "volunteers" for the cocoa islands, who were gathered in São Salvador on 25 November for their march to the coast. For the chiefs, this was a first signal that the king represented the interests of the Portuguese government more than he did their own.[15]

When the colonial administration tried to resume recruitment for the Cabinda enclave in November 1913, refusal turned into revolt. Moreira had received an order to draft seventy-five workers for one of the Portuguese plantations in the enclave, but he was only able to bring thirty-nine to São Salvador; defying colonial authority, forty other conscripts had escaped en route. Mediating between the *chefe de posto* and the chiefs, the king also counted on Álvaro Buta to supply workers, a service he had rendered before. This time Buta refused, however, and instead of collaborating with Kiditu he dispatched messengers telling chiefs to prepare for an attack on São Salvador. With thousands of armed rebels stationed south of the capital early in December, Moreira made a last-ditch attempt to restore peace, but to no avail. On the morning of the 10th, Buta and his allies launched the first large-scale assault on Kongo's sacred city in more than half a century. Without even touching the site of the administration, however, they looted and burned down the city's Catholic neighborhoods, including the king's quarter. The motivations behind the uprising, and Buta's reasons for targeting only one part of town, were made public in the days that followed.[16]

The War Palaver

On December 11, a meeting was held in São Salvador between the Kongo rebels and Portugal's local administrator, Paulo Moreira, which continued the following day in Zamba, a few miles south of the capital. About a thousand people came to São Salvador that morning, many armed with guns, their faces covered in war paint, while another thousand flocked in during the day. The rebels were led by their spokesman, Tulante Álvaro Buta, flanked throughout the palaver by Afonso Nkongolo, his army lieutenant, and Afonso Kalanfwa, who officially represented Princess Noso of Mbanza Mputu, an important township in the kingdom. Delegations of the Baptist and the Catholic missions were also present. One of the Portuguese priests, Manuel Rebello, took notes on the palaver with the help of a notable interpreter, António Moreira Cardoso Nensuka, another son of the late Álvaro XIV, who worked for the colonial administration as an assistant (*amanuense*).[17] The Baptist missionaries had been invited on Buta's request to serve as impartial observers. While Buta was a lifelong Catholic, he had lost confidence in the padres during the events leading up to the revolt. Evangelist Miguel Nekaka translated for the English missionaries.

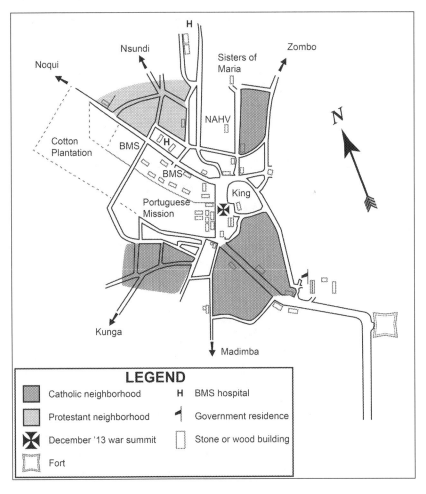

Noqui

Nsundi

Zombo

Sisters of
Maria

NAHV

Cotton
Plantation

BMS

BMS

King

Portuguese
Mission

Kunga

Madimba

LEGEND

■ Catholic neighborhood		H	BMS hospital
■ Protestant neighborhood			Government residence
✚ December '13 war summit		□	Stone or wood building
Fort			

São Salvador, 1913

There are two original transcripts of the meeting, one produced by the Portuguese party, the other by the Baptists, both of which were sent to the district governor in Cabinda. The first is more concise than the second, but it appears truthful and provides details left out of the Baptist transcript. It was signed by Moreira, the priests, as well as the Protestant missionaries. The English transcript, edited by George Claridge and Sidney Bowskill, is lengthier and shows greater attention to the details of Buta's speech. These documents are the closest reflection of the grievances and motives of the Kongo rebels surviving in written form. They demonstrate that the revolt, more than a logical response to colonial exploitation, was the outcome of a series of emotionally charged events that undermined social and political relations in the Kongo community, including the relationship between Kiditu and Buta.[18]

Who was Tulante Álvaro Buta? That he was an "entire stranger" to the British missionaries before the outbreak of the war says more about how little Europeans in São Salvador were aware of what went on outside the capital, or how poorly the Baptist Church had penetrated the traditionally Catholic district of Madimba, than about the status of Buta himself. From his base in Lovo, in the Nsongola region of southern Madimba, Buta governed more than a hundred villages, making him one of the great chiefs in the Kongo heartland.[19] Holding a traditional title, *tulante*, he was deeply involved in the affairs of the kingdom. He belonged to the same matriclan as Manuel Kiditu, whom he seconded at his investiture in 1911 alongside Mfutila of Zamba, an "uncle" of both the king and Álvaro Buta. Because of his position in the kingdom, Buta played a critical role in the government's efforts to extend colonial power from its administrative base in São Salvador. Although Paulo Moreira at one point accused him of participating in a tax revolt and other subversive activities during the reign of Pedro VI (1901–10), the actual report of that revolt brings up the "chief of Lovo" as a mediator between the government and the rebelling chiefs.[20] In exchange for monetary reward, Buta also helped the administration of Faria Leal in the arrest of Fiakete, the insubordinate ruler of Mateca, in 1911. The fact that Buta supported the recruitment of workers for Cabinda until October 1913 confirms his close relationship with the authorities in São Salvador.

Buta addressed his speech specifically to the missionaries, whose role was practically one of jurymen, whereas Paulo Moreira's part in the palaver was, in the absence of the main culprits, limited to that of defendant. Buta opened his testimony with a moral upbraiding: "We have come before you teachers of the Catholic Mission and of the B. M. S. because we know that you are here for our good. You teach us not to kill, not to covet, not to commit adultery, not to steal. . . . Some of us . . . even some of us who do not know how to read or write try to keep your teaching, but some bring shame upon it, about which I am presently going to speak. They rob, they destroy, they compel our women to commit adultery with them, and these things we want [to have] talked [about] before both the Priests and the English Missionaries." This introductory statement expressed the value Kongo elites attached to Christian teaching, both morally and in terms of practical learning, itself a symbol of moral authority. Buta thus emphasized that the exploitation of the Kongo at the hands of colonial agents—whom he would point out by name—constituted an assault on the very morality that Christianity stood for in the kingdom. Those who "brought shame upon it" were locally drafted policemen, court messengers, and officials who had assisted the king and the administrator—always referred to as "Senhor

Paulo"—in the extortion of taxes and manpower. Meanwhile, the missionaries emerged as guardians of the Christian moral standards by which chiefs judged the unprincipled behavior of some community members.

To denote the beginning of moral corruption in the kingdom, Buta pointed to the line of recent Kivuzi and Agua Rosada kings, arguing that under the rule of Henrique II (1842–57), Pedro V (1860–91), and Álvaro XIV (1891–96) "the people were governed by love." But after Henrique Nteyekenge came to power in 1896, the relationship between São Salvador and the outlying districts became strained. Unlike his predecessors, Nteyekenge was a "young man" at the time of his appointment and tended to rule arbitrarily, abusing the alliance between Kongo and the Portuguese government for his own good. His successor, Dom Pedro Mbemba (1901–10) was associated in particular with the introduction of the hut tax. Most chiefs initially resisted colonial taxes, as they had never paid regular tribute to São Salvador, but they were "eventually persuaded that it was good and just to pay them." The military might of the government had swayed them, of course, but having the upper hand on this occasion, they demanded a reduction of the hut tax to its original level.

Buta recalled that after Mbemba died, the Kongo wanted a king who would govern the country "to the satisfaction of the people." The king had to be a good negotiator with the Portuguese government, somebody who was "able to read and to write" and would faithfully represent the wishes of his subjects. To this end, they put the mission-educated Manuel Kiditu on the throne. Under Kiditu's rule, however, conditions in the kingdom and Kongo's relationship with Portugal worsened, especially after the hut tax became tied to colonial campaigns to mobilize labor. On the second day of his palaver, Buta related these developments explicitly to the personnel changes that took place in the colonial administration around 1912. The departing resident, Faria Leal, was locally known and respected as *lemba nsi*, one who keeps the peace in the land. By contrast, under his successor, labor recruitment started and the people did "not drink water or eat quietly" anymore.

To substantiate his claims against the king and other corrupt officials at the royal court, Buta chronicled in meticulous detail the history of labor recruitment in São Salvador in 1912 and 1913. While his reconstruction of crucial episodes in this history corresponds chronologically with government and missionary reports of the same events, it complements them by offering a unique insider's perspective. His account is long; in fact, he spoke for two days, giving himself ample time to criticize the regime in São Salvador, recounting even the most trifling facts. However, certain themes dominated his narrative. Buta first of all remembered the disappointment he and others felt when Kiditu returned from his negotiations with the district governor in Cabinda, in the middle of 1912,

Manuel Martins Kiditu (*bottom right*) with Manuel Lopes de Almeida (*top left*) and José Heliodoro de Faria Leal (*middle*), ca. 1911 (photo by unknown author, private collection, reproduced with permission of José Carlos de Oliveira)

with nothing but a request for workers, consistently called "porters" in reference to the main kind of labor performed in the early colonial economy. Like most chiefs with a stake in the kingdom, Buta used to provide carriers for local employers as well as men for Cabinda when Kiditu asked him. Loyalty to the king, small material rewards, and fear of penalties enticed chiefs like Buta to collaborate with the government. But before long the disastrous effects of government-imposed contract labor became evident: village headmen were taken hostage while policemen took to extortion and rape; workers were chained and beaten; wages were paid late or not at all; and there was uncertainty about the return of migrants from the Cabinda enclave.

Over time, Buta's disappointment in the king's policies became more personal, as the behavior of Kiditu himself became increasingly unreliable. For instance, when Godinho came to São Salvador in October 1913 to contract 1,500 workers for São Tomé and Príncipe, the king himself instructed his chiefs to resist the demands of the "white man"—who was not mentioned by name—and stand firm (*nutoma kanga mpondaku*, "to tighten your belts"), which they did. A month later, however, the king sent messengers to Buta telling him he would be arrested and deported to "Ponta"—Kongo vernacular for a coastal trade point—if he refused to supply fresh workers for Cabinda. According to a Portuguese report, Buta told these messengers that it was only because they were his relatives that he did not have their heads cut off.[21] Other official records indicate that the government had, by that time, reinforced its military posts in the Madimba region and authorized Paulo Moreira to seize Álvaro Buta for his defiance of colonial orders.[22] Buta was aware of the pending threat and narrowly escaped an arrest in Kinganga (Belém), a Catholic mission site in Madimba, where Buta thought he and other chiefs could meet in safety. But one of his followers was killed in the scuffle that took place and this, according to Claridge, was what "really precipitated the conflict."[23] The loss of one of his own men at the hands of soldiers from São Salvador shattered the last bit of trust Buta still had in the integrity of his relative, the king. As normal political relations with the king and his court had broken down, Buta was determined to take military action.

In a later interview, Kiditu passed the blame for this political breakdown to the Portuguese administrator, Paulo Midosi Moreira, while he saw himself as a mediator between the government and the chiefs, someone who should not be held accountable for decisions taken by his superiors. He claimed he knew early on that his involvement in the ongoing recruitment was suspect and that Buta had threatened to kill both Moreira and Kiditu himself if they kept demanding workers from him. So when Moreira informed Kiditu about the government's plan to capture Buta, the king warned him that this would provoke a war, which it did. Moreover, after Buta had announced his intentions to attack São Salvador, Kiditu and several others wanted Bowskill, the Baptist missionary, to broker peace between the government and Buta's rebel army, which Moreira fatefully refused.[24] In short, Kiditu portrayed himself as a conciliator and Moreira as the main architect of the Kongo crisis. To his constituency, however, Kiditu was more than a go-between; as *ntotela*, he was a central player in Kongo politics and ultimately responsible for the current unrest in the kingdom.

Approaching sunset on December 11, Buta explained his motives for attacking São Salvador, and why his rebel group left the reviled *chefe de posto*, Moreira, untouched. While Buta and his allies assembled thousands of warriors a few miles south of the capital, Moreira signaled through the priests that he wished to avoid a full-blown confrontation with the rebels, who far outnumbered the colonial troops at his disposal. Buta had already lost faith in the padres, however, as they had failed to protect him earlier. He responded that he "must go to Kongo and see what is going on. We put the King on the throne to protect the people and as he does not do so I must go and fight him," although he was willing to leave Moreira and the priests out of his conflict with Kiditu if they so wished. Thus Buta assured subsequent embassies from the capital that his army would have their eyes only on Kiditu and his followers.[25] That the *chefe de posto* was so easily dismissed as an irrelevant target in the insurgency demonstrates how much the Kongo chiefs held their king and not Portugal responsible for the nefarious consequences of colonial rule.

Resolutions

On the second day of the palaver, Buta presented the specific charges and demands of his rebel coalition. The first man accused was the king's secretary and counselor, fifty-year-old Manuel Lopes de Almeida, whom Buta described to the missionaries as someone who could read and write but did not "keep your teaching." Almeida was guilty of physical abuse, extortion, kidnapping, and other crimes committed during tax collection, all graphically described and listed in a separate "summary of charges made against certain native officials," which the BMS attached to their report. For his crimes, Almeida had to leave the country to be tried by the Portuguese governor in Cabinda; otherwise Buta's men would kill him. The second major culprit was Afonso Kapitau, an old royal counselor and father of the equally hated colonial officer Ambrósio Divengele. He was "the man who has ruined the King," Buta claimed, expressing particular disappointment in the elder's lack of guidance. "Instead of leading him [the king] in the good way he has misled him." Kapitau seemed to represent Buta's clan in the Kongo government, for Buta said that "he has eaten up my throne" (*umdidi'e kiandu*), an expression signifying the destruction of one's honor. Currently in hiding, he was given three days to leave the country.

Kapitau's son, Ambrósio Augusto Divengele, best exemplified the moral crisis that had descended on the kingdom in recent years. A São Salvador native, Divengele grew up under the auspices of the Portuguese priests and became a proud mission product. He had entered the Catholic school in 1890, when he was about seven years old, and was still with the padres in 1899, by which time he had learned to read, write, and do basic arithmetic. On the occasion of his church's first anniversary, in 1905, Divengele wrote that the missionaries "teach the rules of the good life, [and] do not teach arrogance or the rich to behave haughtily," citing verse 6:17 from 1 Timothy, Paul's final word to the wealthy.[26] When he penned these words, he was working as a stonemason in São Salvador, a respected profession in early colonial Kongo; he later became a clerk (*amanuense*) in the colonial administration, helping the government with the compilation of tax registers. At the palaver in 1913, he was charged with extortion, multiple acts of violence, and rape.

These cases are a potent reminder of how the militarization of power under early colonial rule upset traditional community relations and corresponding ideas of civic virtue. Through the actions of people like Almeida and Divengele, colonialism "posited the issue of contingent human violence," confronting Africans "with the *opaque and murky domain of power*," as the political theorist

Achille Mbembe puts it.[27] It should be noted that the moral corruption induced
by the colonial capacity to command affected Baptist as well as Catholic
members of the Kongo community. To shouts of approval, Buta also accused
one of the Protestant counselors, Pedro Nefwane Talanga, of crooked behavior.
While his crimes were not specified, Talanga was described as a vicious person
(*kimpumbulu*) who "carries pig intestines in his pocket," a Kongo phrase to denote
avarice and greed, that is, witchcraft. Talanga had to drop his public function
but was allowed to return to his home in the country.

But the "big knot" (*ejita diampwena*) in Buta's account concerned the dethronement of Kiditu. The king, who was hiding at the Catholic mission during
the palaver, was accused of political weakness, betrayal, and greediness. As
Buta explained, since Kiditu had been in power, he had done nothing good for
his people; everything he did was done for Paulo Moreira, the Portuguese
administrator. To illustrate this point, Buta explained that when chiefs supplied
workers at the request of São Salvador, "they are sent for in the name of the
King but when they come it is not the King who wants them but Sr. Paul."
This statement reveals the murkiness of the recruitment business, as colonial
demands for workers were met not through transparent contracting but
through the king's ability to command supplies on the basis of coercion, loyalty,
and material rewards. Kiditu's erratic behavior during his two years in government suggests that the king himself was torn between his role as representative
of the people and his position as middleman in the colonial system.[28] For instance, Buta reproached him for personally providing the government with
workers for São Tomé and Príncipe after first telling chiefs to stand firm against
new Portuguese demands for labor. But the strongest condemnation of Kiditu's
behavior was related to his complicity in the violence of local government
agents, who operated in the king's name.

While for Buta the corruption of the royal office was a personal affront,
symbolized by the king's authorization of his capture, other chiefs expressed
unhappiness with Kiditu's alleged avarice. They complained that the king had
taken judicial powers away from them by insisting that all legal disputes be settled
in the capital, only to "ensure that all the [goat] legs came to his *lumbu* [royal
enclosure]" (goat legs were payment chiefs received for settling disputes).
Possibly Kiditu had convinced others that the system of customary law that
Portugal had recently introduced was a kind of centralized jurisprudence,
which theoretically it was not. It is also possible that more and more Kongo
citizens, including women, brought their legal and marital questions directly to
São Salvador to circumvent the control of village authorities.[29] But whatever
reality lay behind the sensed loss of jurisdictional authority, the chiefs clearly
perceived it as an illegitimate extension of royal power at their expense.

"Kiditu we dethrone" (*tunkunkwidi*), shouted the insurgents repeatedly after Buta had finished listing the charges against the king and his associates. Deposing the king was the main objective of the Kongo uprising in December 1913. But in addition to sending Kiditu and two of his senior advisors, Kapitau and Almeida, into exile, the insurgents also demanded changes from the district governor in Cabinda. At this stage of the revolt, ousting the Portuguese from the kingdom was not yet on their agenda. Instead, the chiefs tried to renegotiate their relationship with the colonial government, demanding a reduction of the hut tax and an end to the recruitment of workers for Cabinda and São Tomé. While rebel forces regrouped outside the capital, a ceasefire remained in effect until Governor Cardoso's reply—promising a suspension of labor recruitment but no tax reduction—finally arrived in the middle of January 1914.[30]

While the dust of Buta's attack on São Salvador was still settling, a dispute about the succession of Kiditu began. At the end of the war palaver on December 12, the rebels decided that Kiditu, being dethroned, had to leave the country or face decapitation. To clarify this form of political sanitization to their European audience, the rebels drew a parallel with the Republican upheavals in Portugal, where one king, Dom Carlos I (1889–1908), was murdered, while his son and successor, Dom Manuel II (1908–10), was sent into exile. When Buta demanded that the regalia be taken from Kiditu, others warned that they should under no circumstances be taken out of São Salvador, for that would imply a removal of the government's seat from the kingdom's spiritual center. That same night, therefore, the rebels entrusted the Portuguese priests with the royal robes and insignia. While Kiditu and Kapitau fled to Belgian Congo, the rebel leaders informed the Baptist missionaries that they wanted Noso, the princess of Mbanza Mputu, to occupy the empty throne.[31] Her selection signaled a break on the part of some ruling elites with the long tradition of Madimba kings in São Salvador, which had started with Henrique II in 1842 and had since been cultivated by the Kivuzi and Agua Rosada families with Portuguese support. The last time Mbanza Mputu had tried to claim the Kongo throne was in 1891, when their leader Garcia Mbumba was declared unelectable for being Protestant and received the title of *noso* as compensation. Pressured by Afonso Kalanfwa, also a member of the Baptist Church, the rebels now supported the candidacy of Mbumba's niece, who had received the title of princess from the king upon her uncle's death in 1912.[32] According to the Catholic priests, however, Buta himself preferred to see his uncle Mfutila, the chief of Zamba, on the throne. Buta and Mfutila both represented the Madimba faction in Kongo politics; for them the coup against Kiditu was above all an intra-factional affair driven by emotions of betrayal and deceit. Although Mfutila had initially tried to broker peace between Buta and Kiditu, he joined the uprising later in December. The safe-conducts he then issued to travelers in rebel-controlled areas were marked with a signature that clearly conveyed his ambitions: "Mfutila, king of the whole world."[33] However, further escalation of the insurgency made both Noso and Mfutila unelectable, and when the war ended, in July 1915, Portugal appointed one of its own favorites as king.

Conclusion

The transformation of the Kongo kingdom into a mechanism to expand Portuguese hegemony in northern Angola proved politically catastrophic. The arbitrary implementation of colonial tax and labor laws provoked a popular uprising against the regime in São Salvador, causing the downfall of King Manuel III and pulling Kongo into a protracted guerrilla war against the colonial government. Extant documentation of the revolt indicates that Kongo's political class experienced colonial exploitation first and foremost as an illegitimate extension of royal authority, and this chapter has shown how the revolt was originally orchestrated as a renewal movement aimed to restore responsible kingship. But the rebellion quickly created a platform for the articulation of anti-Portuguese sentiments, even if Kongo intellectuals did not yet see colonial rule—a system of outside domination—as a concrete political problem.

There is some evidence to suggest that opposition to Portuguese rule in Kongo was growing in the Baptist community, where many saw England rather than Portugal as the kingdom's ideal European patron. As the rebel chiefs cordoned off São Salvador, awaiting the governor's response to their demands, they exchanged strategic information and news about the progress of their campaign in written form. From a set of letters intercepted by the colonial authorities, it is clear that members of the Baptist Church were instrumental in communicating messages between the rebel lines. One letter in particular holds important clues as to what the revolt meant to Kongo elites outside the predominantly Catholic district of Madimba. It was written from Mbanza Mputu in the days after Buta's war palaver by the Baptist evangelist António Nlekai, addressing his brother-in-law, Chief Noso of Lungezi.

Nlekai's letter conveyed a perspective on the revolt that was absent from Buta's narrative. On the one hand, Nlekai reminded his relative of the resolutions adopted in Zamba on December 12 regarding the restoration of order in the country. He had "instructed all brothers that the black man [*ndombe*] leaves the other black man [in peace]," saying that "as of now we are all united and there will be no more treason because treason brought harm [*lutovoko*] to our country." Nlekai seemed to refer directly to the corrupt behavior of Kiditu and his associates, but he must have been aware, too, of the potentially damaging consequences of factional rivalry in the process of electing Kiditu's successor.

On the other hand, Nlekai clearly presented the revolt as a movement against the colonial government and its African agents, although at the time of his writing the rebels were not yet at war with the Portuguese authorities. In his words, "we are all together now and our country is already at war with the white men [*vita a mindele*], whom we will confront. We no longer put up with the white man [*nemputu*], who has become unbearable for us. As for the policemen [*mapulisi*], the truth must be told now, they brought so much cruelty and suffering to the country, they stole produce from Madimba and captured the people and chiefs [*mfumu*] of the villages." Nlekai explicitly mentioned *cipaio* Afonso Cupessa, who was "the worst of all" and therefore deserved strong physical punishment. He furthermore described Ambrósio Divengele and Almeida, the royal secretary, as "worse than the devil; they and their policemen are the worst of all bad people."[31] The contents of this letter suggest that for some the revolt was from the beginning an attempt to oust both local evildoers and the Portuguese authorities from the Kongo realm, even if this only meant replacing the latter with another European overlord.

Conclusion

In terms of intrusiveness and brutality, colonial rule in the kingdom of Kongo entailed a sequence of widely divergent experiences. Kongo's colonial history began around 1860, when Dom Pedro V occupied São Salvador with military support from the Portuguese in Angola. In the ensuing decades, the kingdom witnessed the rise of new export trades in ivory and rubber—replacing the old slave trade—the arrival of a new generation of Christian missionaries, and the establishment of formal colonial rule in 1888. While the growth of Atlantic commerce and mission churches ushered in a period of rapid social change, the kingdom lived through five decades of remarkable political stability. For many Kongolese families this was a time of relative economic prosperity, based on their active and widespread involvement in the Central African rubber boom. Meanwhile government interference in the everyday affairs of the Kongo remained extremely limited. In fact, in this early period, the inhabitants of the kingdom barely experienced the new colonial order as a system of outside political, economic, and ideological exploitation.[1] They rather saw it as another episode in their kingdom's continuing engagement with European trade and culture.

Around 1910, however, Kongolese fortunes changed dramatically. The rubber factories that had for decades strengthened the position of São Salvador in the economy of northern Angola, creating employment opportunities for thousands of carriers every year, suddenly closed. As the local export economy collapsed, incomes throughout the region declined, leaving many households struggling to pay the colonial hut tax. Moreover, just when the time of rubber-induced plenty came to an end, the recently installed Republican government

144

in Lisbon began to make serious work of ruling Portugal's colonial possessions in Africa.[2] In Angola, the colonial government introduced laws to mobilize migrant workers from Kongo to labor elsewhere in the Portuguese empire. As always, however, colonial administrators were dependent on the king at São Salvador to put the new labor laws into effect. The incumbent ruler, Manuel Martins Kiditu, agreed to use his influence among fellow chiefs to help the government conscript workers for plantations in Cabinda, north of the Congo River, as well as São Tomé and Príncipe, hoping that the financial benefits of contract labor would alleviate hardship in the kingdom. But Kiditu's decision to assist the government in executing its ambitious migration scheme proved catastrophic for both himself and his people, as soldiers, policemen, and other recruitment agents began to unleash unprecedented levels of violence on Kongo villages. In 1913, these abuses caused some of the most senior chiefs in the kingdom to revolt against their king and depose him.

But even as levels of colonial exploitation deepened in the kingdom, the Kongo did not relate the causes of the ensuing violence to the state's encroachment on society. Instead of seeing policy-makers in Lisbon, Luanda, or Cabinda as the main architects of colonial coercion, the chiefs held the king responsible for their suffering: he had negotiated the Cabinda recruitment with the kingdom's overlord, while men coming from his court to engage workers violated, beat, and captured their kinfolk. The behavior of Kiditu and his associates was mainly seen as a betrayal of traditional notions of good governance, to which all Kongo kings pledged obedience. From a local viewpoint, in other words, the crisis of 1913 was caused not so much by the fact of "being colonized" as by the growing corruption of the royal office and other positions of power in the kingdom under Portuguese tutelage. Hence the solution for this crisis lay not in overthrowing colonial rule but in restoring order in the kingdom, which meant replacing the king and renegotiating colonial rule with Portugal.[3]

The uprising in 1913 marked a turning point in Kongo's colonial history. First, the revolt signaled the end of the era of the carrying trade, which had transformed the lives of many Kongo men and their families since the abolition of the Atlantic slave trade. Declining global rubber prices after 1913 dealt a blow to the African transport business, which had already begun to crumble in São Salvador some years earlier. The colonial government tried to force a transition to wage labor by mobilizing contract workers for plantations overseas, but with such disastrous consequences that after the revolt the government delayed further attempts to impose coerced migration on the Congo District. Second, by the time of the revolt, the new Christian churches had become integral to public life in the kingdom, with mission-educated elites gaining significant social and political power at the expense of the old trading elites.

Some of them used their missionary training to occupy functions in the colonial government, while others found in their writing skills and church membership novel ways to mobilize communities against colonial oppression. Third, the uprising was the culmination of a labor scandal that brought to light the extensive and often illegal activities of Kongo's colonial intermediaries, whose presence went generally unnoticed in the archival record. The African employees of the Portuguese government in São Salvador, while often literate, hardly ever left behind written documents and received little mention in the reports of their white superiors. The Kongo protests against colonial atrocities in 1912 and 1913, however, revealed the unlimited potential of these agents to "expand on their official duties," as one historian has put it.[1]

A number of lessons about the Kongo monarchy and its fate under foreign rule can be drawn from the early colonial experience. To begin with, the uprising against the regime in São Salvador in 1913 is proof that contemporary Kongo kings were not mere "figments of the collective imagination," as a notable scholar once argued.[5] The historian Susan Herlin Broadhead proposed, some time ago, that if we want to understand how the old kingdom survived a pattern of continuous political fragmentation, it is important to think about the Kongo polity in terms "beyond decline."[6] She suggested that size was not the issue, as political relations between chiefdoms in the kingdom were based not on the kind of centralized territorial control claimed by modern states but rather on a shared recognition of São Salvador as a religious center.[7] Chiefs all over the Kongo region tapped into the spiritual power residing in São Salvador to enforce their authority along the trade routes, settle disputes, and regulate other community affairs. This book has carried Broadhead's project forward into the post–slave trade era, a period in which she and others after her have been reluctant to acknowledge the kingdom as an important factor in the everyday lives of the Kongo people.

Around 1860, the kingdom was still a corporation of aristocrats who used the spiritual power emanating from São Salvador to legitimize their control over people, land, and trade routes. The membership of this corporation diminished toward the end of the century as many of its regulatory functions, related to the regional trade in slaves and ivory, became obsolete under colonial rule. But contrary to what is often believed, the kingdom did not collapse because of this.[8] Instead of disintegration, the documentary evidence points to renovation. When European commercial and political interests in Central Africa deepened after the end of the slave trade, Kongo's ruling elites transformed the kingdom into a vehicle of colonial expansion. Many European traders, missionaries, and scientific travelers wanting to explore the corridor between the Atlantic coast and the great markets of Malebo Pool, up the Congo River, and Kasongo-Lunda, on the Kwango, were drawn to São Salvador for the logistical support offered by the king, his relatives, and client chiefs. These early visitors were followed by the colonial government, whose rule in northern Angola was most effective in places where members of Kongo's ruling family, the Agua Rosada, could mediate. Stores, churches, and an administrative residence were built in São Salvador, reinforcing the city's reputation as an economic, religious, and political center in northern Angola.[9]

Colonial rule particularly strengthened the position of the royal court in Kongo society. As the European presence in Kongo became more visible, the kingdom became an important network to place relatives and clients in favorable positions in the government, at factories, and in mission schools. São Salvador remained a source of political power and prestige, transmitted by traditional titles—especially investitures in the Order of Christ—as well as new colonial military ranks. Many clans, even if they participated little in the affairs of the kingdom, still referred to São Salvador to legitimize land holdings and political positions. The colonial government itself depended on forces supplied by the king and other powerful men in São Salvador to provide safety on the caravan routes and, later, extract resources from the Kongolese population. While Pedro V (1860–91) never had the authority to demand regular tribute from his subjects, his successors abused colonial laws—especially those relating to tax and labor—to enhance their extractive powers. In short, the kingdom remained into the twentieth century an arena where powerful agents, both African and European, competed for political and social influence.

Kiditu's installation in 1911 and his dethronement in 1913 brought yet another side of Kongo's monarchical tradition to light. Co-opted by the Portuguese empire, the kingdom continued to exist as a political community, based on specific notions of accountability and centered on the king as the highest spiritual power in the land. The king was a source and symbol of social harmony, but he was also expected to use his secular skills—his knowledge of the white man's ways—to effectively negotiate with Kongo's European partners. In 1913, a crisis about the constitution of this community culminated in revolt. This was a moral crisis in more than one sense. The abuse of political power by the king and his associates constituted not only a transgression of the rules of political legitimacy in the kingdom but also an assault on widely shared beliefs about proper social conduct. In fact, from a Kongolese perspective, the social and the political were connected, as political turmoil was commonly explained as resulting from the malevolence of particular individuals in the community. On a spiritual level, therefore, restoring order meant the return of peace to the kingdom.

Finally, it should be emphasized that the Kongo uprising in 1913 did not come about simply because the colonial state became ever more intrusive and oppressive, as if resistance was the inevitable outcome of increased exploitation.

The political impact of colonial rule on Kongo society was shaped by local moral economies and determined by local contingencies. A micro-analysis of the origins of the Kongo revolt has specifically revealed the importance of interpersonal relations in Kongo politics in the early colonial period. As has been shown, rebels and culprits were often related to one another through kinship, church bonds, or other social networks. It is possible, therefore, that strains on the affective bonds within the Kongo community drove rebels to action as much as did political principles. Álvaro Buta's account of the crisis indicates, in fact, that experiences of betrayal and deceit not only defined postcolonial memories of European rule in Africa, as Johannes Fabian has suggested, but were lived emotions at the time and strong motivators of political action.[10] What if in the final days before the revolt Kiditu had asked forgiveness from Buta for his treacherous behavior? In that case, according to one local eyewitness, this cataclysmic event could have been avoided.[11]

Epilogue

The idea of a Kongo "moral order" to which the subtitle of this book alludes has been borrowed from the anthropologist Wyatt MacGaffey, who used it to reflect on calls for a restoration of the Kongo kingdom heard around Malebo Pool in the late 1950s. In the colonial twin cities of Léopoldville and Brazzaville, Kongo independence movements such as ABAKO (Alliance des Bakongo) and UDDIA (Union de Défense des Intérêts Africains) made resurrecting the ancient monarchy a central tenet of their political programs, as it still is for Bundu dia Kongo today. MacGaffey argued that "for most people to this day 'Mbanza Kongo' is primarily a political and moral order. Independence, in 1959, meant the restoration of the kingdom, that is, of chiefship . . . as a moral principle."[1] Thus talk of restoring the kingdom was part of an ongoing discourse about the meaning of independence, which many people saw as a redemptive moment that would usher in a new era of responsible leadership and general welfare.

In a very different context, John Thornton has shown how Kongo ideas about monarchy influenced the ideology of the Haitian revolution.[2] In Saint Domingue, as in Kinshasa 150 years later, rebel leaders constructed a subversive royalist discourse out of mythical ties to the ancient kingdom of Kongo and an African political morality centered on the binary concepts of witchcraft and social harmony. In Haiti as well as Kinshasa, the kingdom was conceived as a moral order that stood in opposition to different forms of European exploitation, namely slavery and colonialism. While in these diasporic contexts, Kongo royalist discourses were thus mainly utopian expressions of a new political order, they still provide a prism through which to study the genuine restoration movement that emerged within the kingdom in 1913.

Although the revolt of Tulante Álvaro Buta was first and foremost a movement aiming to restore harmony within the kingdom of Kongo, it quickly developed into an insurgency against the incumbent colonial regime. Portugal broke the truce that was agreed in December in the middle of January 1914, when the new military commander in São Salvador, Joaquim Gama, arrested four prominent members of the Baptist community for the illegal possession and trade of firearms. This was a clear signal to Buta that the Portuguese could not be trusted. At this point, according to later eyewitness accounts, Buta decided to focus the war on driving out the Portuguese in order to let another European nation rule the kingdom. For several weeks, rebel forces carried out daily attacks on São Salvador, burning homes and exchanging fire with government troops until the city was liberated near the end of February by a colonial army under the command of interim governor Jayme de Moraes. From that point, Buta had to shift his war to the countryside.[3]

The revolt had started as a feud between related clans based in the Madimba district south of São Salvador, but with the help of several Protestant evangelists, who had license to travel across rebel lines, it quickly spread to areas east, north, and west of the capital. As the war expanded in scale, it laid bare many internal divisions in Kongo society. Coercion and witchcraft were used to persuade chiefs to join the uprising, with Buta sending out warnings that those who refused to adhere would be killed on his command. Villages were burned and people taken hostage, including the family of Álvaro de Agua Rosada Tangi, who fought on the Portuguese side. Especially chiefs of the older generation, who had grown up and risen to power under the rule of Pedro V (1860–91), were reluctant to join the revolt. The elders of Kimalu, a village in Madimba on the rebel side, declared later that they had not originally wanted to fight the government, as their ancestors had never made war against São Salvador. As the war escalated, in short, Kongo's moral crisis deepened.[4]

Buta also tried, often unsuccessfully, to involve other Kongo regions in his revolt against the colonial regime, especially after the siege of São Salvador was broken in late February and Buta was forced to fight his battles away from the capital. His new anti-Portuguese discourse provided a platform for cooperation with chiefs outside the kingdom, and soon there was widespread talk of bringing the English in as new colonial overlords.[5] But some rulers, like the chief of Maquela do Zombo, remained loyal to Portugal. Others, particularly in areas closer to the coast, were fighting their own battles with the colonial government and did not see Buta's program of restoring the kingdom in São Salvador as relevant to their own political strategies.[6] While rebellions sprang up in all corners of the Portuguese Congo District in 1914, Buta's War never became a pan-Kongo or proto-nationalist movement capable of uniting rebels across northern Angola, as some have suggested.

Toward the end of 1914, the colonial government slowly regained control of the kingdom. One of Tulante Buta's main allies, Nkongolo, was captured in October, and government troops seized control of the road between Noqui and São Salvador. Many chiefs were growing tired of war. Baptist evangelists proved to be as important in negotiating peace on behalf of the government as they had been in mobilizing rebel populations a year earlier. Beginning in December 1914, they convinced several chiefs around São Salvador to lay down their arms and negotiate their capitulation in the capital. Buta and many of the remaining rebels, including his most senior ally, Mfutila of Zamba, conceded defeat in São Salvador in July 1915.[7] Portuguese officials, however, were unwilling to bargain with the most important rebel leaders, who upon their surrender were all arrested and deported to Luanda. Buta died in prison shortly after his deportation, reportedly of influenza. In pacified areas, the government immediately set to collecting the hut tax and recruiting young males as carriers and soldiers for war operations against Germany in southern Angola, provoking a wave of Kongo migration north to Belgian Congo. Meanwhile, the installation of a new king in August marked the official end of a civil war that had lasted twenty months. A committee of chiefs, church representatives, and the counselors of the deposed Manuel Kiditu elected as his successor the chief of Mpondani, Noso Álvaro Nzingu (1915–23). Nzingu, an elderly Kivuzi who had received his title from Dom Pedro V and remained neutral during the war, represented a return to stability.[8]

Buta's War was the last concerted effort by Kongo elites to regain control of an institution that had governed the lives of traders, peasants, and aristocrats in this part of West Central Africa for more than five centuries. By the end of the revolt, the balance of power in the kingdom had shifted strongly in favor of the Portuguese government. At the same time, the kingdom was losing its important hinge function in the European colonization of northern Angola, as more and more Kongo-speaking populations with few or no connections to São Salvador came under colonial control. Had decline perhaps finally set in?

That is not the impression one gets from a snapshot of the reign of Dom Pedro VII, alias John Lengo, former elephant hunter and chief of Palabala, in Belgian Congo, who ruled from 1923 to 1955. In his younger days, Lengo had been a student of American and English Baptist missionaries in the Congo and Angola, but during the war of 1913–15 he was part of the auxiliary troops defending the regime in São Salvador. To receive his kingship, he converted to Catholicism, divorced his eight wives, and married in the Church to Ana

Tussamba, a descendant of Kongo nobility like himself. His income in São Salvador derived from a government salary, the arbitration of legal disputes, and tribute paid by lesser chiefs, which came in abundantly during the Feast of the Sacred Heart, held annually in June to celebrate the king and bless the land.[9] Thus Pedro VII still reaped the benefits of São Salvador's religious importance to the wider Kongo populace. The city's continued spiritual attraction was further evidenced by Angolan migrants in Belgian Congo, who often returned to São Salvador to marry and to baptize their newborns, and even sent their children to be educated at the local Catholic mission.[10]

Throughout the colonial period, São Salvador remained home for many Kongo families who for economic reasons had moved from Angola to urban centers across the border. From these multilingual, cosmopolitan migrant communities emerged the political class responsible for creating some of the early Angolan independence movements. Education at the Catholic mission in São Salvador or at one of the lower Congo stations of the Baptist Missionary Society was an important factor in shaping the group identities of these urban intellectuals. Two Protestant factions, one based in Matadi, whose figurehead was Manuel Kiditu, nephew of the former king, and the other in Léopoldville, led by Manuel Barros Nekaka, son of pioneer evangelist Miguel Nekaka, merged in 1957 into the União das Populações do Norte de Angola (UPNA), a forerunner of the Frente Nacional de Libertação de Angola (FNLA). Around the same time, a group of exiled Catholic monarchists in Léopoldville founded Ngwizani a Kongo, or Ngwizako, under the leadership of José dos Santos Kasakanga. In the words of John Marcum, both groups wanted to "revive the authority of the crown so as to create a political instrument through which to work for social and economic reform" in northern Angola, where once again forced labor was an issue of concern for the local population. As Portugal seemed unresponsive to demands for improved colonial governance, Kongo political discourse was quickly oriented to the question of independence, by which party leaders meant a restoration of the ancient kingdom, to be placed under the protection of the United Nations. This was clearly a utopian ideal, although it took a visit of Miguel Nekaka's grandson, Holden Roberto, to the All-African Peoples' Conference in Ghana in 1958 before UPNA sacrificed its "tribal anachronism" for a more inclusive political platform.[11]

NOTES

Abbreviations

AA	Ministère des Affaires étrangères, Archives africaines (Belgium)
AAL	Arquivo do Arçobispado de Luanda (Angola)
AHD	Ministério dos Negócios Estrangeiros, Arquivo Histórico Diplomático (Portugal)
AHM	Arquivo Histórico Militar (Portugal)
AHNA	Arquivo Histórico Nacional de Angola
AHR	*American Historical Review*
AHU	Arquivo Histórico Ultramarino (Portugal)
ALA	Angus Library and Archive, Regent's Park College, Baptist Missionary Society (UK)
BMS	Baptist Missionary Society
BO	*Boletim Oficial de Angola*
BSGL	*Boletim da Sociedade de Geografia de Lisboa*
IJAHS	*International Journal of African Historical Studies*
JAH	*Journal of African History*
MH	*Missionary Herald of the Baptist Missionary Society*
MSENMU	Ministro e secretário de Estado dos Negócios da Marinha e Ultramar
NA	Nationaal Archief (Netherlands)
SGL	Sociedade de Geografia de Lisboa (Portugal)
TNA	The National Archives of the United Kingdom

Introduction

1. Voyages: The Transatlantic Slave Trade Database, voyage id 5052, accessed 20 August 2014, http://www.slavevoyages.org.

2. The kingdom's capital was also known as Mbanza Kongo, but from 1570 to 1975 its official name was São Salvador. This book defines the Kongo as a group of people who were politically affiliated with São Salvador. Kongo language and culture are shared by a larger population in northern Angola and southwest Congo, known since colonial times as the Bakongo.

3. While some historians currently aim to "decentralize" the African past by moving their analytical lens away from centers of political power, the role of court politics in shaping colonial history is sometimes hard to ignore. Compare David Newbury, *The*

Land beyond the Mists: Essays on Identity and Authority in Precolonial Congo and Rwanda (Athens: Ohio University Press, 2009), 1–8; Alison Liebhafsky Des Forges, *Defeat Is the Only Bad News: Rwanda under Musinga, 1896–1931* (Madison: University of Wisconsin Press, 2011); Michael Twaddle, *Kakungulu and the Creation of Uganda, 1868–1928* (London: James Currey, 1993); Jan Vansina, *Being Colonized: The Kuba Experience in Rural Congo, 1880–1960* (Madison: University of Wisconsin Press, 2010).

4. David Van Reybrouck, *Congo: Een geschiedenis* (Amsterdam: Bezige Bij, 2011), 36; Daniel Metcalfe, *Blue Dahlia, Black Gold: A Journey into Angola* (London: Random House, 2013), 256, 265–66.

5. Roger Anstey, *Britain and the Congo in the Nineteenth Century* (Oxford: Clarendon Press, 1962); Eric Axelson, *Portugal and the Scramble for Africa, 1875–1891* (Johannesburg: Witwatersrand University Press, 1967); Françoise Latour da Veiga Pinto, *Le Portugal et le Congo au XIXe siècle: Étude d'histoire des relations internationales* (Paris: Presses universitaires de France, 1972); René Pélissier, *História das campanhas de Angola: Resistência e revoltas 1845–1941*, 2nd ed. (Lisbon: Editorial Estampa, 1997). Existing histories of the kingdom generally end before the colonial period. See, for instance, Anne Hilton, *The Kingdom of Kongo* (Oxford: Clarendon Press, 1985); William G. L. Randles, *L'ancien royaume du Congo des origines à la fin du XIXème siècle* (Paris: Mouton, 1968).

6. For recent overviews, see Jill R. Dias, "Angola," in *O império africano, 1825–1890*, ed. Valentim Alexandre and Jill Dias (Lisbon: Editorial Estampa, 1998), 319–556; Aida Freudenthal, "Angola," in *O império africano, 1890–1930*, ed. António Henrique de Oliveira Marques (Lisbon: Editorial Estampa, 2001), 259–452.

7. William Gervase Clarence-Smith, *Slaves, Peasants and Capitalists in Southern Angola, 1840–1926* (Cambridge: Cambridge University Press, 1979); Linda M. Heywood, *Contested Power in Angola, 1840s to the Present* (Rochester, NY: University of Rochester Press, 2000). For the metropolitan perspective, see Douglas L. Wheeler and René Pélissier, *Angola* (London: Pall Mall Press, 1971), translated into Portuguese as *História de Angola* (Lisbon: Tinta-da-China, 2009); Valentim Alexandre, *Velho Brasil, novas Áfricas: Portugal e o império (1808–1975)* (Porto: Edições Afrontamento, 2000); Gabriel Paquette, *Imperial Portugal in the Age of Atlantic Revolutions: The Luso-Brazilian World, c. 1770–1850* (Cambridge: Cambridge University Press, 2013), ch. 5. For the relation between policy and practice, see Roquinaldo do Amaral Ferreira, "Abolicionismo *versus* colonialismo: Rupturas e continuidades em Angola (século XIX)," in *África: Brasileiros e portugueses, séculos XVI–XIX*, ed. Roberto Guedes (Rio de Janeiro: Mauad, 2013), 95–112.

8. In general, Kongo's incorporation in the Portuguese empire fits the patron-client framework proposed by Colin Newbury, *Patrons, Clients, and Empire: Chieftaincy and Over-rule in Asia, Africa, and the Pacific* (Oxford: Oxford University Press, 2003).

9. For recent discussions of early exchanges, see Linda Heywood and John Thornton, "Central African Leadership and the Appropriation of European Culture," in *The Atlantic World and Virginia, 1550–1624*, ed. Peter C. Mancall (Chapel Hill: University of North Carolina Press, 2007), 194–224; David Northrup, *Africa's Discovery of Europe: 1450–1850*, 3rd ed. (New York: Oxford University Press, 2013), 20–22, 36–43.

10. For insider descriptions of the revolt, see George Cyril Claridge, *Wild Bush Tribes of Tropical Africa* (London: Seeley, Service & Co., 1922), 39–55; Robert H. C. Graham, *Under Seven Congo Kings* (London: Carey Press, 1930), 136–72.

11. Pélissier, *História das campanhas*, 1:240.

12. For a recent discussion, see Eric Allina, *Slavery by Any Other Name: African Life under Company Rule in Early Colonial Mozambique* (Charlottesville: University of Virginia Press, 2012), introduction.

13. Catherine Higgs, *Chocolate Islands: Cocoa, Slavery, and Colonial Africa* (Athens: Ohio University Press, 2012).

14. James Duffy, *A Question of Slavery: Labour Policies in Portuguese Africa and the British Protest, 1850–1920* (Oxford: Clarendon Press, 1967); Kevin Grant, *A Civilised Savagery: Britain and the New Slaveries in Africa, 1884–1926* (New York: Routledge, 2005), ch. 4.

15. See AHU, SEMU/MU-DGU/DGC, Angola, maço 1081.

16. Frederick Cooper, *Decolonization and African Society: The Labor Question in French and British Africa* (Cambridge: Cambridge University Press, 1996), 34.

17. John Marcum, *The Angolan Revolution*, vol. 1, *The Anatomy of an Explosion (1950–1962)* (Cambridge, MA: MIT Press, 1969), 51–53; Pélissier, *História das campanhas*, 1:243–44, 294; Wheeler and Pélissier, *Angola*, 89; Allen F. Isaacman and Jan Vansina, "African Initiatives and Resistance in Central Africa, 1880–1914," in *General History of Africa*, vol. 7, *Africa under Colonial Domination, 1880–1935*, ed. A. Boahen (London: Heinemann, 1985), 185–87.

18. António Setas, *História do Reino do Kongo* (Luanda: Editorial Nzila, 2007), 221–31.

19. William Beinart and Colin Bundy, *Hidden Struggles in Rural South Africa: Politics and Popular Movements in the Transkei and Eastern Cape, 1890–1930* (Berkeley: University of California Press, 1987), 33–34. See also Karen Fields, *Revival and Rebellion in Colonial Central Africa* (Princeton, NJ: Princeton University Press, 1985), 14–21.

20. See, for example, Michelle Moyd, *Violent Intermediaries: African Soldiers, Conquest, and Everyday Colonialism in German East Africa* (Athens: Ohio University Press, 2014).

21. Frederick Cooper, "Conflict and Connection: Rethinking Colonial African History," *AHR* 99, no. 5 (1994): 1534. For "primary resistance," see Terence O. Ranger, "Connexions between 'Primary Resistance' Movements and Modern Mass Nationalism in East and Central Africa," *JAH* 9, nos. 3–4 (1968): 437–53, 631–41; and his auto-critique in "The People in African Resistance: A Review," *Journal of Southern African Studies* 4, no. 1 (1977): 125–46. For subsequent developments in the literature, see Donald Crummey, ed., *Banditry, Rebellion and Social Protest in Africa* (London: James Currey, 1986), introduction; Jon Abbink et al., eds., *Rethinking Resistance: Revolt and Violence in African History* (Leiden: Brill, 2003), ch. 1. For similar developments in the study of political contention in Europe, see Charles Tilly, "The Modernization of Political Conflict in France" and "Parliamentarization of Popular Contention in Great Britain, 1758–1834," in *Roads from Past to Future* (Lanham, MD: Rowman and Littlefield, 1997), 51–108, 217–44.

22. See Edward P. Thompson, "The Moral Economy of the English Crowd in the Eighteenth Century," in *Customs in Common* (London: Penguin Books, 1993), 185–258.

23. Steven Feierman, *Peasant Intellectuals: Anthropology and History in Tanzania* (Madison: University of Wisconsin Press, 1990); Jonathon Glassman, *Feasts and Riot: Revelry, Rebellion, and Popular Consciousness on the Swahili Coast, 1856–1888* (Portsmouth, NH: Heinemann, 1995). The encroaching market idea still informed John Iliffe's interpretation of the Maji Maji rebellion in *A Modern History of Tanganyika* (Cambridge: Cambridge University Press, 1979), ch. 6.

24. John Lonsdale, "The Moral Economy of Mau Mau: The Problem," in *Unhappy Valley: Conflict in Kenya and Africa*, vol. 2, *Violence and Ethnicity*, by Bruce Berman and John

Lonsdale (London: James Currey, 1992), 294. Lonsdale borrows his terminology from Barrington Moore, *Injustice: The Social Basis of Obedience and Revolt* (London: MacMillan, 1979).

25. Sean Redding, *Sorcery and Sovereignty: Taxation, Power, and Rebellion in South Africa, 1880–1963* (Athens: Ohio University Press, 2006), ch. 4.

26. Thomas Spear, *Mountain Farmers: Moral Economies of Land and Agricultural Development in Arusha and Meru* (Oxford: James Currey, 1997). See also Stephen Ellis and Gerrie Ter Haar, *Worlds of Power: Religious Thought and Political Practice in Africa* (New York: Oxford University Press, 2004), 149–50. For a definition of moral economy based on a peasantry's "right to subsistence," see Michael Watts, *Silent Violence: Food, Famine, and Peasantry in Northern Nigeria* (Berkeley: University of California Press, 1983), 104–39. Watts builds on James C. Scott, *Moral Economy of the Peasant: Rebellion and Subsistence in Southeast Asia* (New Haven, CT: Yale University Press, 1976). Worldview is understood as a practical attitude to explain events, focused on healing. See Louis Brenner, "'Religious' Discourses in and about Africa," in *Discourse and Its Disguises: The Interpretation of African Oral Texts*, ed. Karin Barber and P. F. de Moraes Farias (Birmingham, UK: Birmingham University Centre of West African Studies, 1989), 87–105.

27. Glassman, *Feasts and Riot*, 19–20.

28. See Portugal, Ministério dos Negócios da Marinha e Ultramar, Dirrecção Geral do Ultramar, *Annuário estatístico dos domínios ultramarinos portugueses, 1899 e 1900* (Lisbon: Imprensa Nacional, 1905), 83–84.

29. Terence Ranger, "Europeans in Black Africa," *Journal of World History* 9, no. 2 (1998): 255–68; Johannes Fabian, *Out of Our Minds: Reason and Madness in the Exploration of Central Africa* (Berkeley: University of California Press, 2000).

30. See Osumaka Likaka, *Naming Colonialism: History and Collective Memory in the Congo, 1870–1960* (Madison: University of Wisconsin Press, 2009), who interprets naming as a way of defying the authority of colonial agents.

31. Daniel Ladeiras, "Notícia sobre a Missão de S. Salvador do Congo," *O missionário católico* 3, no. 30 (1927): 117–19; W. Holman Bentley, *Pioneering on the Congo* (New York: Fleming H. Revell Co., 1900), 1:210; F. De Bas, "Een Nederlandsch reiziger aan den Congo," *Tijdschrift van het Nederlandsch Aardrijkskundig Genootschap*, 2nd series, 3, no. 2 (1887): 358.

32. Clifton Crais, "Chiefs and Bureaucrats in the Making of Empire: A Drama from the Transkei, South Africa, October 1880," *AHR* 108, no. 4 (2003): 1036, 1055. See also Newbury, *Patrons, Clients, and Empire*, 3 ("how was it that so few could rule so many without general revolt for so long"). For the colonizers' need to create difference, see George Steinmetz, *The Devil's Handwriting: Precoloniality and the German Colonial State in Qingdao, Samoa, and Southwest Africa* (Chicago: University of Chicago Press, 2007), 36–37.

33. On prestige-place associations, see Paul S. Landau, *Popular Politics in the History of South Africa, 1400–1948* (New York: Cambridge University Press, 2010), ch. 2.

34. On Kongo title associations, see Wyatt MacGaffey, *Kongo Political Culture: The Conceptual Challenge of the Particular* (Bloomington: Indiana University Press, 2000).

35. Susan Herlin Broadhead, "Beyond Decline: The Kingdom of Kongo in the Eighteenth and Nineteenth Centuries," *IJAHS* 12, no. 4 (1979): 615–50.

36. Jean Cuvelier, "Traditions congolaises," *Congo* (1930): 480.

37. Faintly echoing Paul S. Landau, *The Realm of the Word: Language, Gender, and Christianity in a Southern African Kingdom* (Portsmouth, NH: Heinemann, 1995), who shows

how Tswana rulers used the arrival of Christian missionaries to forge a new, ecclesiastical polity under British tutelage.

38. Anthony H. M. Kirk-Greene, "The Thin White Line: The Size of the British Colonial Service in Africa," *African Affairs* 79, no. 314 (1980): 25–44. See Jeffrey Herbst, *States and Power in Africa: Comparative Lessons in Authority and Control* (Princeton, NJ: Princeton University Press, 2000), ch. 3, for the notion of "broadcasting," which means "projecting" or "extending" power, but with the connotation of distribution from a center (e.g., São Salvador).

39. Moses E. Ochonu, *Colonial Meltdown: Northern Nigeria in the Great Depression* (Athens: Ohio University Press, 2009).

40. Michael Mann, "The Autonomous Power of the State: Its Origins, Mechanisms and Results," *European Journal of Sociology* 25, no. 2 (1984): 185–213; "Infrastructural Power Revisited," *Studies in Comparative International Development* 43, no. 3 (2008): 355–65.

41. On the fundamental role of violence in the creation of colonial society, see Toyin Falola, *Colonialism and Violence in Nigeria* (Bloomington: Indiana University Press, 2009); Clifton Crais, *Poverty, War, and Violence in South Africa* (New York: Cambridge University Press, 2011).

42. Phyllis M. Martin, "The Violence of Empire," in *History of Central Africa*, vol. 2, ed. David Birmingham and Phyllis M. Martin (London: Longman, 1983), 15; Sara Berry, *No Condition Is Permanent: The Social Dynamics of Agrarian Change in Sub-Saharan Africa* (Madison: University of Wisconsin Press, 1993), ch. 2.

43. Justin Willis, "'Men on the Spot,' Labor, and the Colonial State in British East Africa: The Mombasa Water Supply, 1911–1917," *IJAHS* 28, no. 1 (1995): 25–48.

44. Benjamin N. Lawrance et al., eds., *Intermediaries, Interpreters, and Clerks: African Employees in the Making of Colonial Africa* (Madison: University of Wisconsin Press, 2006). African agents are insignificant in Steinmetz's analysis of the modern colonial state; see *Devil's Handwriting*, 66 (native policy relied on a "rudimentary willingness on the part of the colonized to play their assigned parts"). For a contrasting view, see Richard Price, *Making Empire: Colonial Encounters and the Creation of Imperial Rule in Nineteenth-Century Africa* (Cambridge: Cambridge University Press, 2008).

45. Mahmood Mamdani, *Citizen and Subject: Contemporary Africa and the Legacy of Late Colonialism* (Princeton, NJ: Princeton University Press, 1996). For commentary, see Herbst, *States and Power*, 60–61, 81–84, 88–93; Thomas Spear, "Neo-Traditionalism and the Limits of Invention in British Colonial Africa," *JAH* 44, no. 1 (2003): 9. See also Newbury, *Patrons, Clients, and Empire*, 259.

46. John Lonsdale, "Political Accountability in African History," in *Political Domination in Africa: Reflections on the Limits of Power*, ed. Patrick Chabal (Cambridge: Cambridge University Press, 1986), 151–52; Bruce J. Berman, "Ethnicity, Patronage and the African State: The Politics of Uncivil Nationalism," *African Affairs* 97, no. 388 (1998): 317; Justin Willis, "Violence, Authority, and the State in the Nuba Mountains of Condominium Sudan," *Historical Journal* 46, no. 1 (2003): 89–114.

47. John Lonsdale, "The Politics of Conquest in Western Kenya, 1894–1908," in *Unhappy Valley: Conflict in Kenya and Africa*, vol. 1, *State and Class* (Oxford: James Currey, 1992), 64; Vansina, *Being Colonized*, 326. See also Sherry B. Ortner, "Resistance and the Problem of Ethnographic Refusal," *Comparative Studies in Society and History* 37, no. 1 (1995): 173–93.

Chapter 1. The Kingdom of Kongo
after the Slave Trade

1. H. Grattan Guinness, *The New World of Central Africa: With a History of the First Christian Mission on the Congo* (New York: Fleming H. Revell, 1890), 178–79, 192–93 (citing T. J. Comber).

2. Thomas Lewis, "The Ancient Kingdom of Kongo: Its Present Position and Possibilities," *Geographical Journal* 19, no. 5 (1902): 549.

3. For instance, Onno Zwier van Sandick, *Herinneringen van de zuid-westkust van Afrika: Eenige bladzijden uit mijn dagboek* (Deventer: Van Sandick, 1881), 20. For earlier Portuguese imagery of kingdoms in West Central Africa, see Mariana P. Candido, *An African Slaving Port and the Atlantic World: Benguela and Its Hinterland* (New York: Cambridge University Press, 2013), 33.

4. António Brásio, ed., *Angola*, vol. 1, *1596–1867* (Pittsburgh, PA: Duquesne University Press, 1966), 571–72, Governador geral to Ministro de Ultramar, Luanda, 31 January 1867.

5. W. G. Grandy, "Report of the Proceedings of the Livingstone Congo Expedition," *Proceedings of the Royal Geographical Society of London* 19, no. 2 (1874–75): 89–90.

6. *MH* (1879), 16.

7. Susan Herlin Broadhead, "Trade and Politics on the Congo Coast: 1770–1870" (PhD diss., Boston University, 1971); Anne Hilton, *The Kingdom of Kongo* (Oxford: Clarendon Press, 1985), 210–25; Wyatt MacGaffey, *Kongo Political Culture: The Conceptual Challenge of the Particular* (Bloomington: Indiana University Press, 2000). "Collective strategy" is borrowed from Paul S. Landau, "Political Systems, African," in *The Princeton Companion to Atlantic History*, ed. Joseph C. Miller (Princeton, NJ: Princeton University Press, 2015), 376–79.

8. Broadhead, "Beyond Decline," 619. On Kongo's civil wars, see John K. Thornton, *The Kingdom of Kongo: Civil War and Transition, 1641–1718* (Madison: University of Wisconsin Press, 1983). On the relation between economic and political decentralization after 1700, see Broadhead, "Trade and Politics."

9. MacGaffey, *Kongo Political Culture*, 13, 215.

10. Broadhead, "Beyond Decline," 616.

11. Ibid., 620.

12. Hilton, *Kingdom of Kongo*, 215 (for "trade corporation"), 218. See also Broadhead, "Beyond Decline," 620, 623–27; MacGaffey, *Kongo Political Culture*, 11–12.

13. On Pedro V, see François Bontinck, "Pedro V, roi de Kongo, face au partage colonial," *Africa* (Roma) 37, nos. 1–2 (1982): 1–53; John K. Thornton, "Master or Dupe? The Reign of Pedro V of Kongo," *Portuguese Studies Review* 19, nos. 1–2 (2011): 115–32.

14. See the correspondence in Brásio, *Angola*, 1:54, 97–99, 110–11; and *BO* 539 (1856), Henrique II to Governador geral, S Salvador, 11 and 12 October 1955, and Governador geral to Henrique II, Luanda, 25 January 1956.

15. SGL, Reservados 2, maço 5, doc. 33; José Tavares da Costa e Moura, Lisboa, 16 September 1857. Another member of the expedition was Alfredo de Sarmento; see his *Os sertões d'Africa (apontamentos de viagem)* (Lisbon: F. A. da Silva, 1880).

16. Thornton, "Master or Dupe," 119.

17. Adolf Bastian, *Ein Besuch in San Salvador, der Hauptstadt des Königsreichs Congo* (Bremen: Heinrich Strack, 1859), 119–58 (quotations on 138 and 147). Bastian suggests

Mikiliama as the family's "hometown" (122 and 189), probably Kimiala. There had been a third pretender, who had attacked São Salvador three months before Bastian's visit, burning much of the city before he was chased out by Isabel's sons and disappeared from the record.

18. António Joaquim de Castro, "O Congo em 1845: Roteiro da viagem ao reino do Congo," *BSGL* 2, no. 2 (1880): 64.

19. Zacharias da Silva Cruz, "Relatório duma viagem a S. Salvador do Congo," *BO* 690, 691 (1858); 692, 695, 696, 701,702, 710, 711 (1859), transcribed by Arlindo Correia, http://www.arlindo-correia.com/020907.html (accessed 22 January 2014). On *gente da igreja*, see Cécile Fromont, *The Art of Conversion: Christian Visual Culture in the Kingdom of Kongo* (Chapel Hill: University of North Carolina Press, 2014), 220–24.

20. John H. Weeks, *Among the Primitive Bakongo* (London: Seeley, Service & Co., 1914), 33; Daniel Ladeiras, "Notícia sobre a Missão," no. 28 (1926): 72.

21. Thornton, "Master or Dupe," 116–21. See also Broadhead, "Beyond Decline," 630, 645–48, suggesting an Agua Rosada affiliation for Henrique II. Note that several of his sons were named Agua Rosada e Sardónia.

22. Jean Cuvelier, "Traditions congolaises," *Congo* (1931): 205–8. See also Graham, *Under Seven Congo Kings*, 69; Rino Vezzu and Francisco Ntanda, *O centenário: Resenha histórica da evangelização em Mbanza Kongo* (Luanda: Editorial Nzila, 2007), 158. John K. Thornton ("Kongo's Incorporation into Angola: A Perspective from Kongo," in *A África e a instalação do sistema colonial (c. 1885–c. 1930)*, ed. Maria Emília Madeira Santos [Lisbon: Instituto de Investigação Científica Tropical, 2000], 352) questions the alleged Kimpanzu origin of Ndongo.

23. According to administrator José Heliodoro de Faria Leal, "Memórias d'África," *BSGL* 32 (1914): 315–18, the Agua Rosada family occupied the Kongo throne from Pedro V up to Pedro VI. Pedro's official death record states he was born in Quilele (Madimba) to Dona Isabel ne Vuzi dia Nimo. Arquivo do Arçobispado de Luanda (AAL), S Salvador, Assentos de óbitos, 1891, no. 16. Baptist missionaries believed Pedro V was a Kivuzi. *MH* (1885), 378–81; Lewis, "Ancient Kingdom," 548–49.

24. According to W. Holman Bentley, *Pioneering*, 1:142, Pedro's older brother was a "simple quiet man of little energy."

25. Thornton, *Kingdom of Kongo*, 49–51, 88–90; Broadhead, "Beyond Decline," 636. On houses, matrilineality, and clans in Kongo, see also Jan Vansina, *Paths in the Rainforest: Toward a History of Political Tradition in Equatorial Africa* (Madison: University of Wisconsin Press, 1990), 74–77, 152–58, 220–21; Hilton, *Kingdom of Kongo*, 19–23, 43–44, 212–14; Wyatt MacGaffey, "Changing Representations in Central African History," *JAH* 46, no. 2 (2005): 195–201; "A Note on Vansina's Invention of Matrilinearity," *JAH* 54, no. 2 (2013): 268–80.

26. AHU, SEMU-DGU, Angola, no. 1111/1112, doc. 169, Brig Villa Flor, Treaty, Porto da Lenha, 22 November 1855.

27. AHU, SEMU-DGU, Angola, no. 1111/1112, doc. 203, Henrique II to Governador geral, S Salvador, 29 June 1855.

28. Bastian, *Besuch*, 130–31. On the Vili, see Phyllis M. Martin, *The External Trade of the Loango Coast, 1576–1870: The Effects of Changing Commercial Relations on the Vili Kingdom of Loango* (Oxford: Clarendon Press, 1972).

29. Jelmer Vos, "'Without the Slave Trade No Recruitment': From Slave Trading to 'Migrant Recruitment' in the Lower Congo, 1830–1890," in *Trafficking in Slavery's*

Wake: Law and the Experience of Women and Children in Africa, ed. Benjamin N. Lawrance and Richard L. Roberts (Athens: Ohio University Press, 2012), 45–64.

30. AHNA, caixa 3496, Francisco Mendes dos Santos to Governador do Ambriz, no. 60, Banza-a-Puto, 8 September 1860.

31. Sebastião Lopes de Calheiros e Menezes, *Relatório do Governador Geral da Província de Angola, referido ao anno de 1861* (Luanda: Imprensa Nacional, 1867).

32. AAL, São Salvador, Livro de baptismo, 1858–62.

33. Broadhead, "Beyond Decline," 637, 641, 643; *BO* 611 (1957), "Repressão do tráfico de escravos, 2: Opinião do governador do Ambriz."

34. Brásio, *Angola*, 1:138–39. For another vassal treaty signed in 1859, archived in a village south of Bembe, see Henrique Manoel Collaço Fragoso, *Diário de uma viagem do Ambriz a S. Salvador do Congo* (Luanda: Typ. Luso Africana, 1891), 23–24.

35. Thornton, "Master or Dupe," 122–23; Brásio, *Angola*, 1:147–48; Weeks, *Primitive Bakongo*, 37.

36. The following paragraphs build on Richard Gray, *Black Christians and White Missionaries* (New Haven, CT: Yale University Press, 1990), ch. 3; Wyatt MacGaffey, *Religion and Society in Central Africa: The BaKongo of Lower Zaire* (Chicago: University of Chicago Press, 1986), 198–211; and John K. Thornton, *The Kongolese Saint Anthony: Dona Beatriz Kimpa Vita and the Antonian Movement, 1684–1706* (Cambridge: Cambridge University Press, 1998).

37. Castro, "O Congo em 1845," 64.

38. John M. Janzen, *Lemba, 1650–1930: A Drum of Affliction in Africa and the New World* (New York: Garland Publishing, 1982).

39. Raimundo de Dicomano, "Informação sobre o Reino do Congo," Italian original in AHU, SEMU-DGU, Angola, caixa 823, trans. Arlindo Correia, http://www.arlindo-correia.com/101208.html (accessed 22 January 2014). See also António Brásio "Informação do Reino do Congo de Frei Raimundo de Dicomano," *Studia* 34 (1972): 19–42.

40. Hilton, *Kingdom of Kongo*, 60–65; Georges Balandier, *La vie quotidienne au royaume de Kongo du XVIe au XVIIIe siècle* (Paris: Hachette, 1965), 34. Defining Kongo Christianity as a political cult is not denying the truly religious dimension of conversion. For a recent examination of this conversion, see John K. Thornton, "Afro-Christian Syncretism in the Kingdom of Kongo," *JAH* 54, no. 1 (2013): 53–77.

41. Bastian, *Besuch*, 96.

42. For a more exhaustive reading of these accounts, see Fromont, *Art of Conversion*, ch. 5.

43. James K. Tuckey, *Narrative of an Expedition to Explore the River Zaire, Usually Called the Congo, in South Africa, in 1816* (London: John Murray, 1818), 80, 165.

44. Richard F. Burton, *Two Trips to Gorilla Land and the Cataracts of the Congo* (London: Sampson Low, Marston, Low & Searle, 1876), 2:76.

45. *BO* 608 (1857), José Taveres da Costa e Moura to Governador geral, Luanda, 15 May 1857; AHNA, caixa 2041, António Castanheira Nunes to Governador geral, no. 12, Bembe, 20 November 1872; António Brásio, ed., *Angola*, vol. 2, *1868–1881* (Pittsburgh, PA: Duquesne University Press, 1968), 210, Bishop of Angola and Congo to Pedro V, Luanda, 31 July 1872.

46. Louis Jadin, "Recherches dans les archives et bibliothèques d'Italie et du Portugal sur l'Ancien Congo," *Bulletin des Séances de l'Académie Royal des Sciences Coloniales* 2, no. 6

(1956): 951–90; Bentley, *Pioneering*, 35, 36 (quotation), 123; Weeks, *Primitive Bakongo*, 240; Fragoso, *Diário de uma viagem*, 21–22; Francisco António Pinto, *Angola e Congo* (Lisbon: Livraria Ferreira, 1888), 185; Lewis, "Ancient Kingdom," 547–48. See also David M. Gordon, *Invisible Agents: Spirits in a Central African History* (Athens: Ohio University Press, 2012), ch. 2.

47. Sarmento, *Os sertões d'Africa*, 49.

48. Burton, *Two Trips*, 2:144, 223–25; Josef Chavanne, *Reisen und Forschungen im alten und neuen Kongostaate* (Jena: Hermann Costenoble, 1887), 268, 302; Bentley, *Pioneering*, 59; Weeks, *Primitive Bakongo*, 176. See also Norm Schrag, "Mboma and the Lower Zaire: A Socioeconomic Study of a Kongo Trading Community, c. 1785–1885" (PhD diss., Indiana University, 1985), 64–65.

49. John H. Weeks, "Notes on Some Customs of the Lower Congo People," *Folk-Lore* 20 (1909): 193. See also António Brásio, ed., *D. António Barroso: Missionário, cientista, missiólogo* (Lisbon: Centro de Estudos Históricos Ultramarinos, 1961), 74, 78; Thomas Lewis, *These Seventy Years: An Autobiography* (London: Carey Press, 1930), 199; José Heliodoro Corte Real de Faria Leal, "Congo Portuguez: De S. Salvador ao Rio Cuilo," *Revista Portugueza Colonial e Marítima* (1901–2): 204, 257.

50. AHU, SEMU-DGU, Angola, no. 1111/1112, doc. 203, Henrique II to Governador geral, S Salvador, 29 June 1855.

51. AHU, SEMU-DGU, Angola, 2ª Rep., pasta 1 (no. 828), Pedro V to Governador geral, S Salvador, 8 June 1873, enclosed in Governador geral interino to MSENMU, no. 173, Luanda, 1 July 1873. Smallpox had first broken out in 1863–64. See also Jill R. Dias, "Famine and Disease in the History of Angola, c. 1830–1930," *JAH* 22, no. 3 (1981): 349–78.

52. Grandy, "Report," 102.

53. Weeks, *Primitive Bakongo*, 60–61; Bentley, *Pioneering*, 291.

54. AHU, SEMU-DGU, Angola, no. 1111/1112, doc. 203, Henrique II to Governador geral, S Salvador, 29 June 1855.

55. Cruz, "Relatório."

56. "Angola: Notícias extrahidas dos Boletins Officiaes da mesma Província do anno de 1861," *Annaes do Conselho Ultramarino*, parte não oficial, série 3 (1862): 41.

57. AHU, SEMU-DGU, Angola, 1ª Rep., pasta 8, Governador do Congo to MSENMU, no. 483, Cabinda, 18 August 1888; Brásio, *António Barroso*, 482; *MH* (1886), 316; *MH* (1888), 456. Dona Ana died in 1899 at the age of thirty-nine. AAL, São Salvador, Assentos de óbitos, 1899, no. 40; Leal, "Congo Portuguez," 257. Some speculated she was the mother of Pedro's successor, Mfutila. ALA, A/46/18, [Gwen Lewis], S Salvador, 30 July 1888.

58. Weeks, *Primitive Bakongo*, 40; Jadin, "Recherches," 988; ALA, A/12, Comber to Baynes, 9 August 1878; Beatrix Heintze, *Ethnographische Aneignungen: Deutsche Forschungsreisende in Angola* (Frankfurt am Main: Verlag Otto Lembeck, 2007), 197–98, 410; De Bas, "Een Nederlandsch reiziger," *Tijdschrift van het Nederlandsch Aardrijkskundig Genootschap*, 2nd series, 3, no. 2 (1887): 352–53; Chavanne, *Reisen und Forschungen*, 272, 275. On marriage as a political tool, see Anne Hilton, "Family and Kinship among the Kongo South of the Zaire River from the Sixteenth to the Nineteenth Centuries," *JAH* 24, no. 2 (1983): 191–92; *Kingdom of Kongo*, 223 (arguing that marriages no longer served to build trade alliances).

59. Sarmento, *Os sertões d'Africa*, 49, 51, 58; Cruz, "Relatório." An engraving inserted in Charles de Martrin-Donos, *Les Belges dans l'Afrique central* (Brussels: P. Maes, 1886),

2:182–83, shows King Plenty, the chief of Porto Rico on the south bank of the lower Congo in the 1880s, dressed in a light-colored robe with an embroidered red-colored cross and wearing an embroidered cap. See also the photograph of chief Mazamba in ch. 4.

60. Louis Jadin, "Les survivances chrétiennes au Congo au XIXe siècle," *Études d'histoire africaine* 1 (1970): 158; SGL, Reservados, maço 3, doc. 33, José Tavares da Costa e Moura, Lisboa, 16 September 1857.

61. Jadin, "Recherches," 973; Brásio, *António Barroso*, 23–24, 51–52; Sebastião José Alves, "Remexendo no passado: Memória de um antigo missionário," *O missionário católico* 2, no. 23 (1926): 212–13.

62. Daniel Ladeiras, "Notícia sobre a missão de S. Salvador do Congo," *O missionário católico* 3, no. 30 (1927): 117–19. On Kongo's iron swords of honor, see Cécile Fromont, "By the Sword and the Cross: Power and Faith in the Arts of the Christian Kongo," in *Kongo across the Waters*, ed. Susan Cooksey et al. (Gainesville: University Press of Florida, 2013), 28–31.

63. Simon Bockie, *Death and the Invisible Powers: The World of Kongo Belief* (Bloomington: Indiana University Press, 1993).

64. Jan Vansina, "Kings in Tropical Africa," in *Kings of Africa: Art and Authority in Central Africa*, ed. Erna Beumers and Hans-Joachim Koloss (Maastricht: Foundation Kings of Africa, 1992), 24. Similarly, Joseph C. Miller, "Political Systems, Collective Consensual," in *The Princeton Companion to Atlantic History*, ed. Joseph C. Miller (Princeton, NJ: Princeton University Press, 2015), 379–83, argues that political power in precolonial Africa emanated from the community and operated by consensus rather than compulsion. By contrast, Jeffrey Herbst, *States and Power in Africa: Comparative Lessons in Authority and Control* (Princeton, NJ: Princeton University Press, 2000), ch. 2, argues that precolonial states used centralized coercion to "broadcast" power, even if they were not concerned with territorial control.

65. AHU, SEMU-DGU, Angola, 1ª Rep., pasta 1 (no. 785), Pedro V to Bispo (also in Brásio, *Angola*, 2:535); Weeks, "Notes," *Folk-Lore* 19 (1908): 427; *Primitive Bakongo*, 42; Brásio, *António Barroso*, 367, 373; Chavanne, *Reisen und Forschungen*, 277.

66. *MH* (1880), 121; Weeks, "Notes," *Folk-Lore* 19 (1908): 427; 20 (1909): 44; Grandy, "Report," 85, 90, 97; Fragoso, *Diário de uma viagem*, 15–17, 41–42.

67. Joachim John Monteiro, *Angola and the River Congo* (London: Cass, 1968), 1:212–13. In the 1880s some coastal communities north of Ambriz, while independent from São Salvador in almost every sense, still recognized the king as the ultimate authority in legal disputes. AHU, SEMU-DGU, Angola, 2ª Rep., pasta 12, Delegado to Residente do Ambrizete, no. 16, Quicembo, 10 August 1888; Charles Jeannest, *Quatre années au Congo* (Paris: G. Charpentier et Cie., 1883), 49.

68. Lewis, *These Seventy Years*, 133–49.

69. *MH* (1896), 470–72. For the earlier case, see AHU, SEMU-DGU, Angola, 1ª Rep., pasta 3 (no. 787), Pedro V to Governador geral, S Salvador, 30 January 1883, encl. in Governador geral to MSENMU, no. 68, Luanda, 9 March 1883; AHNA, caixa 212, Pedro V to Governador geral, S Salvador, 8 May 1883; Mário António Fernandes de Oliveira, ed., *Angolana (Documentação sobre Angola) I (1783–1883)* (Luanda: Instituto de Investigação Científica de Angola, 1968), 600–601. On the origins of *nkanu*, see Vansina, *Paths in the Rainforest*, 147.

70. Weeks, *Primitive Bakongo*, 41; Bentley, *Pioneering*, 72.

71. Weeks, *Primitive Bakongo*, 42–49. On the origins of *ntotela* ("king"), see Vansina, *Paths in the Rainforest*, 156. On the title of "prince," see Leal, "Memórias d'África," *BSGL* 32 (1914): 319–20; Cuvelier, "Traditions congolaises" (1931), 203; Hilton, *Kingdom of Kongo*, 219–20. On *dom* and *dona*, see Leo Bittremieux, "Overblijfselen van den katholieken Godsdienst in Lager Kongoland," *Anthropos* 21 (1926): 799–800; Chavanne, *Reisen und Forschungen*, 302.

72. Chavanne, *Reisen und Forschungen*, 273. See also Dicomano, "Informação"; Sarmento, *Os sertões d'Africa*, 63; Oliveira, *Angolana*, 537; Weeks, *Primitive Bakongo*, 42–48. Before 1800, according to Hilton, *Kingdom of Kongo*, 221, five out of six counselors came from outside the traditional nobility.

73. *MH* (1879), 71, 97; *MH* (1880), 197, 231; *MH* (1887), 258; *MH* (1888), 454; BMS, Annual Report (1889), 41; Annual Report (1890), 42–43, both in ALA; T. J. Comber, "Explorations Inland from Mount Cameroons, and Journey through Congo to Makuta," *Proceedings of the Royal Geographical Society* 1, no. 4 (1879): 236; Bentley, *Pioneering*, 167–68; Graham, *Under Seven Congo Kings*, 12; Weeks, *Primitive Bakongo*, 70 (photograph of Dom Álvaro Matoko and Kapitau), 268.

74. Bentley, *Pioneering*, 123, 169n; MH (1880), 15, 197; T. J. Comber, "Brief Account of Recent Journeys in the Interior of Congo," *Proceedings of the Royal Geographical Society* 3, no. 1 (1881): 22; Weeks, *Primitive Bakongo*, 268–69; Oliveira, *Angolana*, 459.

75. See the letters in Brásio, *António Barroso*, 403–5, 410, 419, 446–47.

76. Broadhead, "Beyond Decline," 633.

77. Oliveira, *Angolana*, 565–57; Brásio, *António Barroso*, 3, 4, 15–16, 37, 170, 390–91, 403–4; Bentley, *Pioneering*, 58, 123, 167–69.

78. AHU, SEMU-DGU, Angola, pasta 32–1 (no. 633), Governador geral to MSENMU, no. 61, Luanda, 21 March 1863.

79. AHU, SEMU-DGU, Angola, 2ª Rep., pasta 2 (no. 889), Governador geral interino to MSENMU, no. 280, Luanda, 25 October 1873; ibid., pasta 1 (no. 828), Relatório com relação ao ano de 1873, encl. in Governador geral interino to MSENMU, no. 282, Luanda, 29 October 1873.

80. Brásio, *Angola*, 2:3–4, Governador geral to Ministro do Ultramar, Luanda, 19 January 1868.

81. According to António Marciano Ribeiro da Fonseca, "O rei do Congo," *Revista Militar* 43, no. 11 (1891): 325, in the early 1860s, Ndongo's clan tried to obstruct trade and once threatened to attack São Salvador. See also Bentley, *Pioneering*, 142–43.

82. Brásio, *Angola*, 1:571–72, Governador geral to Ministro do Ultramar, 31 January 1867; ibid., 434–37, Governador geral to Ramos de Carvalho, Luanda, 20 May 1866.

83. Brásio, *Angola*, 2:21–22, António Leite Mendes to Governador geral, Ambriz, 29 November 1868.

84. Leal, "Memórias d'África," *BSGL* 32 (1914): 305, 383–84; AHU, SEMU-DGU, Angola, 1ª Rep., pasta 8, Governador geral to MSENMU, no. 273, Luanda, 13 July 1888.

85. Cuvelier, "Traditions congolaises" (1931), 206.

86. AHNA, caixa 3374, Alferes José Crisóstomo Ribeiro Guimarães to Secretário geral, no. 2, S Salvador, 5 January 1870.

87. Leal, "Memórias d'África," *BSGL* 32 (1914): 314–15. See also Ana Paula Tavares and Catarina Madeira Santos, eds., *Africae Monumenta: A apropriação da escrita pelos Africanos*, vol. 1, *Arquivo Caculo Cacahenda* (Lisbon: Instituto de Investigação Científica Tropical, 2002), esp. 331–35. On the cultural context of the Dembos' vassal treaties with Portugal,

see Linda M. Heywood, "Portuguese into African: The Eighteenth-Century Central African Background to Atlantic Creole Cultures," in *Central Africans and Cultural Transformations in the American Diaspora*, ed. Linda M. Heywood (Cambridge: Cambridge University Press, 2002), 105–11; Catarina Madeira Santos, "Écrire le pouvoir en Angola: Les archives ndembu (XVIIe–XXe siècles)," *Annales: Histoire, Sciences Sociales* 64, no. 4 (2009): 767–95.

88. António de Almeida, "Mais subsídios para a história dos reis do Congo," in *Congresso do mundo português*, ed. Comissão executiva dos centenários (Lisbon: Comissão executiva dos centenários, secçao dos congressos, 1940), 8:643–96. In 1902, Dembo Dom Gracia Ngombe-a-Muquiama provided protection to a Kongo embassy traveling to Luanda. AHNA, caixa 3308, no. 11.1.1, Guia, Banza de Lemvo, 9 January 1902.

89. Full correspondence in AHNA, caixa 2041, Relatório da missão do Congo feito pelo Padre António Castanheira Nunes sobre D Pedro V, Rei de Congo. Citations from António Castanheira Nunes to Pedro V, no. 8, S Salvador, 3 October 1872; Pedro V, S Salvador, 29 October 1872. Also AHU, SEMU-DGU, Angola, 2ª Rep., pasta 2 (no. 889), Concelho dos Dembos, Manoel Pereira dos Santos, no. 8, Trombeta, 31 March 1873. Portugal awarded Dom Garcia a salary in 1877. Brásio, *Angola*, 2:372, 377.

90. Brásio, *Angola*, 2:21–22.

91. SGL, Reservados 2, maço 4, doc. 58, Relatório feito pelo missionário Boaventura dos Santos tendo voltado da missão do reino do Congo, anno de 1876 e 1877.

92. Bentley, *Pioneering*, 139.

93. Broadhead, "Beyond Decline," 650.

94. Chavanne, *Reisen und Forschungen*, 276.

95. Brásio, *Angola*, 2:372, 377. In 1882, for being the son of a "vassal" chief, Dom Miguel requested an extra allowance on top of the monthly salary of ten thousand *reis* he already received from the colonial treasury. The government went along, not wanting a member of the African elite to defect and seek the patronage of British agents in Angola. AHU, SEMU-DGU, Angola, 1ª Rep., pasta 3 (no. 787), Governador geral to MSENMU, no. 436, Luanda, 18 December 1882.

96. Douglas L. Wheeler, "Nineteenth-Century African Protest in Angola: Prince Nicolas of Kongo (1830?–1860)," *African Historical Studies* 1, no. 1 (1968): 40–59; François Bontinck, "Notes Complémentaires sur Dom Nicolau Agua Rosada e Sardonia," *African Historical Studies* 2, no. 1 (1969): 101–19. Another son of Pedro V, Dom Pedro de Agua Rosada, became corporal in the colonial infantry in 1868. AHNA, caixa 2041, Pedro V to Governor, n.d.

Chapter 2. Carrying Trade

1. For French Congo, see Catherine Coquery-Vidrovitch, *Le Congo au temps des grandes compagnies concessionaires, 1898–1930* (Paris: Mouton, 1972); Tamara Giles-Vernick, *Cutting the Vines of the Past: Environmental Histories of the Central African Rain Forest* (Charlottesville: University Press of Virginia, 2002). For the Congo Free State, see Robert Harms, "The End of Red Rubber: A Reassessment," *JAH* 16, no. 1 (1975): 73–88; Adam Hochschild, *King Leopold's Ghost: A Story of Greed, Terror, and Heroism in Colonial Africa* (Boston: Houghton Mifflin, 1998).

2. Raymond Dumett, "The Rubber Trade of the Gold Coast and Asante in the Nineteenth Century: African Innovation and Market Responsiveness," *JAH* 12, no. 1 (1971): 79–101.

3. Peter Geschiere, "'Tournaments of Value' in the Forest Area of Southern Cameroon: 'Multiple Self-Realization' versus Colonial Coercion during the Rubber Boom (1900–1913)," in *Commodification: Things, Agency, and Identities*, ed. Wim M. J. van Binsbergen and Peter L. Geschiere (Münster: Lit, 2005), 243–63. In Cameroon, the rubber boom introduced a market economy to communities that had never before participated in export production; it was an economic activity that elders were unable to control; and it created new monetary values undermining established principles of social organization.

4. Kwame Arhin, "The Ashanti Rubber Trade with the Gold Coast in the Eighteen-Nineties," *Africa* 42, no. 1 (1972): 32–43; "The Economic and Social Significance of Rubber Production and Exchange on the Gold and Ivory Coasts, 1880–1900," *Cahiers d'études africaines* 20, nos. 77–78 (1980): 49–62; Emily Lynn Osborn, "'Rubber Fever,' Commerce and French Colonial Rule in Upper Guinée, 1890–1913," *JAH* 45, no. 3 (2004): 445–65.

5. Jelmer Vos, "Of Stocks and Barter: John Holt and the Kongo Rubber Trade, 1906–1910," *Portuguese Studies Review* 19, nos. 1–2 (2011): 153–75. Ralph Austen, *African Economic History* (Oxford: James Currey, 1987), 85, 96–97, highlights a more sinister continuity between slave and commodity trading, predatory production (*Raubwirtschaft*).

6. Robin Law, ed., *From Slave Trade to "Legitimate" Commerce: The Commercial Transition in Nineteenth-Century West Africa* (Cambridge: Cambridge University Press, 1995).

7. Jean-Luc Vellut, "The Congo Basin and Angola," in *General History of Africa*, vol. 6, *Africa in the Nineteenth Century until the 1880s*, ed. J. F. Ade Ajayi (Paris: UNESCO, 1989), 294–324.

8. Josef Chavanne, *Reisen und Forschungen*, 392, 398; Burton, *Two Trips*, 2:212–14; Wyatt MacGaffey, *Religion and Society*, 25.

9. Among the many contemporary descriptions of agricultural life in Kongo, see esp. Jaime Pereira de Sampaio Forjaz de Serpa Pimentel, "Um anno no Congo," *Portugal em África* 6 (1899): 390–404, 425–47, 465–72; Brásio, *António Barroso*, 59–68, 113–20; Grandy, "Report," 78–105.

10. According to the military commander António Marciano Ribeiro da Fonséca, "O rei do Congo," *Revista Militar* 43, no. 11 (1891): 327, peasants in the vicinity of São Salvador began to cultivate peanuts for export in the 1860s.

11. John H. Weeks, "The Congo and Its People," *MH* (1911), 139; Wyatt MacGaffey, "Economic and Social Dimensions of Kongo Slavery," in *Slavery in Africa: Historical and Anthropological Perspectives*, ed. Suzanne Miers and Igor Kopytoff (Madison: University of Wisconsin Press, 1977), 243. On rubber production, see J. Moraes e Castro, "De Noqui ao Cuango: Notas de viagem," *BSGL* 21, no. 3 (1903): 84; Leal, "Memórias d'África," *BSGL* 33 (1915): 164–65.

12. Cruz, "Relatório"; Bastian, *Besuch*, 51, 107.

13. Grandy, "Report," 104. The Zombo had run the caravan routes between the Pool and the Atlantic coast south of the Congo estuary since the mid-eighteenth century. See Hilton, *Kingdom of Kongo*, 211–12. On the role of the Tio in the ivory trade, see Jan Vansina, *The Tio Kingdom of the Middle Congo, 1880–1892* (London: Oxford University Press, 1973), 247–312. A well-known Kongo entrepreneur was Makito, a chief of slave origin in the district of Lutete, who purchased ivory from Tio merchants near the Pool and organized caravans, sometimes in partnership with other traders, to carry tusks down to the coast. See F. De Bas, "Een Nederlandsch reiziger aan den Congo," *Tijdschrift van het Nederlandsch Aardrijkskundig Genootschap*, 2nd series, 3, no. 2 (1887): 366–67;

Éduard Dupont, *Lettres sur le Congo: Récit d'un voyage scientifique entre l'embouchure du fleuve et le confluent du Kassai* (Paris: C. Reinwald, 1889), 149–50; MacGaffey, *Religion and Society*, 40, 213.

14. Hendrik Blink, *Het Kongo-land en zijne bewoners in betrekking tot de Europeesche staatkunde en den handel* (Haarlem: Tjeenk Willink, 1891), 174–75; Van Sandick, *Herinneringen*, 37–43, 67–69; Hugh McNeile Dyer, *The West Coast of Africa as Seen from the Deck of a Man-of-War* (London: J. Griffin & Co., 1876), 113, 128–29, 148; Jeannest, *Quatre années*, 55–56, 63, 121–22. Jeannest (p. 63) estimated annual exports from the coast between Ambriz and the Congo estuary around 1869 at a hundred metric tons or five thousand to six thousand tusks. A Dutch visitor to the coast in 1860 found a caravan of four hundred men in Quicembo, where they had just delivered about a hundred tusks. J. F. Koopman, "Verslag van eene reize naar de Westkust van Afrika, Rio de Janeiro en Rio de la Plata," *Verhandelingen en berigten betrekkelijk het zeewezen, de zeevaartkunde, de hydrographie, de kolonien en de daarmee in verband staande wetenschappen* 23, no. 3 (1863): 319–21.

15. ALA, A/12, Comber to Baynes, 17 August 1878 and 24 November 1878; *MH* (1879), 11.

16. Chavanne, *Reisen und Forschungen*, 289.

17. Beatrix Heintze, *Afrikanische Pioniere: Trägerkarawanen im westlichen Zentralafrika (ca. 1850–1890)* (Frankfurt am Main: Lembeck, 2002), 95–102.

18. AHU, SEMU-DGU, Angola, 3ª Rep., no. 1091, D. Paulo do Congo to Henrique de Carvalho, 17 November 1887; no. 1157 (livro 4633), 4, Auto de inauguração da Estação Luciano Cordeira; ibid., 63, Henrique de Carvalho to MSENMU, Lisboa, 27 May 1890.

19. Brásio, *António Barroso*, 172.

20. AHU, SEMU-DGU, Angola, 2ª Rep., Pasta 4 (no. 831-1), Governador geral to MSENMU, confidencial, no. 23, Luanda, 24 November 1879.

21. Leal, "Congo Portuguez," 260. The transition from ivory to rubber trading is reflected in export statistics from the end of the decade. In 1889, in total just twenty-six metric tons of ivory were exported from the lower Congo River and the coast south of the estuary, compared to ninety-six tons from the upper Congo, where the Congo Free State controlled the trade. By contrast, rubber exports were heavily concentrated in the lower Congo region, particularly in outlets on the south bank and the Atlantic coast under official Portuguese control; independent European trade houses, followed by the great concessionary companies, were only beginning to exploit the rubber sources of the vast interior Congo basin. See Blink, *Kongo-land*, 164–65.

22. Brásio, *António Barroso*, 484; AHNA, caixa 4012, Residente interino to Secretário do governo do Congo, no. 122, S Salvador, 31 December 1894. The most common rubber plants west of the Kwango were the *Landolphia owariensis* and the *Landolphia florida*, both climbers. The lower-value *Landolphia thollonii* was typical of regions east of the Kwango. See Pimentel, "Um anno no Congo," 439–42; Júlio A. Henriques, "Das plantas productoras da borracha," *Portugal em Africa* 3, no. 33 (1896): 360–61. The aggressive economic policies pursued by the Congo Free State in the 1890s—in particular the granting of a concession to the Comptoir Commercial Congolais for rubber extraction east of the Kwango and the construction of the railway between Matadi and Léopoldville—inhibited further expansion of the Kongo rubber trade. See Jelmer Vos, "The Economics of the Kwango Rubber Trade, c. 1900," in *Angola on the Move: Transport Routes, Communications and History*, ed. Beatrix Heintze and Achim von Oppen (Frankfurt am Main: Verlag Otto Lembeck, 2008), 85–98.

23. Bentley, *Pioneering*, 2:36.

24. João Mesquita, *Dados estatísticos para o estudo das pautas de Angola: Exportação pelas alfândegas do círculo e do Congo nos anos de 1888 a 1913* (Luanda: Imprensa Nacional, 1918); Chavanne, *Reisen und Forschungen*, 291. Export statistics are rare for precolonial Kongo, but according to Robidé van der Aa, *Afrikaansche studiën: Koloniaal bezit en partikuliere handel op Afrika's westkust* (The Hague: M. Nijhoff, 1871), 129, the Afrikaanse Handelsvereniging imported seventy tons of rubber through its factories north of the Dande River in 1870.

25. Jeannest, *Quatre années*, 33, 47, 78; Grandy, "Report," 83; Alexandre Delcommune, *Vingt années de vie africaine: Récits de voyages, d'aventures et d'exploration au Congo Belge, 1874–1893* (Brussels: Larcier, 1922), 36.

26. Weeks, "Notes," *Folk-Lore* 20 (1909): 43, 46.

27. AHNA, caixa 3628, Sebastião José Pereira, Breve notícia d'uma viagem ao rio Lunda, S Salvador, 31 October 1883; De Bas, "Nederlandsch reiziger aan den Congo," *Tijdschrift van het Nederlandsch Aardrijkskundig Genootschap*, 2nd series, 3, no. 2 (1887): 354; Chavanne, *Reisen und Forschungen*, 258, 291–92.

28. Weeks, *Primitive Bakongo*, 201; Chavanne, *Reisen und Forschungen*, 295–96; Grandy, "Report," 94, 99; Bentley, *Pioneering*, 1:43.

29. Dieudonné de Thulin, "Les Capucins au Congo: L'esclavage et la traite des noirs au Congo," *Études Franciscaines* 35 (1923): 630. For the Kimbubuge-Ambrizete connection, see AHNA, caixa 3548, Governador do Congo to Secretaria geral, no. 456, Cabinda, 24 August 1900; AHNA, caixa 4724, doc. 11.2.3, Capitão Magalhães to Governador do distrito, no. 13, Cabinda, 27 January 1895; ibid., Delegação da Mucula to Residência do Ambrizete, no. 118, 1895; João Jardim, "A expedição a Quincunguila na circunscrição de Ambrizette (janeiro a março de 1902)," *Revista Portugueza Colonial e Marítima* 12 (1903): 61.

30. Leal, "Memórias d'África," *BSGL* 33 (1915): 67–68; Hermenegildo Capello and Roberto Ivens, *From Benguella to the Territory of the Yacca* (New York: Negro Universities Press, 1969), 2:123–26; *Arquivos de Angola*, 2nd series, 26 (1969): 92–93. See also Joseph C. Miller, *Way of Death: Merchant Capitalism and the Angolan Slave Trade, 1730–1830* (Madison: University of Wisconsin Press, 1988), 209, 213, 260, 617–18.

31. Van Sandick, *Herinneringen*, 102–6; Blink, *Kongo-land*, 172, 175; Weeks, *Primitive Bakongo*, 206.

32. Brásio, *António Barroso*, 20–21, 37.

33. Ibid., 73–83; Oliveira, *Angolana*, 537.

34. Grandy, "Report," 93–97; Bentley, *Pioneering*, 1:77–81; *MH* (1879), 11–12; *MH* (1880), 227–30.

35. Beatrix Heintze, "As construções de parentesco e sua retórica na política da África Centro-Ocidental do século XIX," in *A África Centro-Ocidental no século XIX (c. 1850–1890): Intercâmbio com o mundo exterior, apropriação, exploração e documentação* (Luanda: Kilombelombe, 2013), 39–99.

36. AAL, Livro de baptismos administrados no Reino do Congo e povos do norte d'Angola, 1876.

37. AHU, SEMU-DGU, Angola, 2ª Rep., pasta 1 (no. 828), Pedro V to Governador geral, S Salvador, 8 June 1873, encl. in Governador geral interino to MSENMU, no. 173, Luanda, 1 July 1873, reporting on Grandy's intentions to visit Sundi. See also Grandy, "Report," 91–92.

38. AHNA, caixa 212, Barroso to Secretaria geral, no. 29, Missão do Congo, 15 December 1883.

39. AHNA, caixa 212, Barroso to Secretaria geral, no. 11, S Salvador, 22 April 1885. On Kasongo-Lunda, see Heintze, *Ethnographische Aneignungen*, 184–86, 411–16.

40. Willy Wolff, in Heintze, *Ethnographische Aneignungen*, 405.

41. Grandy, "Report," 101, 104.

42. Claridge, *Wild Bush Tribes*, 104; *MH* (1892), 130; *MH* (1895), 14. On Zombo chiefs stocking capital, see *Portugal em África* 9 (1902): 320–20A (letter from Maquela do Zombo, 27 March 1902), 500.

43. Josef Chavanne, "Reisen im Gebiete der Muschi-congo im portugiesischen Westafrika," *Petermanns Mitteilungen aus Justus Perthes' Geographischer Anstalt* 32 (1886): 99; Thomas Lewis, "The Old Kingdom of Kongo," *Geographical Journal* 31, no. 6 (1908): 608.

44. Dupont, *Lettres sur le Congo*, 148.

45. Albert Thys, *Au Congo et au Kassaï* (Brussels: P. Weissenbruch, 1888), 44–45.

46. Grandy, "Report," 94. In interviews conducted by Luzolo Kiala in 2001, four Zombo elders born in the 1910s and '30s discuss how during the rubber boom carriers were recruited and paid, confirming the evidence gleaned from historical documents. Luzolo Kiala, "Comércio e sociedade: Subsídios para a história dos Bazombo, c. 1880–c. 1925" (Licenciatura, Universidade Agostinho Neto, Luanda, 2005), 111–38. See also Stephen J. Rockel, *Carriers of Culture: Labor on the Road in Nineteenth-Century East Africa* (Portsmouth, NH: Heinemann, 2006); Linda M. Heywood, "Porters, Trade, and Power: The Politics of Labor in the Central Highlands of Angola, 1850–1914," in *The Workers of African Trade*, ed. Catherine Coquery-Vidrovitch and Paul E. Lovejoy (Beverly Hills, CA: Sage Publications, 1985), 243–67. For the view that carriers were mostly slaves, see Vansina, *Tio Kingdom*, 260n32, 276–77, 300.

47. Linda M. Heywood, "Slavery and Forced Labor in the Changing Political Economy of Central Angola, 1850–1949," in *The End of Slavery in Africa*, ed. Suzanne Miers and Richard Roberts (Madison: University of Wisconsin Press, 1988): 415–36.

48. AHU, SEMU-DGU, Angola, pasta 32-1 (no. 633), Governador geral to MSENMU, confidencial, no. 32, Luanda, 26 February 1863.

49. Prosper Augouard, *28 années au Congo* (Poitiers: Société Française d'Imprimerie et de Librairie, 1905), 1:198, 229, 244; De Bas, "Een Nederlandsch reiziger aan den Congo," *Tijdschrift van het Nederlandsch Aardrijkskundig Genootschap*, 2nd series, 4, no. 1 (1887): 172; Blink, *Kongo-land*, 137, 139; Chavanne, *Reisen und Forschungen*, 403; Grandy, "Report," 102; Weeks, "Notes," *Folk-Lore* 20 (1909): 33; Sarmento, *Os sertões d'Africa*, 94–95.

50. AHU, SEMU-DGU, Angola, 1ª Rep., maço 898, Confidential, José de Mello Gouvêa, 27 July 1877 ("All factories . . . receive their *serviçaes* from local chiefs, who supply them to serve for a short or indefinite time against an agreed upon remuneration in goods or other values").

51. Van Sandick, *Herinneringen*, 3, 10, 44, 50–51, 57, 95–96, 100, 107; Pieter J. Veth and Johannes F. Snelleman, eds., *Daniël Veth's reizen in Angola, voorafgegaan door eene schets van zijn leven* (Haarlem: Tjeenk Willink, 1887), 134, 136; Jeannest, *Quatre années*, 7, 25, 50; Delcommune, *Vingt années*, 44–46; Chavanne, *Reisen und Forschungen*, 261.

52. TNA, FO 881/3317, no. 1, Consul Hopkins to the Earl of Derby, 28 April 1877.

53. In the early 1900s, coastal factories still acquired slaves and traded them illegally or as contract workers to Ambriz and possibly to São Tomé and Príncipe. Ana Flávia

Cicchelli Pires, "Comércio e trabalho em Cabinda durante a ocupação colonial portuguesa, c.1880–c.1915" (PhD diss., Universidade Federal Fluminense, 2010), 170–84. Higgs, *Chocolate Islands*, 90, 95, also mentions Ambrizete as an illegal shipping point of contract labor for São Tomé and Príncipe.

54. AHU, SEMU-DGU, Angola, 2ª Rep., pasta 4 (no. 831-1), Curador geral to MSENMU, no. 46, Luanda, 25 February 1880.

55. AHU, SEMU-DGU, Angola, 2ª Rep., pasta 10 (no. 837), Curador geral, no. 88, Luanda, 14 April 1886; ibid., Curador geral, no. 119, Luanda, 14 July 1886; ibid., Curadoria geral, no. 213, Luanda, 13 November 1886.

56. Delcommune, *Vingt années*, 46–49; De Bas, "Een Nederlandsch reiziger aan den Congo," *Tijdschrift van het Nederlandsch Aardrijkskundig Genootschap*, 2nd series, 3, no. 2 (1887): 340–41.

57. For Álvaro, see Brásio, *António Barroso*, 3, 15–16, 27, 170, 403–5, 520, 522; C. J. Rooney, "As missões do Congo e Angola," *Portugal em África* 7 (1900): 231, 548; Heintze, *Ethnographische Aneignungen*, 184 (Büttner). For Manuel, see AHU, SEMU-DGU, Angola, 2ª Rep., pasta 7 (no. 834), Convention, Né Pereira, 1 June 1884, encl. in Governador geral to MSENMU, no. 330, Luanda, 14 June 1884.

58. De Bas, "Een Nederlandsch reiziger aan den Congo," *Tijdschrift van het Nederlandsch Aardrijkskundig Genootschap*, 2nd series, 3, no. 2 (1887): 342; Chavanne, *Reisen und Forschungen*, 295–96; Pinto, *Angola e Congo*, 392; L. Du Verge, "How Affairs Are Now Conducted on the Congo," *Journal of the American Geographical Society* 16 (1884): 148.

59. AHU, SEMU-DGU, Angola, 2ª Rep., pasta 6 (no. 833), Governador geral to MSENMU, no. 19, Luanda, 12 December 1882; ibid., pasta 7 (no. 834), Governador geral to MSENMU, confidencial, Luanda, 12 September 1882. In 1892, Daumas, Béraud & Compagnie sold all their Lower Congo factories to the Société Anonyme Belge. See Heinrich Jakob Waltz, *Das Konzessionswesen im belgischen Kongo* (Jena: G. Fischer, 1917), 1:29.

60. AHU, SEMU-DGU, Angola, 2ª Rep., pasta 6 (no. 833), Governador geral to MSENMU, no. 414, Luanda, 13 October 1883; De Bas, "Een Nederlandsch reiziger aan den Congo," *Tijdschrift van het Nederlandsch Aardrijkskundig Genootschap*, 2nd series, 3, no. 2 (1887): 353.

61. Mário António Fernandes de Oliveira and Carlos Alberto Mendes do Couto, eds., *Angolana (Documentação sobre Angola) II (1883–1887)* (Luanda: Instituto de Investigação Científica de Angola, 1971), 49; *BO* 29 (1885), Portaria 325-B, 29 July 1883; Brásio, *António Barroso*, 105–7. Chavanne, *Reisen und Forschungen*, 276, estimated the king's revenue from the factories in 1885 at twenty thousand francs. The NAHV sold mainly flintlock guns manufactured in Liège out of old French percussion rifles. See NA, NAHV (2.18.10.09), 145/364, Schalwijk & De Bloeme, Rotterdam, 18 January 1889.

62. AHU, SEMU-DGU, Angola, 1ª Rep., pasta 3 (no. 787), Governador geral to MSENMU, confidencial, no. 51, Luanda, 20 June 1883; *BO* 29 (1885).

63. Cruz, "Relatório"; *MH* (1878), 89; *MH* (1879), 288; Bentley, *Pioneering*, 1:68–69; Oliveira, *Angolana*, 537.

64. John H. Weeks, *Among Congo Cannibals* (London: Seeley, Service & Co., 1913), 22–23.

65. Chavanne, *Reisen und Forschungen*, 260; Grandy, "Report," 104; *MH* (1879), 163; Bentley, *Pioneering*, 1:184. Jeannest, *Quatre années*, 57, argued that previously most carriers had only possessed knives.

66. De Bas, "Een Nederlandsch reiziger aan den Congo," *Tijdschrift van het Nederlandsch Aardrijkskundig Genootschap*, 2nd series, 3, no. 2 (1887): 342–46; Chavanne, *Reisen und Forschungen*, 270, 296; Grandy, "Report," 81.

67. AHU, SEMU-DGU, Angola, 2ª Rep., pasta 7 (no. 834), Pedro V to Governador geral, S Salvador, 18 February 1884, encl. in Governador geral to MSENMU, no. 157, Luanda, 18 March 1884.

68. Blink, *Kongo-land*, 164.

69. Chavanne, *Reisen und Forschungen*, 272; AHNA, caixa 212, Barroso to Secretaria geral, no. 24, S Salvador, 30 September 1883.

70. Bentley, *Pioneering*, 1:137.

71. *MH* (1880), 120; Chavanne, *Reisen und Forschungen*, 268, 300; De Bas, "Een Nederlandsch reiziger aan den Congo," *Tijdschrift van het Nederlandsch Aardrijkskundig Genootschap*, 2nd series, 3, no. 2 (1887): 354; Blink, *Kongo-land*, 134.

72. Phyllis M. Martin, *Leisure and Society in Colonial Brazzaville* (Cambridge: Cambridge University Press, 1995), 160. See also James A. Pritchett, "Christian Mission Stations in South-Central Africa: Eddies in the Flow of Global Culture," in *Christianity and Public Culture in Africa*, ed. Harri Englund (Athens: Ohio University Press, 2011), 36–38.

73. *MH* (1888), 453; Bentley, *Pioneering*, 1:42, 139; Brásio, *António Barroso*, 104–8, 369, 372, 485; Chavanne, *Reisen und Forschungen*, 272; Leal, "Memórias d'África," *BSGL* 33 (1915): 69; Thomas Lewis, "Ancient Kingdom," 545.

74. *MH* (1883), 136; Burton, *Two Trips*, 201–2; SGL, Reservados 2, maço 4, no. 58, Relatório feito pelo missionário Boaventura dos Santos tendo voltado da missão do reino do Congo, anno de 1876 e 1877.

75. Grandy, "Report," 99; Brásio, *António Barroso*, 108; Dupont, *Lettres sur le Congo*, 146–48; *MH* (1879), 71; *MH* (1890), 294.

76. Thomas Lewis, "Life and Travel among the People of the Congo," *Scottish Geographical Magazine* 18, no. 7 (1902): 361–63.

77. *MH* (1883), 79. See also Vansina, *Tio Kingdom*, 276–78. Although Vansina does not mention it, the expansion of slavery at the Pool was probably closely related to the growing production of foodstuffs. For methods of enslavement, see Jelmer Vos, "Slavery in Southern Kongo in the Late Nineteenth Century," in *Trabalho forçado africano: Experiências coloniais comparadas*, ed. Centro de Estudos Africanos da Universidade do Porto (CEAUP) (Porto: Campo das Letras, 2006), 315–36.

78. Justin Willis and Suzanne Miers, "Becoming a Child of the House: Incorporation, Authority and Resistance in Giryama Society," *JAH* 38, no. 3 (1997): 480.

79. Brásio, *António Barroso*, 138–39; Claridge, *Wild Bush Tribes*, 138–39; Augouard, *28 années*, 492.

80. Weeks, *Primitive Bakongo*, 67.

81. Delcommune, *Vingt années*, 105–30.

82. AHNA, caixa 2041, Auto de investigação, São Salvador do Congo, 19 November 1894.

83. For another example from Central Africa, see Vansina, *Being Colonized*, 57.

84. Thornton, *Kingdom of Kongo*, 54–55. On Angolan naming practices, see John Thornton, "Central African Names and African-American Naming Patterns," *William and Mary Quarterly* 50, no. 4 (1993): 727–42; Heywood, "Portuguese into African," 102–3, 108–9.

85. *BO* 593 (1857), supplement, Francisco Teixeira da Silva to Governador geral, Ambriz, 4 February 1857.

86. See also Candido, *African Slaving Port*, 133–39.

87. Pinto, *Angola e Congo*, 381 (quotation); Pimentel, "Um anno no Congo," 338–39. On Noqui's role in the slave trade, see Tuckey, *Narrative of an Expedition*, 135, 138; Burton, *Two Trips*, 132–50, 201–41.

88. Leal, "Memórias d'África," *BSGL* 32 (1914): 384–85; *Portugal em África* 8, no. 93 (1901): 499, letter from Zaire, 12 August 1901; ibid., 9, no. 101 (1902): 320, letter from Maquela do Zombo, 27 March 1902.

89. Castro, "De Noqui ao Cuango," 92. The lack of resistance is remarkable in light of earlier encounters. Kongo and Zombo caravan leaders who traveled to the Pool objected to Stanley's settlement in Tio territory in 1881, as they feared European competition in the carrying trade. See Henry M. Stanley, *The Congo and the Founding of Its Free State: A Story of Work and Exploration* (New York: Harper & Brothers, 1885), 1:309; Grandy, "Report," 101.

90. AHNA, caixa 3910, Delegação de Noqui, Mapas dos caravanas entrados durante Outubro-Dezembro 1902, encl. in Governador Pinheiro to Secretaria geral, no. 84, Cabinda, 24 March 1903.

91. AHU, SEMU-MU/DGU-DGC, Angola, maço 1076. The wages for a single journey to Noqui were either calculated on the basis of carried weight or consisted of a flat rate for loads of thirty-five kilograms. In the first case, a journey from São Salvador paid eighty *reis* per kilogram, and a journey from Maquela between 120 and 150 *reis*. If a single tariff was applied, carriers earned two thousand *reis* for a journey from São Salvador, and three thousand *reis* for a journey from Maquela. The same rates applied to return journeys. Note that these wages were lower than those stipulated for government carriers in 1896. See *BO* 5 (1896), portaria 58.

92. AHNA, caixa 3413, Santo António, Estatística geral de importação, 1902; ibid., Santo António, Estatística geral de importação, 1905; ibid., Santo António, Alfândega, mapa no. 30, importação por países de procedência, 1910; AHNA, caixa 3374, Circunscrição administrativa de S Salvador do Congo, Estatística aduaneira, 1908; AHNA, caixa 3672, Distrito do Congo, Circunscrição civil de S Salvador, Importação por paizes de procedência, 1911; AHNA, caixa 3910, Circumscrição civil de Maquela do Zombo, Estatísticas de importação e exportação, 1912.

93. On early colonial clothing traditions, consumer demands, and European suppliers, see Martin, *Leisure and Society*, 155–65.

94. Leal, "Memórias d'África," *BSGL* 33 (1915): 67–68; AHNA, caixa 3496, Relatório sobre a organisação dos serviços aduaneiros do districto do Congo, 1904.

95. AHNA, caixa 3374, Residência de S. Salvador do Congo, Relatório, Novembro de 1903. The report for October 1903 (in caixa 3910) stated that they had to be forced. In 1906, no *serviçaes* were contracted in São Salvador. AHNA, caixa 3910, Concelho de S Salvador, Serviçaes contratados em 1906.

96. AHNA, caixa 3672, Districto do Congo, Indicações . . . em harmonia com a circular no. 37 de 21 de Agosto de 1906.

97. In 1910, wild rubber, such as that produced in Brazil and Africa, still accounted for nearly 90 percent of global rubber production, but in 1923 this percentage had dropped to less than 10. See José Carlos de Macedo Soares, *A borracha: Estudo economico e estatístico* (Paris: Pedone, 1927), 41. Only two tons were expedited from stores in São

Salvador in 1911. AHNA, caixa 3672, Distrito do Congo, Circumscrição de S Salvador, Exportação geral e exportação por paízes de destino, 1911.

Chapter 3. Christian Revival in São Salvador

1. See Brian Stanley, *The History of the Baptist Missionary Society, 1792–1992* (Edinburgh: T & T Clark, 1992), for general background on the BMS Congo mission; F. James Grenfell, *História da Igreja Baptista em Angola, 1879–1975* (Queluz: Núcleo, 1998), for a history of the Baptist Church in Angola. For the support from the Royal Geographical Society, see TNA, FO 541/47, no. 182, letters by Comber (1879).

2. AHU, SEMU-DGU, Angola, 1ª Rep., pasta 1 (no. 785), Pedro V to Bispo (cópia, no. 68 [1881]).

3. Adrian Hastings, *The Church in Africa, 1450–1950* (Oxford: Clarendon Press, 1994), 385, 387–88.

4. *MH* (1879), 16. See also ALA, A/12, Comber to Baynes, 24 November 1878.

5. ALA, A/12, Comber papers, Pedro V to Comber, 31 July 1878. Pedro had communicated earlier with French Holy Ghost Fathers. See Brásio, *Angola*, 2:26–27, 92, 440.

6. Brásio, *Angola*, 1:518; Claridge, *Wild Bush Tribes*, 67.

7. *MH* (1900), 93. See also BMS Annual Report (1901), 90, at ALA; Brásio, *Angola*, 2:540.

8. George Hawker, *An Englishwoman's Twenty-Five Years in Tropical Africa: Being the Biography of Gwen Elen Lewis, Missionary to the Cameroons and the Congo* (London: Hodder and Stoughton, 1911), 233–34.

9. Wyatt MacGaffey, "The West in Congolese Experience," in *Africa and the West: Intellectual Responses to European Culture*, ed. Phillip D. Curtin (Madison: University of Wisconsin Press, 1972), 56; Gray, *Black Christians*, 60.

10. MacGaffey, *Religion and Society*, 6–7; Simon Bockie, *Death and the Invisible Powers*, 43–48; Weeks, "Notes," *Folk-Lore* 19 (1908): 416–19; 20 (1909): 35–36, 182.

11. MacGaffey, "The West," 54–57; Bentley, *Pioneering*, 1:252; Weeks, "Notes," *Folk-Lore* 20 (1909): 479; *MH* (1890), 96. See also ALA, A/27, Hartland to Mother, 6 June 1880.

12. Weeks, *Primitive Bakongo*, 207; Weeks, "Notes," *Folk-Lore* 20 (1909): 45, 471. See also Brásio, *António Barroso*, 483; De Bas, "Een Nederlandsch reiziger aan den Congo," *Tijdschrift van het Nederlandsch Aardrijkskundig Genootschap*, 2nd series, 3, no. 2 (1887): 366.

13. *MH* (1909), 5.

14. Weeks, "Notes," *Folk-Lore* 20 (1909): 46.

15. Claridge, *Wild Bush Tribes*, 58.

16. *MH* (1879), 14 (quotation); *MH* (1892), 51; *MH* (1898), 393.

17. Dias, "Famine and Disease," 349–78.

18. *MH* (1890), 438; *MH* (1896), 15, 597–98.

19. *MH* (1906), 346.

20. *MH* (1905), 504.

21. ALA, A/94, "Memorandum on Mabaya Station," Congo, 1 March 1915.

22. MacGaffey, *Religion and Society*, 193–95, 203–5; "Dialogues of the Deaf: Europeans on the Atlantic Coast of Africa," in *Implicit Understandings: Observing, Reporting, and Reflecting on the Encounters between Europeans and Other People in the Early Modern Era*, ed. Stuart B. Schwartz (Cambridge: Cambridge University Press, 1994), 257, 264.

23. Jadin, "Recherches," 981–83.

24. Hawker, *Englishwoman*, 99.

25. Graham, *Under Seven Congo Kings*, 33.

26. See also Phyllis M. Martin, "Life and Death, Power and Vulnerability: Everyday Contradictions at the Loango Mission, 1883–1904," *Journal of African Cultural Studies* 15, no. 1 (2002): 71–74.

27. *MH* (1880), 198; *MH* (1883), 64; *MH* (1888), 40–41; *MH* (1892), 15 (Tungwa).

28. Lewis, *These Seventy Years*, 168.

29. BMS, Annual Reports, at ALA.

30. Hawker, *Englishwoman*, 159.

31. Samuël Coghe, "Population Politics in the Tropics: Demography, Health and Colonial Rule in Portuguese Angola, 1890s–1940s" (PhD diss., European University Institute, 2014), 121. As Coghe (p. 122) explains, by 1913 the medical infrastructure of the BMS included a dispensary for outpatients, surgery, pharmacy, laboratory, general hospital, and, outside São Salvador, a special hospital for the treatment of sleeping sickness patients.

32. *MH* (1938), 118.

33. Hawker, *Englishwoman*, 136. On the mission's later maternal and infant health care, see Coghe, "Population Politics," 302–5.

34. Lewis, *These Seventy Years*, 154. See also Nancy Rose Hunt, *A Colonial Lexicon of Birth Ritual, Medicalization, and Mobility in the Congo* (Durham, NC: Duke University Press, 1999), esp. 227 ("A woman in childbearing crisis, seen as particularly open to conversion, could make a good parable").

35. See also Norman Etherington, "Education and Medicine," in *Missions and Empire*, ed. Norman Etherington (Oxford: Oxford University Press, 2005), 275–84; Pritchett, "Christian Mission Stations," 30.

36. *MH* (1896), 60. See also *MH* (1890), 59.

37. *MH* (1889), 305–7; *MH* (1896), 265.

38. Hawker, *Englishwoman*, 169.

39. Weeks, "Notes," *Folk-Lore* 20 (1909): 57–58; MacGaffey, *Religion and Society*, 192, 199–200, 211–16.

40. Delcommune, *Vingt années*, 114; De Bas, "Een Nederlandsch reiziger aan den Congo," *Tijdschrift van het Nederlandsch Aardrijkskundig Genootschap*, 2nd series, 3, no. 2 (1887): 358. On the meaning of *mfumu*, see Vansina, *Paths in the Rainforest*, 73–74, 274–75; and the discussion in Kathryn M. de Luna, "Affect and Society in Precolonial Africa," *IJAHS* 46, no. 1 (2013): 133–40.

41. *MH* (1881), 366.

42. *MH* (1893), 306–7; *MH* (1897), 479–80; *MH* (1905), 500–501; *MH* (1906), 214; Sebastião José Alves, "Remexendo no passado," 196–98.

43. For examples, see Bentley, *Pioneering*, 196–98; Brásio, *Angola*, vol. 3, *1882–1889* (Pittsburgh: Duquesne University Press, 1969), 382–84.

44. *MH* (1898), 381; Lewis, *These Seventy Years*, 181; BMS Annual Report (1901), 91, at ALA. See also Ruth Slade, *King Leopold's Congo: Aspects of the Development of Race Relations in the Congo Independent State* (London: Oxford University Press, 1962), 164.

45. Roland Oliver, *The African Experience: From Olduvai Gorge to the 21st Century* (London: Weidenfeld & Nicolson, 1991), 237–38. See also Roland Oliver, *The Missionary Factor in East Africa* (London: Longmans, Green & Co., 1952), esp. 50–81, 172–222; Robert I.

Rotberg, "Plymouth Brethren and the Occupation of Katanga, 1886–1907," *JAH* 5, no. 2 (1964): 285–97; Thomas O. Beidelman, "Contradictions between the Sacred and the Secular Life: The Church Missionary Society in Ukaguru, Tanzania, East Africa, 1876–1914," *Comparative Studies in Society and History* 23, no. 1 (1981): 73–95.

46. Gray, *Black Christians*, 95–96; Slade, *King Leopold's Congo*, 163; Etherington, "Education and Medicine," 261. On the danger of overemphasizing instrumental reasons for conversion, see Thomas Spear, "Toward the History of African Christianity," in *East African Expressions of Christianity*, ed. Thomas T. Spear and Isaria N. Kimambo (Oxford: James Currey, 1999), 3–24.

47. John K. Thornton, "The Development of an African Catholic Church in the Kingdom of Kongo, 1491–1750," *JAH* 25, no. 2 (1984): 147–67.

48. Gray, *Black Christians*, 62–65.

49. Hawker, *Englishwoman*, 158. See also Lewis, *These Seventy Years*, 169–70.

50. *MH* (1881), 404, 443.

51. *MH* (1895), 445; *MH* (1896), 62; *MH* (1898), 386.

52. *MH* (1899), 93–94; *MH* (1907), 125; BMS Annual Report (1908), 59; Annual Report (1911), 63; Annual Report (1912), 74, all at ALA; ALA, A/64, Logbook "Comber Memorial Station" (Kibokolo), correspondence from 1900 and 3 January 1907; ibid., Letter book (Zombo 1902–12), Pinnock, Report for 1907, 31 January 1908; ibid., Letter book (Zombo 1907–12), Zombo Station, Report for 1911; Hawker, *Englishwoman*, 251–69.

53. MacGaffey, *Religion and Society*, 213, referring to Mbanza Manteke. For a similar critique, see Justin Willis, "The Nature of a Mission Community: The Universities' Mission to Central Africa in Bonde," *Past and Present* 140 (1993): 128.

54. Hawker, *Englishwoman*, 104.

55. Hawker, *Englishwoman*, 195. See also the examples of Kavieke and Mbaki in William Young Fullerton, *The Christ of the Congo River* (London: Carey Press, 1928), 111–15.

56. Pritchett, "Christian Mission Stations," 45.

57. Hawker, *Englishwoman*, 190; Grenfell, *História da Igreja Baptista*, 21; *MH* (1886), 102, 316; François Bontinck, "Domzwau M. D. Nlemvo (c. 1871–1938) et la Bible Kikongo," *Revue africaine de théologie* 2, no. 3 (1978): 19.

58. Weeks, *Among Congo Cannibals*, 20.

59. See Bontinck, "Domzwau," 5–32. Nlemvo recounted his own experience in *MH* (1926), 33–34, 167–69; and *MH* (1938), 118. See also Grenfell, *História da Igreja Baptista*, 92–99.

60. *MH* (1889), 26–27; *MH* (1892), 11; Bentley, *Pioneering*, 35, 200–202; Weeks, *Primitive Bakongo*, 43–46, 196–97.

61. Guinness, *New World*, 191, 431.

62. *MH* (1938), 118.

63. See Thornton, *Kongolese Saint Anthony*.

64. Graham, *Under Seven Congo Kings*, 12; *MH* (1888), 40–41; *MH* (1894), 211.

65. Hawker, *Englishwoman*, 103, 107–8, 119, 121, 133; Grenfell, *História da Igreja Baptista*, 109; Graham, *Under Seven Congo Kings*, 12; *MH* (1887), 258; *MH* (1888), 375.

66. Hawker, *Englishwoman*, 190–91, 103, 122, 135; Grenfell, *História da Igreja Baptista*, 109–10; ALA, A/44/6, Graham, S Salvador, 28 January 1891; Graham, *Under Seven Congo Kings*, 12; *MH* (1886), 533; *MH* (1889), 305–7; *MH* (1892), 339–40.

67. *MH* (1888), 81, 193, 375; *MH* (1896), 15–16.

68. Hawker, *Englishwoman*, 140, 147, 188.

69. Nekaka died in 1944. ALA, Wilson Acc. 223/2, Miguel Nekaka, Autobiography (1931); Grenfell, *História da Igreja Baptista*, 15, 111–14; Graham, *Under Seven Congo Kings*, 121–28; Claridge, *Wild Bush Tribes*, 103; José d'Almeida Mattos, *O Congo Português e as suas riquezas* (Lisbon: Simões, Marques, Santos & Cia., 1924), 203–4.

70. *MH* (1888), 380; Graham, *Under Seven Congo Kings*, 13; Hawker, *Englishwoman*, 192; Lewis, *These Seventy Years*, 153; Grenfell, *História da Igreja Baptista*, 125–28.

71. Hawker, *Englishwoman*, 117–18.

72. Ibid., 104–14, 192, 194.

73. Ibid., 124–25, and photograph inserted at 140–41; *MH* (1897), 479–80. For other problems concerning bridewealth and female converts, see *MH* (1897), 267; *MH* (1898), 245.

74. Etherington, "Education and Medicine," 263.

75. Hawker, *Englishwoman*, 148.

76. *MH* (1887), 258; *MH* (1896), 265.

77. *MH* (1896), 612; *MH* (1907), 251; Graham, *Under Seven Congo Kings*, 87; Hawker, *Englishwoman*, 135, 138, 147; Claridge, *Wild Bush Tribes*, 61–62.

78. Hawker, *Englishwoman*, 113–14.

79. Ibid., 160.

80. BMS Annual Report (1901), 89, at ALA; *MH* (1898), 474–75.

81. Terence Ranger, "The Invention of Tradition in Colonial Africa," in *The Invention of Tradition*, ed. Eric Hobsbawm and Terence Ranger (Cambridge: Cambridge University Press, 1983), 254–59; Giles-Vernick, *Cutting the Vines*, 109; John Iliffe, *Honour in African History* (New York: Cambridge University Press, 2005), ch. 12.

82. Hawker, *Englishwoman*, 240–41, 252–53.

83. TNA, FO 541/47, no. 182, enclosure 2, Pedro V to Menezes, S Salvador, 29 June 1879.

84. AHU, SEMU-DGU, Angola, 1ª Rep., pasta 2 (no. 786), Pedro V to Governador geral, S Salvador, 10 July 1880.

85. Brásio, *Angola*, 2:442–43, Ministro do Ultramar to Bispo de Angola e Congo, 28 July 1880.

86. *MH* (1882), 214.

87. AHNA, caixa 5442, 11.1.3, Residente to Secretário interino do governo do Congo, S Salvador, 14 September 1889; ALA, A/46/18, [Gwen Lewis], S Salvador, 30 July 1888; De Bas, "Een Nederlandsch reiziger aan den Congo," *Tijdschrift van het Nederlandsch Aardrijkskundig Genootschap*, 2nd series, 3, no. 2 (1887), 350.

88. Brásio, *António Barroso*, 482. There was a rumor that Pedro V at one point divided the population of São Salvador between both missions to steady the flux. Daniel Ladeiras, "Notícia sobre a Missão de S. Salvador do Congo," *O missionário católico* 3, no. 28 (1926): 72–75.

89. Brásio, *Angola*, 2:442–43, Ministro do Ultramar to Bispo de Angola e Congo, 28 July 1880.

90. AHNA, caixa 2041, Pedro V to "Meus Paes Espirituaes," S Salvador, 17 March 1881.

91. AHNA, caixa 2041, Barroso to Pedro V, S Salvador, 1 April 1881.

92. António Brásio, ed., *Angola*, vol. 4, *1890–1903* (Pittsburgh: Duquesne University Press, 1970), 53.

93. AHN, caixa 2041, Barroso to Bispo, no. 6, S Salvador, 10 April 1883; Brásio, *António Barroso*, 405–6.

94. Ladeiras, "Notícia sobre a Missão," no. 31 (1927): 134–37.

95. TNA, FO 84/1616, Cohen to Granville, slave trade no. 8, Luanda, 16 August 1882; ibid., FO 84/1807, Herbert Dixon to Cohen, S Salvador, 8 September 1882, encl. in Cohen to Foreign Office, no. 38, Luanda, 15 October 1883. A few convicts still lived in São Salvador in 1884. See AHNA, caixa 212, Barroso to Secretário da Junta da Fazenda, no. 11, S Salvador, 21 July 1884; Chavanne, *Reisen und Forschungen*, 293.

96. AHNA, caixa 212, Commissão projecto reorganisação da Missão do Congo, no. 275, Luanda, 14 January 1883; Oliveira, *Angolana*, 541, 585–89, 675.

97. Jelmer Vos, "Child Slaves and Freemen at the Spiritan Mission in Soyo, 1880–1885," *Journal of Family History* 35, no. 1 (2010): 71–90.

98. Chavanne, "Reisen im Gebiete," 102; *Reisen und Forschungen*, 278.

99. AHU, SEMU-DGU, Angola, 1ª Rep., pasta 7 (no. 791), Administração ecclesiástica (14 December 1886).

100. AHNA, caixa 3672, Residente Leal to Secretaria do governo do Congo, confidencial, no. A, S Salvador, 8 March 1896, and no. D, S Salvador, 6 July 1896.

101. Both cases are described in AHNA, caixa 2041, Auto de investigação, São Salvador do Congo, 19 November 1894.

102. AHNA, caixa 212, Barroso to Secretaria geral, no. 29, Missão do Congo, 15 December 1883.

103. AAL, Baptismos administrados no Reino do Congo e povos do norte d'Angola, 1876.

104. AHNA, caixa 2041, António Barroso to Bispo, S Salvador, 6 May 1887.

105. AHNA, caixa 2041, António Barroso to Bispo, S Salvador, 17 October 1887 and 3 January 1888.

106. AAL, São Salvador, Casamentos, 1890–1909.

107. AHNA, caixa 3672, Residente Leal to Secretaria do governo do Congo, confidencial, no. A, S Salvador, 8 March 1896.

108. AAL, São Salvador, Casamentos, 1929, no. 7.

109. AHNA, caixa 3643, Escolas, São Salvador, 1899.

110. AHNA, caixa 2041, Barroso to Bispo, no. 16, S Salvador, 21 July 1883.

111. AHNA, caixa 212, Barroso to Secretaria geral, no. 5, S Salvador, 10 April 1883; Brásio, *António Barroso*, 170, 403–5.

112. AHNA, caixa 212, Barroso to Secretaria geral, no. 12, S Salvador, 22 April 1885; AHU, SEMU-MU/DGU-DGC, Angola, maço 864, Relatório do superior local da missão de S José de Belém na Madimba (10 January 1908).

113. AHU, SEMU-MU/DGU-DGC, Angola, maço 864, Relatório do superior local da missão de S José de Belém na Madimba (10 January 1908); AAL, S José de Belém na Madimba, Casamentos 1907–9; Chavanne, *Reisen und Forschungen*, 293.

114. Pedro Lukanga d'Agua Rosada, "As nossas escholas," in *A Maria Immaculada: Homenagem da Missão Portugueza de S. Salvador do Congo, 8 de Dezembro de 1905* (San Salvador: Missão, 1905).

115. AHU, SEMU-MU/DGU-DGC, Angola, maço 864, Relatório do superior da circunscrição missionária de S Salvador do Congo, 1906–7; ibid., Relatório do superior local da missão de S Salvador do Congo, 21 January 1908.

116. AHNA, caixa 3590, Missão Portuguesa to Governador do Congo, no. 32, S Salvador, 19 September 1904, and no. 24, S Salvador, 6 May 1905; ibid., Governador do Congo to Secretário geral, no. 8, Cabinda, 28 March 1905; AHU, SEMU-MU/DGU-DGC, Angola, maço 864, Relatório do superior da circunscrição missionária de S Salvador do Congo, 1906–7.

117. BMS, Annual Report (1909), at ALA; AHU, SEMU-MU/DGU-DGC, Angola, maço 864, Mapa estatístico do pessoal e de algumas obras missionárias, 1906–7 e 1907–8.

118. AHNA, caixa 3672, Residente interino Santana to Governo do Congo, no. 40, S Salvador, 22 February 1896; David Birmingham, *Empire in Africa: Angola and Its Neighbors* (Athens: Ohio University Press, 2006), 30; Michael Twaddle, "The Emergence of Politico-Religious Groupings in Late Nineteenth-Century Buganda," *JAH* 29, no. 1 (1988): 81–92.

119. AHU, SEMU-DGU, Angola, 1ª Rep., pasta 12, Superior da Missão de S Salvador to Governador geral, Luanda, 28 November 1891 (original in pasta 11).

120. Ladeiras, "Notícia sobre a Missão," no. 30 (1927): 117–19.

121. Affonso Fernando Nimi, "A Missão de S. Salvador," in *A Maria Immaculada.*

122. BMS Annual Report (1907), 49, at ALA; Graham, *Under Seven Congo Kings*, 81; Leal, "Memórias d'África," *BSGL* 32 (1914): 394.

123. AHU, SEMU-DGU, Angola, 1ª Rep., pasta 20, Residente to Secretaria do governo do Congo, S Salvador, 20 February 1900.

124. Hawker, *Englishwoman*, 184–87.

125. Chavanne, *Reisen und Forschungen*, 274, 278; Hawker, *Englishwoman*, 138.

126. AHU, SEMU-DGU, Angola, 1ª Rep., pasta 6 (no. 790), Pedro V to Governador geral, S Salvador, 25 November 1885, encl. in Governador geral to MSENMU, no. 9, Luanda, 13 January 1886.

127. P. Gonçalves, "A acção das nossas missões," in *A Maria Immaculada.*

128. AHNA, caixa 4147, doc. 38, Bispo de Angola e Congo to Governador geral, no. 167, Luanda, 9 October 1912.

129. Ladeiras, "Notícia sobre a Missão," no. 31 (1927): 134–37; idem, no. 32 (1927): 161–63; José Manuel da Costa, "S. Salvador do Congo, as suas missões e o seu rei," *Boletim Geral das Colónias* 7, no. 77 (1931): 119.

Chapter 4. Portugal and the Agua Rosada

1. The kingdom of Kongo was incorporated in the Portuguese Congo District, whose headquarters were in Cabinda north of the Congo River.

2. Colin Newbury, "Patrons, Clients, and Empire: The Subordination of Indigenous Hierarchies in Asia and Africa," *Journal of World History* 11, no. 2 (2000): 232 ("the key element for a European 'paramount' was the kinds of indigenous service groups in the hierarchy that could be made to ensure access to resources and political stability, in return for legitimacy and continuity in office").

3. Terence Ranger, "The Invention of Tradition in Colonial Africa," in *The Invention of Tradition*, ed. Eric Hobsbawm and Terence Ranger (Cambridge: Cambridge University Press, 1983), 229.

4. See also Vansina, *Being Colonized*, 48; Newbury, *Land beyond the Mists*, ch. 7.

5. John Iliffe, *Honour in African History* (New York: Cambridge University Press, 2005), chs. 12 and 14.

6. See the discussion in Andrew Porter, "An Overview, 1700–1914," in *Missions and Empire*, ed. Norman Etherington (Oxford: Oxford University Press, 2005), 40–63.

7. Brásio, *Angola*, 2:3, Governador geral to Ministro das Colónias, 19 January 1868. For imperial expansion and contraction in Angola, see Wheeler and Pélissier, *História de Angola*, 89–104.

8. William Gervase Clarence-Smith, *The Third Portuguese Empire, 1825–1975: A Study in Economic Imperialism* (Manchester, UK: Manchester University Press, 1985), 77, 81–83. For the international dimension, see also Pinto, *Le Portugal*; Anstey, *Britain and the Congo*.

9. AHU, SEMU-DGU, Angola, 2ª Rep., pasta 4 (no. 831–1), confidencial, no. 23, Luanda, 24 November 1879; ibid., 1ª Rep., pasta 1 (no. 785), Governador geral to MSENMU, no. 16, Luanda, 25 August 1879. See also the Portuguese reaction to the arrival of the Livingstone Inland Mission in 1878 in Oliveira, *Angolana*, 133–35; Brásio, *Angola*, 2:397.

10. Brásio, *António Barroso*, 352–53.

11. AHNA, caixa 212, Pedro V to Governador geral, S Salvador, 16 June 1884, and statement by D. Álvaro de Agua Rosada, S Salvador 16 June 1884; AHU, SEMU-DGU, Angola, 2ª Rep., pasta 7 (no. 834), Brito Capelo to Barroso, 4 June 1884, and Agência política do governo português no Zaire, no. 10, Banana, 2 July 1884, encl. in Governador geral to MSENMU, no. 330, Luanda, 14 June 1884; ibid., pasta 8 (no. 835), Governador geral to MSENMU, no. 586, Luanda, 13 December 1884; De Bas, "Een Nederlandsch reiziger aan den Congo," *Tijdschrift van het Nederlandsch Aardrijkskundig Genootschap*, 2nd series, 3, no. 2 (1887): 356.

12. AHU, SEMU-DGU, Angola, 2ª Rep., pasta 8 (no. 835), doc. 51, Governador geral to Commandante da divisão naval, Luanda, 21 January 1885, encl. in Governador geral to Ministro da Marinha e Ultramar, confidencial, no. 4, Luanda, 6 February 1885; AHNA, caixa 2041, letters from Pedro V, S Salvador, 28 January 1885 and 5 February 1885; AHNA, caixa 3910, Folga to Secretaria do governo, Banana, 20 February 1885. On coastal patron-client relationships, see Jean-Luc Vellut, "L'économie internationale des côtes de Guinée inférieure au XIXe siècle," in *I Reunião Internacional de História de África: Relação Europa-África no 3º quartel do séc. XIX*, ed. Maria Emília Madeira Santos (Lisbon: Instituto de Investigação Científica e Tropical, 1989), 135–206.

13. AHNA, caixa 212, Commissão projecto reorganisação da Missão do Congo, no. 275, Luanda, 14 January 1883. According to the Angolan bishop, the gifts of the British missionaries were even more lavish. AHU, SEMU-DGU, Angola, 1ª Rep., pasta 7 (no. 791), Administração ecclesiástica (14 December 1886).

14. AHNA, caixa 212, Pedro V to Governador geral, S Salvador, 8 May 1883; AHU, SEMU-DGU, Angola, 2ª Rep., pasta 7 (no. 834), Pedro V to Governador geral, S Salvador, 18 February 1884, encl. in Governador geral to MSENMU, no. 157, Luanda, 18 March 1884.

15. AHNA, caixa 212, Dom Pedro to Governador geral, S Salvador, 15 November 1884. For canned food, see AHU, SEMU-DGU, Angola, 1ª Rep., pasta 6 (no. 790), Governador geral to MSENMU, no. 9, Luanda, 6 October 1886.

16. AHU, SEMU-DGU, Angola, 1ª Rep., pasta 3 (no. 787), Pedro V to Governador geral, S Salvador, 3 June 1883, encl. in Governador geral to MSENMU, confidencial,

no. 45, Luanda, 17 July 1883; original letter in AHNA, caixa 212. See also Brásio, *António Barroso*, 413–14, 463–64.

17. AHU, SEMU-DGU, Angola, 1ᵃ Rep., pasta 6 (no. 790), Governador geral to MSENMU, no. 364, Luanda, 10 August 1885; idem, no. 9, Luanda, 6 October 1886 (quotation).

18. Chavanne, *Reisen und Forschungen*, 276.

19. According to Fragoso, *Diário de uma viagem*, 40, "the king does nothing without his approval and advice." Administrators in Luanda thought of Barroso as the "real interpreter of the king's wishes." See AHU, SEMU-DGU, Angola, 1ᵃ Rep., pasta 8, Secretário geral to MSENMU, no. 396, Luanda, 14 September 1888.

20. AHU, SEMU-DGU, Angola, 1ᵃ Rep., pasta 7 (no. 791), Bispo to MSENMU, Luanda, 14 January 1887.

21. AHU, SEMU-DGU, Angola, 1ᵃ Rep., pasta 8, Governador geral to MSENMU, no. 273, Luanda, 13 July 1888 and no. 483, Cabida, 18 August 1888; *MH* (1888), 456; Leal, "Memórias d'África," *BSGL* 32 (1914): 304.

22. AHNA, caixa 3672, Residente Leal to Secretaria do governo do Congo, confidencial, no. A, S Salvador, 8 March 1896, and no. D, S Salvador, 6 July 1896.

23. AHNA, caixa 2041, Auto de investigação, São Salvador do Congo, 19 November 1894.

24. AHNA, caixa 4724, 11.1.12, Governo do districto do Congo, no. 133, reservado, 10 July 1892.

25. The operation is also described in AHNA, caixa 4724, Francisco João de França, 9 July 1892.

26. AHNA, caixa 212, Barroso to Secretaria geral, Missão do Congo, no. 3, 3 March 1884. See also Brásio, *António Barroso*, 441; Oliveira and Couto, *Angolana II*, 418–22.

27. Bentley, *Pioneering*, 1:168; AHU, SEMU-DGU, Angola, 1ᵃ Rep., pasta 7 (no. 791), Mapa demonstrativa das escolas primárias no ano de 1885 (Luanda, 14 February 1887); *BO* 11 (1887), portaria 95; AHNA, caixa 3658, Letter from Henrique de Agua Rosada, Calumbo, 12 March 1890. Henrique died in 1898 at the age of 45. AAL, S Salvador, Óbitos, 1898, no. 27.

28. Bentley, *Pioneering*, 123, 171; Hawker, *Englishwoman*, 92; AHU, SEMU/MU-DGU/DGC, Angola, maço 1081, doc. 26.

29. Brásio, *António Barroso*, 15–16, 520, 522; Leal, "Congo Portuguez," 206–9; "Memórias d'África," *BSGL* 32 (1914): 384. A photograph from 1881 reproduced in *Almanaque de O Missionário Católico* 2 (1927): 39, shows a young Álvaro Tangi dressed in a dark suit with two brothers and Padres António Barroso and Sebastião Pereira.

30. Vos, "Economics," 85–98.

31. Ministère des Affaires étrangères, Archives africaines (AA), 260/294, Gouverneur général to Secrétaire d'État, no. 890, Boma, 12 November 1907.

32. AA, 260/294, Chef de poste to Commissaire de district, no. C/120, Tumba-Mani, 8 January 1905, and C/127, 21 January 1905.

33. AA, 259/293, VIII, Vice-gouverneur général to Secrétaire d'État, no. 778, Boma, 8 August 1901; ibid., District du Kwango Oriental, Rapports mensuels sur la situation générale du district, mois de décembre 1900/janvier 1901.

34. AA, 259/293, VIII and X.

35. AHNA, caixa 3420, Governador do Congo to Secretaria geral, 17 July 1899; caixa 3496, Secretário interino to Secretaria geral, no. 574, Cabinda, 10 November 1899, 2 enclosures; caixa 3643, Escolas, S Salvador, 1899 (the boys were Pedro Vuta, 11, and Nicolau Yenga, 9). Luvaka became part of the Congo State.

36. ALA, A/64, Letter book (Zombo 1899–1911), Lewis to Faria Leal, Kibokolo, 5 March 1904.

37. AHNA, caixa 1755, 11.2.19, Binda, 30 October 1901; AHD, 3ª piso, M25, A9, Secretaria de Estado to Director geral dos Negócios Políticos e Diplomáticos, Lisboa, 20 May 1902; ibid., Relatório do commisário no Noqui-Cuango, no. 34, 16 April 1902; *Portugal em África* 10, no. 109 (1903): 61–62, letter from Maquela do Zombo, 7 November 1902. See also Jean-Luc Vellut, "La violence armée dans l'État Indépendant du Congo: Ténèbres et clartés dans l'histoire d'un état conquérant," *Cultures et développements* 16, nos. 3–4 (1984): 671–707.

38. See Anne Hilton, "Family and Kinship among the Kongo South of the Zaire River from the Sixteenth to the Nineteenth Centuries," *JAH* 24, no. 2 (1983): 189–206; Wyatt MacGaffey, "Lineage Structure, Marriage and the Family amongst the Central Bantu," *JAH* 24, no. 2 (1983): 173–87; MacGaffey, "Changing Representations," 189–207.

39. *MH* (1880), 195–98; *MH* (1891), 254, 287; Bentley, *Pioneering*, 167–68; Leal, "Memórias d'África," *BSGL* 32 (1914): 309. Son of Pedro's maternal sister, Isabel Iadi, Álvaro XIV belonged to same matrilineage as his predecessor. The surnames of two of his own sons, Feliciano dos Santos Rosa Nembamba and António Moreira Cardoso Nensuka, suggest he was allied by marriage to other aristocratic families. Another son, Álvaro Casemiro Dimoche, born in Kimiala, died in 1898 at age twenty. AAL, S Salvador, Óbitos, 1896, no. 20; 1898, no. 21. For details on Álvaro's installation, see AHU, SEMU-DGU, Angola, 1ª Rep., pasta 11.

40. Graham, *Under Seven Congo Kings*, 41–44; AHU, SEMU-DGU, Angola, 2ª Rep., pasta 15, Secretaria do governo do Congo to Direcção Geral do Ultramar, Cabinda, 27 March 1891; *MH* (1891), 287; Leal, "Memórias d'África," *BSGL* 32 (1914): 320.

41. Leal, "Memórias d'África," *BSGL* 32 (1914): 307, 385–86; AHU, SEMU-DGU, Angola, 1ª Rep., pasta 17, Governador geral to MSENMU, Luanda, 15 December 1896.

42. Bentley, *Pioneering*, 168; Graham, *Under Seven Congo Kings*, 50–57; *MH* (1897), 167; AHNA, caixa 3672, Residente Leal to Secretaria do governo do Congo, confidencial, no. A, S Salvador, 8 March 1896; AAL, S Salvador, Óbitos, 1896, no. 20.

43. AHNA, caixa 3590, Reitor interino, Huila, 9 September 1905; ibid., Vigário capitular to Secretário geral, no. 191, Luanda, 11 October 1905; ibid., Governador do Congo to Secretário geral, no. 86, Cabinda, 24 March 1906; ibid., Reitor interino, Huila, 30 May 1906; AHNA, caixa 3500, 10.6, Governador do Congo to Secretaria geral, no. 630, Cabinda, 19 November 1910; ibid., Governo da Huila, no. 73, 20 April 1911; Leal, "Memórias d'África," *BSGL* 32 (1914): 310–13.

44. Leal, "Memórias d'África," *BSGL* 32 (1914): 308, 355; *MH* (1897), 167; Graham, *Under Seven Congo Kings*, 69. Nteyekenge sent his children to the Portuguese mission for education; in 1899, the priests buried the son he had with his "illegitimate" wife, Isabel Duma; but his own death two years later went unrecorded by the Church. AAL, S Salvador, Óbitos, 1899, no. 3. Kalandenda continued his career in the civil service, where he was later promoted to the position of fiscal agent (*guarda fiscal de 2ª classe*), with a salary only slightly below Nteyekenge's official income. AHNA, caixa 3374, Residencia

de S Salvador, Informação referida ao ano de 1900; AHNA, caixa 3590, Auto de notícia, S Salvador, 3 December 1902.

45. AHNA, caixa 3420, Governador do Congo to Secretaria geral, confidencial, no. 22, Cabinda, 17 July 1899; Leal, "Memórias d'África," *BSGL* 32 (1914): 387–90; Leal, "Congo Portuguez," 258.

46. ALA, A/99, Graham, S Salvador, 6 May 1901; ALA A/122 (D), S Salvador Logbook, 1900; BMS Annual Report (1901), 89; Annual Report (1902), 77, both at ALA; Graham, *Under Seven Congo Kings*, 87, 94–95, 103–4; Claridge, *Wild Bush Tribes*, 151–52.

47. In 1910, Kibelongo's candidature was again obstructed by the resident. Leal, "Memórias d'África," *BSGL* 32 (1914): 309. See also Brásio, *Angola*, 2:21–22; Brásio, *António Barroso*, 485–86; *MH* (1888), 412–13.

48. AHNA, caixa 3590, Resident to Secretaria do governo do Congo, no. 147, S Salvador, 1 May 1901; idem, no. 197 and 198, S Salvador, 18 May 1901; ibid., Governo do Congo to Residência de S Salvador, Cabinda, 8 June 1901; AHNA, caixa 3500, 10.6, Governador do Congo to Secretaria geral, no. 630, Cabinda, 19 November 1910; Leal, "Memórias d'África," *BSGL* 32 (1914): 309–10; Graham, *Under Seven Congo Kings*, 97 (quotation); Weeks, *Primitive Bakongo*, 306. Mbemba used the Agua Rosada surname, though some traditions have him as a Kivuzi. See Cuvelier, "Traditions congolaises" (1931), 198.

49. BMS, Annual Report (1902), 77, at ALA; *MH* (1902), 126.

50. AHNA, caixa 3590, Governador do Congo to Secretário geral, no. 8, Cabinda, 28 March 1905; *MH* (1907), 348.

51. AHU, SEMU-DGU, Angola, 1ª Rep., pasta 17, Governador geral to MSENMU, Luanda, 15 December 1896.

52. AHNA, caixa 3590, Governador do Congo to Secretaria geral, no. 86, Cabinda, 24 March 1906.

53. AHNA, caixa 3500, 10.6, Governador do Congo to Secretaria geral, Cabinda, 19 November 1910.

54. Leal, "Memórias d'África," *BSGL* 32 (1914): 314; 33 (1915): 29; AHNA, caixa 3590, Governador do Congo to Secretaria geral, no. 86, Cabinda, 24 March 1906.

55. AHNA, caixa 3308, 11.1.1, Rei do Congo to Governador geral, S Salvador, 25 June 1902; AHNA, caixa 3496, Inspecção de Fazenda, no. 165-1/859, 4 November 1903; AHNA, caixa 3590, Governador do Congo to Secretário geral, no. 86, Cabinda, 24 March 1906; Leal, "Memórias d'África," *BSGL* 32 (1914): 309–10; Leal, "Congo Portuguez," 257.

56. AAL, S Salvador, Óbitos, 1900, no. 36, D André de Souza Soqui.

57. Ranger, "Invention of Tradition," 224–25.

58. AHNA, caixa 3590, Governador do Congo to Secretário geral, no. 8, Cabinda, 28 March 1905; *BO* 29 (1903), oficio no. 349, 3 June 1903. See also André L'Hoist, "L'ordre du Christ au Congo," *Revue de l'Aucam* 7 (1932): 258, noting the continuity between the old and the new military orders.

59. AHNA, caixa 3500, 10.6, Administrador to Secretaria do governo do Congo, no. 300, S Salvador, 8 July 1910.

60. Graham, *Under Seven Congo Kings*, 132, 239.

61. AHNA, caixa 3500, 10.6, Administrador to Secretaria do governo do Congo, no. 301, S Salvador, 8 July 1910.

62. AHNA, caixa 3500, 10.6, Governador do distrito to Secretaria geral, no. 630, Cabinda, 19 November 1910.

63. Graham, *Under Seven Congo Kings*, 120–21.

64. See AHNA, caixa 3672, Governador do Congo to Governador geral, Cabinda, January 1912, encl. in Repartição do gabinete, Processo no. 14, 1912.

65. AHU, SEMU-MU/DGU-DGC, Angola, maço 1081, doc. 57.

66. AHNA, caixa 3500, 10.6, Residente to Secretaria do governo do Congo, no. 44, S Salvador, 27 January 1911.

67. Leal, "Memórias d'África," *BSGL* 32 (1914): 316–17.

68. AHNA, caixa 1334, 11.1.6, Guias de marcha, 1893.

69. AAL, S Salvador, Casamentos 1894 (no. 2), 1899 (no. 1), 1909 (no. 1); AHNA, caixa 1755, 11.2.13, Comandante do posto militar to Residência de S Salvador, no. 24, Maquela, 22 March 1900. In 1912, Kidito & Sobrinho (nephew) were a small import firm in São Salvador, who also employed Manuel Rosa Jinga. In 1956, Kiditu's nephew and Rosa Ginga were known Protestant royalists. AHNA, caixa 3672, Administração de S Salvador, invoice, 30 June 1912.

70. Leal, "Memórias d'África," *BSGL* 32 (1914): 315–18 (quotation on 317).

71. Thornton, "Kongo's Incorporation into Angola," 357.

72. AHNA, caixa 3500, 10.6, Auto, S Salvador, 6 April 1911.

73. John K. Thornton, "The Regalia of the Kings of Kongo," in *Kings of Africa: Art and Authority in Central Africa*, ed. Erna Beumers and Hans-Joachim Koloss (Maastricht: Foundation Kings of Africa, 1992), 57–63. See also António Brásio, "O problema da eleição e coroação dos reis do Congo," *Revista Portuguesa de História* 12, no. 1 (1969): 351–81.

74. On the early origins of Kongo political culture, see Vansina, *Paths in the Rainforest*, 146–52.

75. AHNA, caixa 3308, 11.1.1, Manuel Lopes de Almeida to Governador geral, S Salvador 25 June 1902. Henrique Lunga was named after Dom Henrique II (1842–57).

76. AHNA, caixa 3646, Escolas, S Salvador, 1899; AAL, S Salvador, Casamentos, 1906, no. 1.

77. AHNA, caixa 3500, 10.6, Residente to Secretaria do governo do Congo, no. 148, S Salvador, 7 April 1911; AHNA, caixa 3590, Inspector de Fazenda to Secretário do governo geral, Luanda, 2 January 1912; Leal, "Memórias d'África," *BSGL* 32 (1914): 318–26.

78. Bittremieux, "Overblijfselen," 804–5. For descriptions of *sangamentos* honoring Pedro V, see Bentley, *Pioneering*, 201; Lewis, "Old Kingdom," 596–98.

79. Leal, "Memórias d'África," *BSGL* 33 (1915): 125–27.

80. Leal, "Memórias d'África," *BSGL* 33 (1915): 69–70; Governo Geral da Província de Angola, *Annuário estatístico da Província de Angola, 1897* (Luanda: Imprensa Nacional, 1899), 31.

81. Weeks, *Primitive Bakongo*, 306.

Chapter 5. Forced Labor

1. The classic treatment is Duffy, *Question of Slavery*. For general overviews of Portuguese colonial policies and their implementation in Angola, see Wheeler and Pélissier, *Angola*; Malyn Newitt, *Portugal in Africa: The Last Hundred Years* (London: C. Hurst & Co., 1981); Clarence-Smith, *Third Portuguese Empire*, esp. 107–9, 139–40, 181–83; Jeremy Ball, "Colonial Labor in Twentieth-Century Angola," *History Compass* 3, no. 1 (2005): 1–9, doi: 10.1111/j.1478-0542.2005.00168.x. For colonial labor histories in Angola at the

grassroots level, see Heywood, "Porters, Trade, and Power," 243–67, and "Slavery and Forced Labor," 415–36; Alexander Keese, "Searching for the Reluctant Hands: Obsession, Ambivalence and the Practice of Organising Involuntary Labour in Colonial Cuanza-Sul and Malange Districts, Angola, 1926–1945," *Journal of Imperial and Commonwealth History* 41, no. 2 (2013): 238–58; Todd Charles Cleveland, "Rock Solid: African Laborers on the Diamond Mines of the Companhia de Diamantes de Angola (Diamang), 1917–1975" (PhD diss., University of Michigan, 2008).

    2. *BO* 6 (1900), decree of 9 November 1899. For a discussion of early colonial labor reforms and their limitations, see Newitt, *Portugal in Africa*, 106–12; Adelino Torres, *O império português: Entre o real e o imaginário* (Lisbon: Escher, 1991), 163–89.

    3. Miguel Bandeira Jerónimo, "The 'Civilisation Guild': Race and Labour in the Third Portuguese Empire, c. 1870–1930," in *Racism and Ethnic Relations in the Portuguese-Speaking World*, ed. Francisco Bethencourt and Adrian J. Pearce (Oxford: Oxford University Press, 2012), 173–99.

    4. Frederick Cooper, "Conditions Analogous to Slavery: Imperialism and Free Labor Ideology in Africa," in Frederick Cooper et al., *Beyond Slavery: Explorations of Race, Labor, and Citizenship in Postemancipation Societies* (Chapel Hill: University of North Carolina Press, 2000), 107–49; Alice L. Conklin, "Colonialism and Human Rights, a Contradiction in Terms? The Case of France and West Africa, 1895–1914," *AHR* 103, no. 2 (1998): 437–40.

    5. Newitt, *Portugal in Africa*, 107.

    6. William Gervase Clarence-Smith, "Capital Accumulation and Class Formation in Angola," in *History of Central Africa*, vol. 2, ed. David Birmingham and Phyllis M. Martin (London: Longman, 1983), 168.

    7. On this point, see also David Northrup, "Freedom and Indentured Labor in the French Caribbean, 1848–1900," in *Coerced and Free Migration: Global Perspectives*, ed. David Eltis (Stanford, CA: Stanford University Press, 2002), 208; Frederick Cooper, "Africa and the World Economy," in Frederick Cooper et al., *Confronting Historical Paradigms: Peasants, Labor, and the Capitalist World System in Africa and Latin America* (Madison: University of Wisconsin Press, 1993), 84–204.

    8. Catherine Coquery-Vidrovitch and Paul E. Lovejoy, "The Workers of Trade in Precolonial Africa," in Coquery-Vidrovitch and Lovejoy, *Workers of African Trade*, 15.

    9. Anne Phillips, *The Enigma of Colonialism: British Policy in West Africa* (London: James Currey, 1989), 11.

    10. Barbara Bush and Josephine Maltby, "Taxation in West Africa: Transforming the Colonial Subject into the 'Governable Person,'" *Critical Perspectives on Accounting* 15, no. 1 (2004): 7.

    11. Crawford Young, *The African Colonial State in Comparative Perspective* (New Haven, CT: Yale University Press, 1994), 124–33; John Iliffe, *Africans: The History of a Continent* (Cambridge: Cambridge University Press, 1995), 196–98; Redding, *Sorcery and Sovereignty*, ch. 1; Falola, *Colonialism and Violence*, ch. 4; Ewout Frankema and Marlous van Waijenburg, "Metropolitan Blueprints of Colonial Taxation? Lessons from Fiscal Capacity Building in British and French Africa," *JAH* 55, no. 3 (2014): 371–400.

    12. Beatrix Heintze, "Der portugiesisch-afrikanische Vassallenvertrag in Angola im 17. Jahrhundert," *Paideuma* 25 (1979): 195–223; "Luso-African Feudalism in Angola? The Vassal Treaties of the Sixteenth to the Eighteenth Century," *Revista portuguesa de história* 18 (1980): 111–31.

13. José de Oliveira Ferreira Diniz, "Da política indígena em Angola: Os impostos indígenas," *Boletim Geral das Colónias* 47 (1929): 136–65; *Portugal em África* 8, no. 92 (1901), 444.

14. *BO* 42 (1906), decree of 13 September 1906; *BO* 3 (1909), edict 38 of 16 January 1909; *BO* 36 (1910), edict 766 of 2 September 1910.

15. Leal, "Memórias d'África," *BSGL* 33 (1915): 28; AHU, SEMU/MU-DGU/ DGC, Angola, maço 1081, doc. 26, Paulo Midosi Moreira, Relatório acerca dos acontecimentos passados no Congo, Benguela, 24 October 1914.

16. *BO* 31 (1907), edict 414 of 30 July 1907; *BO* 20 (1912), circular of 14 May 1912.

17. Weeks, *Primitive Bakongo*, 201; Leal, "Memórias d'África," *BSGL* 32 (1914): 319; 33 (1915): 71, 126; Castro, "De Noqui ao Cuango," 92; José Maria da Silva Cardoso, *No Congo Português: Viagem ao Bembe e Damba, considerações relacionadas, Setembro a Outubro de 1912* (Luanda: Imprensa Nacional de Angola, 1914), 37.

18. AHNA, caixa 2041, Governador do Congo to Secretaria geral, no. 268/260, Cabinda, 7 July 1909; ALA, A/46/10, Extract by E. R. Jones (n/d).

19. AHNA, caixa 2041, Governador do Congo to Secretaria geral, Cabinda, 6 February 1911. On tax payments in rubber, see also Jaime Manuel Viana Pedreira, "Relatório do reconhecimento ao Zaza-Lunga-Cuílo: Dezembro de 1915," *Ordem à Força Armada* 2, no. 1 (1918): 95; "Relatório do percurso de 600 kilometros atravez da capitania: Março de 1916," *Ordem à Força Armada* 2, no. 1 (1918): 127.

20. AHNA, caixa 3374, Administrador José Antunes dos Santos to Secretário do governo do Congo, no. 332, S Salvador, 22 July 1910.

21. Cardoso, *No Congo Português*, 10; AHNA, caixa 1755, 11.2.28, Governador do Congo to Secretaria geral, no. 40, Cabinda, 4 February 1908; AHNA, caixa 2041, Alferes António de Mattos to Residente do Ambrizete, no. 7, Kinzau, 17 January 1911, encl. in Governador do Congo to Secretaria geral, Cabinda, 2 February 1911.

22. Watts, *Silent Violence*, 136–39.

23. AHU, MU-DGC, Angola, pasta 999, Informação para o Ministro das Colónias de José Cardoso, Lisboa, 21 May 1914; Henrique M. de Paiva Couceiro, *Angola: Dois anos de governo, Junho 1907–Junho 1909; História e comentários* (Lisbon: Gama, 1951), 42–45; Pélissier, *História das campanhas*, 1:221–31.

24. Leigh A. Gardener, "Decentralization and Corruption in Historical Perspective: Evidence from Tax Collection in British Colonial Africa," *Economic History of Developing Regions* 25, no. 2 (2010): 213–36.

25. See also Vansina, *Being Colonized*, 69.

26. Lewis, *These Seventy Years*, 219; Bentley, *Pioneering*, 195–98.

27. AHU, SEMU/MU-DGU/DGC, Angola, maço 1081, doc. 58, Faria Leal, Ocupação da Damba, Relatório, S Salvador, 26 October 1911; ibid., doc. 84, Governador do Congo to Quartel general, Cabinda, 23 April 1912.

28. Camilo Afonso, "O contributo da tradição oral no estudo da história de Angola: Caso dos Bakongo" (Licenciatura, Universidade Agostinho Neto, Lubango, 1991), 90–95.

29. Vos, "Of Stocks and Barter," 153–75.

30. Afonso, "O contributo," 96–110.

31. AHNA, caixa 3590, Administrador to Secretaria do governo do Congo, no. 340, S Salvador, 31 July 1910, and no. 339, S Salvador, 26 July 1910.

32. AHM, caixa 17, no. 17, Relatório; AHU, SEMU/MU-DGU/DGC, Angola, maço 1081, doc. 58; Leal, "Memórias d'África," *BSGL* 32 (1914): 402–10; 33 (1915): 15–28; Cardoso, *No Congo Português*, 32, 39, 50.

33. Lewis, *These Seventy Years*, 263.

34. AHNA, caixa 3643, Escolas, S Salvador, 1899; AAL, S Salvador, Casamentos, 1903, no. 3; AHU, SEMU/MU-DGU/DGC, Angola, maço 1081, doc. 26.

35. AHM, caixa 17, no. 17, Relatório, 35–46; caixa 20, no. 17, 62; Leal, "Memórias d'África," *BSGL* 32 (1914): 400–402, 406–7; 33 (1915): 219–22; Cardoso, *No Congo Português*, 47. On chiefs and *cipaios*, see also Norton de Matos, *Circular do Governo Geral de Angola: Em data de 17 de Abril de 1913* (Ponte de Lima: Tip. Augusto de Sousa, 1952).

36. Falola, *Colonialism and Violence*, 61.

37. BMS, Annual Report (1902), 77, at ALA.

38. *MH* (1902), 47.

39. Jardim, "A expedição a Quincunguila," *Revista Portugueza Colonial e Marítima* 12 (1903): 64; *Portugal em África* 9 (1902): 320 (Maquela do Zombo, 27 March 1902), 500.

40. Castro, "De Noqui ao Cuango," 92; Leal, "Memórias d'África," *BSGL* 33 (1915): 359 (referring to decree 1091, in *BO* 36 [1911]).

41. Lewis, "Ancient Kingdom," 556.

42. AHNA, caixa 3343, Residência de S Salvador, 8 May 1906.

43. *MH* (1899), 381, 460–63; Lewis, *These Seventy Years*, 176–77, 190.

44. ALA, A/64, Letter book (Zombo 1899–1911), Lewis to Baynes, Kibokolo, 2 August 1900, and Pinnock to Graham, Kibokolo, 16 July 1901; ibid., Letter book (Zombo 1902–12), [Pinnock] to Baynes, January 1902; BMS, Annual Report (1902), 80, at ALA.

45. *MH* (1903), 32.

46. Lewis, *These Seventy Years*, 203–8, 214; ALA, A/64, Letter book (Zombo 1899–1911), Lewis to BMS, 10 October 1902, and Lewis to Baynes, 1902 (pp. 336–42); ibid., Letter book (Zombo 1902–12), Lewis to Thomson, 11 November 1902; ibid., Logbook "Comber Memorial Station," Report for 1909, Kibokolo, 26 December 1909; *MH* (1903), 32–35, 95; Annual Report (1903), 62–63; Annual Report (1904), 69; AHNA, códice 797, série 1902, no. 280, Cabinda 17-12-1902; Leal, "Memórias d'África," *BSGL* 32 (1914): 402–3.

47. AHNA, caixa 3496, Governador do Congo to Secretaria geral, no. 386, Cabinda, 25 July 1898; ibid., Obras Publicas, Relatório, Motivo da decadência da agricultura no enclave de Cabinda, 1910; AHU, Angola, 1ª Rep., pasta 23, Governador geral to Ministro das Colónias, no. 1046, Luanda, 24 November 1912. In the early 1900s, colonial authorities in Cabinda tried to restrict labor migration out of the enclave, in hopes of increasing local labor supplies to agricultural firms, but to no avail, as Cabindan migration mainly happened outside official channels. See Pires, "Comércio e trabalho em Cabinda durante a ocupação colonial portuguesa," ch. 5.

48. TNA, FO 367/334, 8547, Drummond-Hay to Grey, Luanda, 28 January 1913.

49. TNA, FO 881/10217, Memorandum regarding labor conditions in the Spanish and Portuguese West African Dominions, May 1913.

50. AHU, SEMU/MU-DGU/DGC, Angola, maço 1081, doc. 26. When Kiditu was questioned in August 1914 about his negotiations with the governor in Cabinda, he suffered a nervous breakdown. Ibid., doc. 145, interview no. 6. For the NAHV, see NA, NAHV (2.18.10.09), 74/178, Accounts 1908–10.

51. Cardoso, *No Congo Português*, 6, 49, 56–57; AHU, Angola, 1ª Rep., pasta 23, List of officials in Congo District, 1912.

52. AHNA, caixa 3496, file 1909, Distrito do Congo, Relação dos residentes, escrivães e delegados, Cabinda, 28 June 1904; AHNA, caixa 3672, Governador to Secretaria geral, no. Extra, Luanda, 23 June 1913; AHU, SEMU/MU-DGU/DGC, Angola, maço 1081, doc. 26.

53. Personal documentation held by José Carlos de Oliveira, Óbidos, Portugal, and shown to author on 27 July 2014.

54. Lewis, *These Seventy Years*, 263.

55. AHU, SEMU/MU-DGU/DGC, Angola, maço 1081, doc. 75, Jayme de Moraes to Governador geral.

56. On the Republican reforms, see Wheeler and Pélissier, *Angola*, ch. 5.

57. José d'Almeida Mattos, *O Congo Português e a suas riquezas* (Lisbon: Simões, Marques, Santos & Cia., 1924), 15–24 (Companhia de Cabinda), 42–43 (Lucola), 55–65 (Hatton & Cookson).

58. TNA, FO 367/334, 8547, Drummond-Hay to Thomas, Luanda, 6 December 1912.

59. TNA, FO 367/334, 8547, Drummond-Hay to Grey, Luanda, 28 January 1913.

60. AHNA, caixa 3374, Negócios Indígenas, Processo no. 221, Estatística dos trabalhadores da Província do Congo (1913).

61. AHNA, caixa 3698, Relação do pessoal empregado na limpeza da povoação no mês de março 1912, encl. in Commissão municipal de S Salvador, ordem de pagamento, no. 67, 1912.

62. TNA, FO 367/334, 8547, Royle to Drummond-Hay, Cabinda, 12 December 1912.

63. AHU, SEMU/MU-DGU/DGC, Angola, maço 1081, doc. 29, Governador do districto to Governador geral, Cabinda, 5 February 1913.

64. TNA, FO 367/335, 18278, Thomas to Drummond-Hay, Matadi, 31 December 1912. Also FO 367/334, 8547, Thomas to Smallbones, S Salvador, 8 September 1912.

65. AHU, SEMU/MU-DGU/DGC, Angola, maço 1081, doc. 35, Administrador Pinto to Governador Cardoso, Relatório, S Salvador, 8 March 1913.

66. BMS, Annual Reports of 1908–12, at ALA.

67. TNA, FO 367/334, 8547, António Mesakala Makaya to BMS, Cabinda, 27 October 1912 (translated).

68. Ibid., Letter to Lungezi, Kunku and Mwingu, Cabinda, 27 October 1912 (translated).

69. Ibid., Royle to Drummond-Hay, Cabinda, 12 December 1912.

70. AHU, SEMU/MU-DGU/DGC, Angola, maço 1081, doc. 35.

71. TNA, FO 367/335, 18278, Thomas to Drummond-Hay, Matadi, 31 December 1912. Also FO 367/334, 2713, BMS to Grey, London, 15 January 1913.

72. AHU, SEMU/MU-DGU/DGC, Angola, maço 1081, doc. 34, Governador Cardoso to Governador geral, Cabinda, 24 February 1913.

73. Leal, "Memórias d'África," *BSGL* 33 (1915): 27–28.

74. Ibid., 394.

75. AHU, SEMU/MU-DGU/DGC, Angola, maço 1081, doc. 36, Governador do districto to Governador geral, Cabinda, 11 July 1913.

76. AHU, SEMU/MU-DGU/DGC, Angola, maço 1081, doc. 35.

77. AHM, caixa 20, doc. 11, 5; *Arquivos de Angola*, 2nd series, 16, nos. 63–66 (1959), 9–10.

78. AHU, SEMU/MU-DGU/DGC, Angola, maço 1081, doc. 37, Norton de Matos, Luanda, 7 April 1913; *BO* 51 (1912), circular of 20 December 1912.

79. AHU, SEMU/MU-DGU/DGC, Angola, maço 1081, doc. 36.

80. Gareth Austin, "Resources, Techniques, and Strategies South of the Sahara: Revising the Factor Endowments Perspective on African Economic Development, 1500–2000," *Economic History Review* 61, no. 3 (2008): 609–10.

81. Leal, "Memórias d'África," *BSGL* 33 (1915): 372–75.

82. Cooper, *Decolonization and African Society*, 26.

83. AHU, MU-DGC, Angola, pasta 999, "An Account of the War Palaver."

84. Castro, "De Noqui ao Cuango," 89.

85. Cooper, *Decolonization and African Society*, 28.

86. TNA, FO 367/355, 18278, Thomas to Drummond-Hay, Matadi, 31 December 1912; AHNA, caixa 3374, Secretaria geral, Processo no. 1044, 1913, Imigração clandestina para o Congo Belga.

Chapter 6. Political Breakdown

1. For a recent discussion of Kongo renewal movements, see John M. Janzen, "Renewal and Reinterpretation in Kongo Religion," in *Kongo across the Waters*, ed. Susan Cooksey et al. (Gainesville: University Press of Florida, 2013), 132–42. For comparison, see Fields, *Revival and Rebellion*; Vansina, *Being Colonized*, ch. 9.

2. Thornton, *Kongolese Saint Anthony*, 55. The 1913 uprising resembled the Antonian movement in that both were reactions to visible manifestations of violence, which were explained by the selfish behavior of people in positions of power.

3. Joseph-Achille Mbembe, *On the Postcolony* (Berkeley: University of California Press, 2001), 14. See also Lonsdale, "Political Accountability," 150.

4. On the early slave trade from Kongo to São Tomé, see Robert Garfield, *A History of São Tomé Island, 1470–1655: The Key to Guinea* (San Francisco, CA: Mellen Research University Press, 1992), ch. 3; Hilton, *Kingdom of Kongo*, 55–60. For the later slave trade from Angola to São Tomé, see William Gervase Clarence-Smith, "Emigration from Western Africa, 1807–1940," *Itinerario* 14, no. 1 (1990): 45–60; "Cocoa Plantations and Coerced Labor in the Gulf of Guinea, 1870–1914," in *Breaking the Chains: Slavery, Bondage, and Emancipation in Modern Africa and Asia*, ed. Martin A. Klein (Madison: University of Wisconsin Press, 1993), 150–70.

5. TNA, FO 881/10217, Memorandum regarding labor conditions in the Spanish and Portuguese West African Dominions, May 1913. See also William Gervase Clarence-Smith, "Labour Conditions in the Plantations of São Tomé and Príncipe, 1875–1914," *Slavery and Abolition* 14, no. 1 (1993): 149–67. For a recent treatment of the British campaign, see Grant, *Civilised Savagery*, ch. 4.

6. See supplement to *BO* 34 (1909), decree of 17 June 1909; *BO* 25 (1911), decree of 27 May 1911; *BO* 20 (1912), decree of 30 March 1912; *BO* 36 (1912), decree of 20 July 1912; *BO* 51 (1912), circular of 20 December 1912.

7. *BO* 36 (1913), edict 1021 of 3 September 1913; TNA, FO 881/10424, Memorandum regarding labor conditions in the Spanish and Portuguese West African Dominions, May 1914.

8. José de Oliveira Ferreira Diniz, *Negócios Indígenas: Relatório do ano de 1913* (Luanda: Imprensa Nacional de Angola, 1914), 87–88.

9. See the letter of 21 October 1913 in J. Sidney Bowskill, *São Salvador, Portuguese Congo: Mr. Bowskill's Letters on the Native War of 1913-4, and Other Documents* (London: Carey Press, 1914), 15–20; also in TNA, FO 367/337, 57958, Bowskill to Wilson, S Salvador, 21 October 1913.

10. ALA, A/123, Claridge to Wilson, Yakusu, 22 June 1914, 6. In his later memoir, Claridge played up the São Tomé factor. See Claridge, *Wild Bush Tribes*, 44.

11. AHNA, caixa 3910, folder 9-3, Parliamentary Debates, House of Lords, Monday, 27 July, 1914, Official Report, 160.

12. AHU, SEMU/MU-DGU/DGC, Angola, maço 1081, doc. 77, Norton de Matos to Governador do distrito, S Antonio do Zaire, 12 January 1914.

13. AHU, SEMU/MU-DGU/DGC, Angola, maço 1081, doc. 26/12.

14. Heywood, "Slavery and Forced Labor," 415-36; *Contested Power*, 44. On Kongo slavery, see MacGaffey, "Economic and Social Dimensions," 235-57; Wyatt MacGaffey, "Kongo Slavery Remembered by Themselves: Texts from 1915," *IJAHS* 41, no. 1 (2008): 55-76. On lineage slavery and colonial rule, see Paul E. Lovejoy, *Transformations in Slavery: A History of Slavery in Africa*, 2nd ed. (Cambridge: Cambridge University Press, 2000), 262-67.

15. AHU, SEMU/MU-DGU/DGC, Angola, maço 1081, doc. 26, 41, 83; Bowskill, *São Salvador*, 21.

16. For the events described in this paragraph, see AHU, SEMU/MU-DGU/DGC, Angola, maço 1081, doc. 26/6, 26/7, 26/11, 26/12; Bowskill, *São Salvador*, 21-27.

17. Bowskill, *São Salvador*, 28; AHU, SEMU/MU-DGU/DGC, Angola, maço 1081, doc. 144.

18. Both transcripts are located in AHU, MU-DGC, Angola, pasta 999. In a supplement to the Portuguese report, the BMS confirmed its overall accuracy. My citations are from the BMS version, which is also published in Bowskill, *São Salvador*, 32-50. Graham, *Under Seven Congo Kings*, 139, claimed that the district governor never saw the English version.

19. ALA, A/123, Claridge to Wilson, Yakusu, 22 June 1914, 12 (quotation); Bowskill, *São Salvador*, 18-19. According to Hilton, *Kingdom of Kongo*, 20, *mbuta* means "eldest" (of the clan). In 1890, a nineteen-year-old man named Álvaro Mbuta, carpenter in São Salvador, married Graça Zongi from Tuku (Madimba), who died in 1897. The same Mbuta was also married outside the church to Susana Calula, while in 1929, a daughter of Mbuta (then deceased) by another wife, Maria Sangui, got married in São Salvador. AAL, São Salvador, Óbitos, 1897, no. 22 1902, no. 33; Casamentos, 1890, no. 1; 1929, no. 1. But it cannot be confirmed that Álvaro Mbuta and Tulante Buta are one and the same.

20. AHNA, caixa 3590, Residente to Governador do Congo, no. 340, S Salvador, 31 July 1910; AHU, SEMU/MU-DGU/DGC, Angola, maço 1081, doc. 26/6.

21. AHU, SEMU/MU-DGU/DGC, Angola, maço 1081, doc. 26/7. These men were Vatunga and Melandwa, the latter a son of Mfutila, Buta's uncle. Ibid., doc. 145, interview no. 16.

22. AHU, SEMU/MU-DGU/DGC, Angola, maço 1081, doc. 26/8.

23. ALA, A/123, Claridge to Wilson, Yakusu, 22 June 1914, 6.

24. AHU, SEMU/MU-DGU/DGC, Angola, maço 1081, doc. 145, interview no. 6.

25. According to one eyewitness, Buta had told earlier embassies from the court that war could be avoided if Kiditu asked forgiveness for his actions. AHU, SEMU/MU-DGU/DGC, Angola, maço 1081, doc. 145, interview no. 16.

26. Ambrósio Augusto Divengele, "Trabalhos," in *A Maria Immaculada*; AHNA, caixa 3643, Escolas, São Salvador, 1899.

27. Mbembe, *On the Postcolony*, 13–14 (quotation), 72–73.

28. Newbury, "Patrons, Clients, and Empire," 233, mentions the ambiguities surrounding "the position of an indigenous ruler coopted as both a public functionary and a traditional patron with his own client network."

29. Leal, "Memórias d'África," *BSGL* 33 (1915): 372–75.

30. AHU, SEMU/MU-DGU/DGC, Angola, maço 1081, doc. 26/14, 26/16–17, 72, 73.

31. Bowskill, *São Salvador*, 30. During the war of 1914, most of the exiled returned to São Salvador and afterward Almeida apparently became secretary again. See José Manuel da Costa, "S. Salvador do Congo, as suas missões e o seu rei," *Boletim Geral das Colónias* 7, no. 77 (1931): 119.

32. Tulante Buta assisted Kiditu at the ceremony. Claridge, *Wild Bush Tribes*, 91; Weeks, *Primitive Bakongo*, 40 (photographs of installation ceremony).

33. AHU, SEMU/MU-DGU/DGC, Angola, maço 1081, doc. 26/16–17, 83, 103 and 146; AHU, MU-DGU, Angola, pasta 999, doc. 12.

34. AHU, SEMU/MU-DGU/DGC, Angola, maço 1081, doc. 109, A. Nlekai to Noso, Mbanza Mputu, December 1913 (Portuguese translation by Álvaro Tangi in AHM, caixa 21, no. 15). Unlike Almeida, Cupessa later admitted he was guilty of some misdeeds. Ibid., doc. 145, interview nos. 8 and 12.

Conclusion

1. Wolfgang Reinhard, *A Short History of Colonialism* (Manchester, UK: Manchester University Press, 2011), 1.

2. Wheeler and Pélissier, *Angola*, ch. 5.

3. For a comparable case, see Stephen Ellis, *The Rising of the Red Shawls: A Revolt in Madagascar, 1895–1899* (Cambridge: Cambridge University Press, 1985). Vansina, *Being Colonized*, has been inspirational in many ways.

4. Emily Lynn Osborn, "'Circle of Iron': African Colonial Employees and the Interpretation of Colonial Rule in French West Africa," *JAH* 44, no. 1 (2003): 49.

5. Vansina, *Paths in the Rainforest*, 221.

6. Broadhead, "Beyond Decline," 615–50. Broadhead did not mean that the kingdom had reached a stage beyond repair, as Miller, *Way of Death*, 224, seems to suggest. See also Jan Vansina, *Kingdoms of the Savanna* (Madison: University of Wisconsin Press, 1968), 194.

7. In this sense, nineteenth-century Kongo was different from the militarized kingdoms of the Great Lakes region. See Richard Reid, *Political Power in Pre-Colonial Buganda: Economy, Society, and Welfare in the Nineteenth Century* (Oxford: James Currey, 2002); Jan Vansina, *Antecedents to Modern Rwanda: The Nyiginya Kingdom* (Oxford: James Currey, 2004).

8. Hilton, *Kingdom of Kongo*, 222.

9. For a longer perspective on the city's historical development, see John K. Thornton, "Mbanza Kongo/São Salvador: Kongo's Holy City," in *Africa's Urban Past*, ed. David M. Anderson and Richard Rathbone (Oxford: James Currey, 2000), 67–84.

10. Johannes Fabian, *Remembering the Present: Painting and Popular History in Zaire* (Berkeley: University of California Press, 1996), 278–95. See also Barbara H. Rosenwein,

"Problems and Methods in the History of Emotions," *Passions in Context* 1, no. 1 (2010): 1–32; De Luna, "Affect and Society," 123–50.

11. AHU, SEMU/MU-DGU/DGC, Angola, maço 1081, doc. 145, interview no. 16.

Epilogue

1. MacGaffey, "The West," 60–61. See also Ernest Wamba-dia-Wamba, "Bunda dia Kongo: A Congolese Fundamentalist Religious Movement," in *East African Expressions of Christianity*, ed. Thomas Spear and Isaria N. Kimambo (Athens: Ohio University Press, 1999), 213–28.

2. John K. Thornton, "'I Am the Subject of the King of Congo': African Political Ideology and the Haitian Revolution," *Journal of World History* 4, no. 2 (1993): 181–214.

3. SGL, Reservados 1 (Estante 145), pasta M, no. 25, Joaquim Pedro de Magalhaes Gama, Resumo do relatório, Lisboa, 25 March 1943; AHU, SEMU/MU-DGU/DGC, Angola, maço 1081, doc. 72, 73, 87, 88; AHM, caixa 20, no. 11, "Operações no Congo em 1914–15," 6.

4. AHU, SEMU/MU-DGU/DGC, Angola, maço 1081, doc. 73–75, 90, 103, 144–46; Graham, *Under Seven Congo Kings*, 136–37.

5. ALA, A/123, Phillips to Wilson, Matadi, 15 July 1914; ibid., Lewis to Wilson, Kibokolo, 23 July 1914; ibid., Frame to Wilson, Wathen/Thysville, 24 July 1914. For similar rumors elsewhere in Angola, see Heywood, *Contested Power*, 54–55.

6. AHM, caixa 20, no. 9, Victor de Lacerda, Relatório, Maquela do Zombo, 25 February 1914; ibid., no. 16; AHU, SEMU/MU-DGU/DGC, Angola, maço 1081, doc. 81, 83, 153.

7. AHNA, caixa 3413, folder 8–6, Governador interino, no. 294, Informação quinzenal, Cabinda, 10 October 1914; caixa 3496, Governador interino, no. 375, Boletim quinzenal sobre a situação militar [November 1914]; caixa 3910, folder 9–3, telegrams, 1915.

8. AHU, SEMU-DGU, Angola, 1ª Rep., pasta 22, Governador do Congo to Secretário geral, Luanda, 1 October 1915; ALA, Western Sub-Committee, no. 16, pp. 95, 100, 116, 144; Graham, *Under Seven Congo Kings*, 159–73.

9. Costa, "S. Salvador do Congo," 118–20; Graham, *Under Seven Congo Kings*, 201. For a short description of his rule, with images of the king and his regalia, see Hein Vanhee, "King Pedro VII of Kongo (r. 1923–55)," in *Kongo across the Waters*, ed. Susan Cooksey et al. (Gainesville: University Press of Florida, 2013), 26–27.

10. Ladeiras, "Notícia sobre a Missão," 134–37.

11. Marcum, *The Angolan Revolution*, vol. 1, ch. 2 (quotation on 56); Wheeler and Pélissier, *História de Angola*, 244–48; Alexander Keese, "The Constraints of Late Colonial Reform Policy: Forced Labour Scandals in the Portuguese Congo (Angola) and the Limits of Reform under Authoritarian Rule, 1955–61," *Portuguese Studies* 28, no. 2 (2012): 186–200.

Bibliography

Archives

Angola

Arquivo do Arçobispado de Luanda (AAL)
Arquivo Histórico Nacional de Angola (AHNA)

Belgium

Ministère des Affaires étrangères, Archives africaines (AA)

Netherlands

Nationaal Archief (NA)

Portugal

Arquivo Histórico Militar (AHM)
Arquivo Histórico Ultramarino (AHU)
Ministério dos Negócios Estrangeiros, Arquivo Histórico Diplomático (AHD)
Sociedade de Geografia de Lisboa (SGL)

United Kingdom

Angus Library and Archive, Regent's Park College, Baptist Missionary Society (ALA)
National Archives (TNA)

Published Primary Sources

Almanaque de O missionário católico. Couto de Cucujães: Escóla Tipográfrica do Colégio das Missões Religiosas Ultramarinas Portuguesas, 1926–27.
Almeida, António de. "Mais subsídios para a história dos reis do Congo." In *Congresso do mundo português*, vol. 8, edited by Comissão executiva dos centenários, 643–96. Lisbon: Comissão executiva dos centenários, secçao dos congressos, 1940.

Alves, Sebastião José. "Remexendo no passado: Memória de um antigo missionário." *O missionário católico* 2, no. 20 (1926): 155–57; 2, no. 21 (1926): 175–78; 2, no. 22 (1926): 196–98; 2, no. 23 (1926): 212–13; 2, no. 24 (1926): 235–37; 3, no. 25 (1926): 15–16; 3, no. 26 (1926): 23–24.

A Maria Immaculada: Homenagem da Missão Portugueza de S. Salvador do Congo, 8 de Dezembro de 1905. San Salvador: Missão, 1905.

"Angola: Notícias extrahidas dos Boletins Officiaes da mesma Provincia do anno de 1861." *Annaes do Conselho Ultramarino,* parte não oficial, série 3 (1862): 37–42.

Annual Report of the Baptist Missionary Society. London, 1880–.

Arquivos de Angola. 2nd series. Luanda: Museu de Angola, 1943–.

Augouard, Prosper. *28 années au Congo.* 2 vols. Poitiers: Société Française d'Imprimerie et de Librairie, 1905.

Bastian, Adolf. *Ein Besuch in San Salvador, der Hauptstadt des Königsreichs Congo.* Bremen: Heinrich Strack, 1859.

Bentley, W. Holman. *Pioneering on the Congo.* 2 vols. New York: Fleming H. Revell Co., 1900.

Bittremieux, Leo. "Overblijfselen van den katholieken Godsdienst in Lager Kongoland." *Anthropos* 21 (1926): 797–805.

Blink, Hendrik. *Het Kongo-land en zijne bewoners in betrekking tot de Europeesche staatkunde en den handel.* Haarlem: Tjeenk Willink, 1891.

Boletim do Governo Geral da Província de Angola. Luanda: Imprensa do Governo, 1845–1911.

Boletim official da Província de Angola. Luanda: Imprensa Nacional, 1912–14.

Bowskill, J. Sidney. *São Salvador, Portuguese Congo: Mr. Bowskill's Letters on the Native War of 1913–4, and Other Documents.* London: Carey Press, 1914.

Brásio, António, ed. *Angola.* Vol. 1, *1596–1867.* Pittsburgh, PA: Duquesne University Press, 1966.

———, ed. *Angola.* Vol. 2, *1868–1881.* Pittsburgh, PA: Duquesne University Press, 1968.

———, ed. *Angola.* Vol. 3, *1882–1889.* Pittsburgh, PA: Duquesne University Press, 1969.

———, ed. *Angola.* Vol. 4, *1890–1903.* Pittsburgh, PA: Duquesne University Press, 1970.

———, ed. *D. António Barroso: Missionário, cientista, missiólogo.* Lisbon: Centro de Estudos Históricos Ultramarinos, 1961.

———. "Informação do Reino do Congo de Frei Raimundo de Dicomano." *Studia* 34 (1972): 19–42.

———. "O problema da eleição e coroação dos reis do Congo." *Revista Portuguesa de História* 12, no. 1 (1969): 351–81.

Burton, Richard Francis. *Two Trips to Gorilla Land and the Cataracts of the Congo.* 2 vols. London: Sampson Low, Marston, Low & Searle, 1876.

Capello, Hermenegildo, and Roberto Ivens. *From Benguella to the Territory of the Yacca.* 2 vols. New York: Negro Universities Press, 1969.

Cardoso, José Maria da Silva. *No Congo Português: Viagem ao Bembe e Damba, considerações relacionadas, Setembro a Outubro de 1912.* Luanda: Imprensa Nacional de Angola, 1914.

Castro, António Joaquim de. "O Congo em 1845: Roteiro da viagem ao reino do Congo." *BSGL* 2, no. 2 (1880): 53–67.

Castro, J. Moraes e. "De Noqui ao Cuango: Notas de viagem." *BSGL* 21, no. 3 (1903): 81–94.

Chavanne, Josef. "Reisen im Gebiete der Muschi-congo im portugiesischen Westafrika." *Petermanns Mitteilungen aus Justus Perthes' Geographischer Anstalt* 32 (1886): 97–106.

———. *Reisen und Forschungen im alten und neuen Kongostaate.* Jena: Hermann Costenoble, 1887.

Claridge, George Cyril. *Wild Bush Tribes of Tropical Africa.* London: Seeley, Service & Co., 1922.

Comber, T. J. "Brief Account of Recent Journeys in the Interior of Congo." *Proceedings of the Royal Geographical Society* 3, no. 1 (1881): 20–26.

———. "Explorations Inland from Mount Cameroons, and Journey through Congo to Makuta." *Proceedings of the Royal Geographical Society* 1, no. 4 (1879): 225–40.

Costa, José Manuel da. "S. Salvador do Congo, as suas missões e o seu rei." *Boletim Geral das Colónias* 7, no. 77 (1931): 110–22.

Couceiro, Henrique M. de Paiva. *Angola: Dois anos de governo, Junho 1907–Junho 1909; História e comentários.* Lisbon: Gama, 1951.

Cruz, Zacharias da Silva. "Relatório duma viagem a S. Salvador do Congo." *BO* 690, 691 (1858); 692, 695, 696, 701,702, 710, 711 (1859). Transcribed by Arlindo Correia at http://www.arlindo-correia.com/020907.html.

Cuvelier, Jean. "Traditions congolaises." *Congo* (1930): 469–87.

———. "Traditions congolaises." *Congo* (1931): 193–208.

De Bas, F. "Een Nederlandsch reiziger aan den Congo." *Tijdschrift van het Nederlandsch Aardrijkskundig Genootschap,* 2nd series, 3, no. 2 (1887): 339–73.

———. "Een Nederlandsch reiziger aan den Congo." *Tijdschrift van het Nederlandsch Aardrijkskundig Genootschap,* 2nd series, 4, no. 1 (1887): 162–75.

Delcommune, Alexandre. *Vingt années de vie africaine: Récits de voyages, d'aventures et d'exploration au Congo Belge, 1874–1893.* Brussels: Larcier, 1922.

Dicomano, Raimundo de. "Informação sobre o Reino do Congo." Italian original in AHU, SEMU-DGU, Angola, caixa 823. Transcribed by Arlindo Correia at http://www.arlindo-correia.com/101208.html.

Diniz, José de Oliveira Ferreira. "Da política indígena em Angola: Os impostos indígenas." *Boletim Geral das Colónias* 47 (1929): 136–65.

———. *Negócios Indígenas: Relatório do ano de 1913.* Luanda: Imprensa Nacional de Angola, 1914.

Dupont, Éduard. *Lettres sur le Congo: Récit d'un voyage scientifique entre l'embouchure du fleuve et le confluent du Kassai.* Paris: C. Reinwald, 1889.

Du Verge, L. "How Affairs Are Now Conducted on the Congo." *Journal of the American Geographical Society* 16 (1884): 147–51.

Dyer, Hugh McNeile. *The West Coast of Africa as Seen from the Deck of a Man-of-War.* London: J. Griffin & Co., 1876.

Fonseca, António Marciano Ribeiro da. "O rei do Congo." *Revista Militar* 43, nos. 10–11 (1891): 292–302, 324–30.

Fragoso, Henrique Manoel Collaço. *Diário de uma viagem do Ambriz a S. Salvador do Congo.* Luanda: Typ. Luso Africana, 1891.

Fullerton, William Young. *The Christ of the Congo River.* London: Carey Press, 1928.

Governo Geral da Província de Angola. *Annuário estatístico da Província de Angola, 1897.* Luanda: Imprensa Nacional, 1899.

Graham, Robert Haldane Carson. *Under Seven Congo Kings.* London: Carey Press, 1930.

Grandy, W. G. "Report of the Proceedings of the Livingstone Congo Expedition." *Proceedings of the Royal Geographical Society of London* 19, no. 2 (1874–75): 78–105.

Guinness, H. Grattan. *The New World of Central Africa: With a History of the First Christian Mission on the Congo.* New York: Fleming H. Revell, 1890.

Hawker, George. *An Englishwoman's Twenty-Five Years in Tropical Africa: Being the Biography of Gwen Elen Lewis, Missionary to the Cameroons and the Congo.* London: Hodder and Stoughton, 1911.

Heintze, Beatrix. *Ethnographische Aneignungen: Deutsche Forschungsreisende in Angola.* Frankfurt am Main: Verlag Otto Lembeck, 2007.

Henriques, Júlio A. "Das plantas productoras da borracha." *Portugal em Africa* 3, no. 33 (1896): 353–81.

Jadin, Louis. "Recherches dans les archives et bibliothèques d'Italie et du Portugal sur l'Ancien Congo." *Bulletin des Séances de l'Académie Royal des Sciences Coloniales* 2, no. 6 (1956): 951–90.

Jardim, João. "A expedição a Quincunguila na circunscrição de Ambrizette (janeiro a março de 1902)." *Revista Portugueza Colonial e Marítima* 11 (1903): 252–69; 12 (1903): 54–69, 112–25, 160–71, 216–26, 264–69; 13 (1903): 69–79, 129–34, 178–87, 224–37, 278–83; 14 (1903): 18–37, 73–79, 118–28.

Jeannest, Charles. *Quatre années au Congo.* Paris: G. Charpentier et Cie., 1883.

Koopman, J. F. "Verslag van eene reize naar de Westkust van Afrika, Rio de Janeiro en Rio de la Plata." *Verhandelingen en berigten betrekkelijk het zeewezen, de zeevaartkunde, de hydrographie, de kolonien en de daarmee in verband staande wetenschappen* 23, nos. 2–3 (1863): 169–228, 297–363.

Ladeiras, Daniel. "Notícia sobre a Missão de S. Salvador do Congo." *O missionário católico* 3, no. 28 (1926): 72–75; 3, no. 29 (1926): 92–94; 3, no. 30 (1927): 117–19; 3, no. 31 (1927): 134–37; 3, no. 32 (1927): 161–63; 3, no. 33 (1927): 179–81; 3, no. 34 (1927): 190–92.

Leal, José Heliodoro Corte Real de Faria. "Congo Portuguez: De S. Salvador ao Rio Cuilo." *Revista Portugueza Colonial e Marítima* 5 (1901–2): 202–10, 246–61.

———. "Memórias d'África." *BSGL* 32 (1914): 299–339, 343–62, 383–410; 33 (1915): 15–30, 64–79, 113–28, 162–73, 214–31, 357–80.

Lewis, Thomas. "The Ancient Kingdom of Kongo: Its Present Position and Possibilities." *Geographical Journal* 19, no. 5 (1902): 541–57.

———. "Life and Travel among the People of the Congo." *Scottish Geographical Magazine* 18, no. 7 (1902): 358–69.

———. "The Old Kingdom of Kongo." *Geographical Journal* 31, no. 6 (1908): 589–611.

———. *These Seventy Years: An Autobiography.* London: Carey Press, 1930.

Martrin-Donos, Charles de. *Les Belges dans l'Afrique central.* Brussels: P. Maes, 1886.

Matos, Norton de. *Circular do Governo Geral de Angola: Em data de 17 de Abril de 1913.* Ponte de Lima: Tip. Augusto de Sousa, 1952.

Matta, A. "Álbum sobre o Congo português e belga" (1906). Biblioteca Nacional de Portugal, Lisbon. http://purl.pt/22658.

Mattos, José d'Almeida. *O Congo Português e as suas riquezas.* Lisbon: Simões, Marques, Santos & Cia., 1924.

Menezes, Sebastião Lopes de Calheiros e. *Relatório do Governador Geral da Província de Angola, referido ao anno de 1861.* Luanda: Imprensa Nacional, 1867.

Mesquita, João. *Dados estatísticos para o estudo das pautas de Angola: Exportação pelas alfândegas do círculo e do Congo nos anos de 1888 a 1913.* Luanda: Imprensa Nacional, 1918.

Metcalfe, Daniel. *Blue Dahlia, Black Gold: A Journey into Angola.* London: Random House, 2013.

Missionary Herald of the Baptist Missionary Society. London, 1878–.

Monteiro, Joachim John. *Angola and the River Congo*. 2 vols. London: Cass, 1968.

Oliveira, Mário António Fernandes de, ed. *Angolana (Documentação sobre Angola) I (1783–1883)*. Luanda: Instituto de Investigação Científica de Angola, 1968.

Oliveira, Mário António Fernandes de, and Carlos Alberto Mendes do Couto, eds. *Angolana (Documentação sobre Angola) II (1883–1887)*. Luanda: Instituto de Investigação Científica de Angola, 1971.

Pedreira, Jaime Manuel Viana. "Relatório do percurso de 600 kilometros atravez da capitania: Março de 1916." *Ordem à Força Armada* 2, no. 1 (1918): 117–30.

———. "Relatório do reconhecimento ao Zaza-Lunga-Cuílo: Dezembro de 1915." *Ordem à Força Armada* 2, no. 1 (1918): 73–101.

Pimentel, Jaime Pereira de Sampaio Forjaz de Serpa. "Um anno no Congo." *Portugal em África* 6 (1899): 85–109, 142–62, 189–206, 240–57, 289–311, 329–44, 381–404, 425–47, 465–97, 601–35.

Pinto, Francisco António. *Angola e Congo*. Lisbon: Livraria Ferreira, 1888.

Portugal em África. Lisbon, 1900–1903.

Portugal, Ministério dos Negócios da Marinha e Ultramar, Dirrecção Geral do Ultramar. *Annuário estatístico dos domínios ultramarinos portugueses, 1899 e 1900*. Lisbon: Imprensa Nacional, 1905.

Rooney, C. J. "As missões do Congo e Angola." *Portugal em África* 7 (1900): 13–32, 60–85, 127–32, 176, 209–33, 330–35, 378–82, 433–46, 481–92, 532–54.

Sarmento, Alfredo de. *Os sertões d'Africa (apontamentos de viagem)*. Lisbon: F. A. da Silva, 1880.

Soares, José Carlos de Macedo. *A borracha: Estudo económico e estatístico*. Paris: Pedone, 1927.

Stanley, Henry M. *The Congo and the Founding of Its Free State: A Story of Work and Exploration*. New York: Harper & Brothers, 1885.

Tavares, Ana Paula, and Catarina Madeira Santos, eds. *Africae Monumenta: A apropriação da escrita pelos Africanos*. Volume 1, *Arquivo Caculo Cacahenda*. Lisbon: Instituto de Investigação Científica Tropical, 2002.

Thulin, Dieudonné de. "Les Capucins au Congo: L'esclavage et la traite des noirs au Congo." *Études Franciscaines* 35 (1923): 615–31.

Thys, Albert. *Au Congo et au Kassaï*. Brussels: P. Weissenbruch, 1888.

Tuckey, James Kingston. *Narrative of an Expedition to Explore the River Zaire, Usually Called the Congo, in South Africa, in 1816*. London: John Murray, 1818.

Van der Aa, Robidé. *Afrikaansche studiën: Koloniaal bezit en particuliere handel op Afrika's westkust*. The Hague: M. Nijhoff, 1871.

Van Sandick, Onno Zwier. *Herinneringen van de zuid-westkust van Afrika: Eenige bladzijden uit mijn dagboek*. Deventer: Van Sandick, 1881.

Veth, Pieter J., and Johannes F. Snelleman, eds. *Daniël Veth's reizen in Angola, voorafgegaan door eene schets van zijn leven*. Haarlem: Tjeenk Willink, 1887.

Weeks, John H. *Among Congo Cannibals*. London: Seeley, Service & Co., 1913.

———. *Among the Primitive Bakongo*. London: Seeley, Service & Co., 1914.

———. "The Congo and Its People." *MH* (1910), 273–74, 301–2, 331–33, 362–64; (1911), 15–17, 51–52, 75–76, 107–9, 137–39, 173–74, 199–200, 237–38, 275–76, 305–6.

———. "Notes on Some Customs of the Lower Congo People." *Folk-Lore* 19 (1908): 409–37; 20 (1909): 32–63, 181–201, 304–11, 457–80.

BOOKS AND ARTICLES

Abbink, Jon, Mirjam de Bruijn, and Klaas van Walraven, eds. *Rethinking Resistance: Revolt and Violence in African History*. Leiden: Brill, 2003.

Alexandre, Valentim. *Velho Brasil, novas Áfricas: Portugal e o império (1808–1975)*. Porto: Edições Afrontamento, 2000.

Allina, Eric. *Slavery by Any Other Name: African Life under Company Rule in Colonial Mozambique*. Charlottesville: University of Virginia Press, 2012.

Anstey, Roger. *Britain and the Congo in the Nineteenth Century*. Oxford: Clarendon Press, 1962.

Arhin, Kwame. "The Ashanti Rubber Trade with the Gold Coast in the Eighteen-Nineties." *Africa* 42, no. 1 (1972): 32–43.

———. "The Economic and Social Significance of Rubber Production and Exchange on the Gold and Ivory Coasts, 1880–1900." *Cahiers d'études africaines* 20, no. 77–78 (1980): 49–62.

Austen, Ralph. *African Economic History*. Oxford: James Currey, 1987.

Austin, Gareth. "Resources, Techniques, and Strategies South of the Sahara: Revising the Factor Endowments Perspective on African Economic Development, 1500–2000." *Economic History Review* 61, no. 3 (2008): 587–624.

Axelson, Eric. *Portugal and the Scramble for Africa, 1875–1891*. Johannesburg: Witwatersrand University Press, 1967.

Balandier, Georges. *La vie quotidienne au royaume de Kongo du XVIe au XVIIIe siècle*. Paris: Hachette, 1965.

Ball, Jeremy. "Colonial Labor in Twentieth-Century Angola." *History Compass* 3, no. 1 (2005): 1–9. doi: 10.1111/j.1478-0542.2005.00168.x.

Beidelman, Thomas O. "Contradictions between the Sacred and the Secular Life: The Church Missionary Society in Ukaguru, Tanzania, East Africa, 1876–1914." *Comparative Studies in Society and History* 23, no. 1 (1981): 73–95.

Beinart, William, and Colin Bundy. *Hidden Struggles in Rural South Africa: Politics and Popular Movements in the Transkei and Eastern Cape, 1890–1930*. Berkeley: University of California Press, 1987.

Berman, Bruce J. "Ethnicity, Patronage and the African State: The Politics of Uncivil Nationalism." *African Affairs* 97, no. 388 (1998): 305–41.

Berry, Sara. *No Condition Is Permanent: The Social Dynamics of Agrarian Change in Sub-Saharan Africa*. Madison: University of Wisconsin Press, 1993.

Birmingham, David. *Empire in Africa: Angola and Its Neighbors*. Athens: Ohio University Press, 2006.

Bockie, Simon. *Death and the Invisible Powers: The World of Kongo Belief*. Bloomington: Indiana University Press, 1993.

Bontinck, François. "Domzwau M. D. Nlemvo (c. 1871–1938) et la Bible Kikongo." *Revue africaine de théologie* 2, no. 3 (1978): 5–32.

———. "Notes Complémentaires sur Dom Nicolau Agua Rosada e Sardonia." *African Historical Studies* 2, no. 1 (1969): 101–19.

———. "Pedro V, roi de Kongo, face au partage colonial." *Africa* (Roma) 37, nos. 1–2 (1982): 1–53.

Brenner, Louis. "'Religious' Discourses in and about Africa." In *Discourse and Its Disguises: The Interpretation of African Oral Texts*, edited by Karin Barber and P. F. de Moraes

Farias, 87–105. Birmingham, UK: Birmingham University Centre of West African Studies, 1989.

Broadhead, Susan Herlin. "Beyond Decline: The Kingdom of Kongo in the Eighteenth and Nineteenth Centuries." *IJAHS* 12, no. 4 (1979): 615–50.

Bush, Barbara, and Josephine Maltby. "Taxation in West Africa: Transforming the Colonial Subject into the 'Governable Person.'" *Critical Perspectives on Accounting* 15, no. 1 (2004): 5–34.

Candido, Mariana P. *An African Slaving Port and the Atlantic World: Benguela and Its Hinterland*. New York: Cambridge University Press, 2013.

Clarence-Smith, William Gervase. "Capital Accumulation and Class Formation in Angola." In *History of Central Africa*, vol. 2, edited by David Birmingham and Phyllis M. Martin, 163–99. London: Longman, 1983.

———. "Cocoa Plantations and Coerced Labor in the Gulf of Guinea, 1870–1914." In *Breaking the Chains: Slavery, Bondage, and Emancipation in Modern Africa and Asia*, edited by Martin A. Klein, 150–70. Madison: University of Wisconsin Press, 1993.

———. "Emigration from Western Africa, 1807–1940." *Itinerario* 14, no. 1 (1990): 45–60.

———. "Labour Conditions in the Plantations of São Tomé and Príncipe, 1875–1914." *Slavery and Abolition* 14, no. 1 (1993): 149–67.

———. *Slaves, Peasants and Capitalists in Southern Angola, 1840–1926*. Cambridge: Cambridge University Press, 1979.

———. *The Third Portuguese Empire, 1825–1975: A Study in Economic Imperialism*. Manchester, UK: Manchester University Press, 1985.

Conklin, Alice L. "Colonialism and Human Rights, a Contradiction in Terms? The Case of France and West Africa, 1895–1914." *AHR* 103, no. 2 (1998): 419–42.

Cooper, Frederick. "Africa and the World Economy." In Frederick Cooper, Allen F. Isaacman, Florencia C. Mallon, William Roseberry, and Steve J. Stern, *Confronting Historical Paradigms: Peasants, Labor, and the Capitalist World System in Africa and Latin America*, 84–204. Madison: University of Wisconsin Press, 1993.

———. "Conditions Analogous to Slavery: Imperialism and Free Labor Ideology in Africa." In Frederick Cooper, Thomas C. Holt, and Rebecca J. Scott, *Beyond Slavery: Explorations of Race, Labor, and Citizenship in Postemancipation Societies*, 107–49. Chapel Hill: University of North Carolina Press, 2000.

———. "Conflict and Connection: Rethinking Colonial African History." *AHR* 99, no. 5 (1994): 1516–45.

———. *Decolonization and African Society: The Labor Question in French and British Africa*. Cambridge: Cambridge University Press, 1996.

Coquery-Vidrovitch, Catherine. *Le Congo au temps des grandes compagnies concessionaires, 1898–1930*. Paris: Mouton, 1972.

Coquery-Vidrovitch, Catherine, and Paul E. Lovejoy. "The Workers of Trade in Precolonial Africa." In *The Workers of African Trade*, edited by Catherine Coquery-Vidrovitch and Paul E. Lovejoy, 9–24. Beverly Hills, CA: Sage Publications, 1985.

Crais, Clifton. "Chiefs and Bureaucrats in the Making of Empire: A Drama from the Transkei, South Africa, October 1880." *AHR* 108, no. 4 (2003): 1034–56.

———. *Poverty, War, and Violence in South Africa*. New York: Cambridge University Press, 2011.

Crummey, Donald, ed. *Banditry, Rebellion and Social Protest in Africa*. London: James Currey, 1986.

De Luna, Kathryn M. "Affect and Society in Precolonial Africa." *IJAHS* 46, no. 1 (2013): 123–50.

Des Forges, Alison Liebhafsky. *Defeat Is the Only Bad News: Rwanda under Musinga, 1896–1931*. Madison: University of Wisconsin Press, 2011.

Dias, Jill R. "Angola." In *O império africano, 1825–1890*, edited by Valentim Alexandre and Jill Dias, 319–556. Lisbon: Editorial Estampa, 1998.

———. "Famine and Disease in the History of Angola, c. 1830–1930." *JAH* 22, no. 3 (1981): 349–78.

Duffy, James. *A Question of Slavery: Labour Policies in Portuguese Africa and the British Protest, 1850–1920*. Oxford: Clarendon Press, 1967.

Dumett, Raymond. "The Rubber Trade of the Gold Coast and Asante in the Nineteenth Century: African Innovation and Market Responsiveness." *JAH* 12, no. 1 (1971): 79–101.

Ellis, Stephen. *The Rising of the Red Shawls: A Revolt in Madagascar, 1895–1899*. Cambridge: Cambridge University Press, 1985.

Ellis, Stephen, and Gerrie Ter Haar. *Worlds of Power: Religious Thought and Political Practice in Africa*. New York: Oxford University Press, 2004.

Etherington, Norman. "Education and Medicine." In *Missions and Empire*, edited by Norman Etherington, 261–84. Oxford: Oxford University Press, 2005.

Fabian, Johannes. *Out of Our Minds: Reason and Madness in the Exploration of Central Africa*. Berkeley: University of California Press, 2000.

———. *Remembering the Present: Painting and Popular History in Zaire*. Berkeley: University of California Press, 1996.

Falola, Toyin. *Colonialism and Violence in Nigeria*. Bloomington: Indiana University Press, 2009.

Feierman, Steven. *Peasant Intellectuals: Anthropology and History in Tanzania*. Madison: University of Wisconsin Press, 1990.

Ferreira, Roquinaldo do Amaral. "Abolicionismo *versus* colonialismo: Rupturas e continuidades em Angola (século XIX)." In *África: Brasileiros e portugueses, séculos XVI–XIX*, edited by Roberto Guedes, 95–112. Rio de Janeiro: Mauad, 2013.

Fields, Karen. *Revival and Rebellion in Colonial Central Africa*. Princeton, NJ: Princeton University Press, 1985.

Frankema, Ewout, and Marlous van Waijenburg. "Metropolitan Blueprints of Colonial Taxation? Lessons from Fiscal Capacity Building in British and French Africa." *JAH* 55, no. 3 (2014): 371–400.

Freudenthal, Aida. "Angola." In *O império africano, 1890–1930*, edited by António Henrique de Oliveira Marques, 259–452. Lisbon: Editorial Estampa, 2001.

Fromont, Cécile. *The Art of Conversion: Christian Visual Culture in the Kingdom of Kongo*. Chapel Hill: University of North Carolina Press, 2014.

———. "By the Sword and the Cross: Power and Faith in the Arts of the Christian Kongo." In *Kongo across the Waters*, edited by Susan Cooksey, Robin Poynor, and Hein Vanhee, 28–31. Gainesville: University Press of Florida, 2013.

Gardener, Leigh A. "Decentralization and Corruption in Historical Perspective: Evidence from Tax Collection in British Colonial Africa." *Economic History of Developing Regions* 25, no. 2 (2010): 213–36.

Garfield, Robert. *A History of São Tomé Island, 1470–1655: The Key to Guinea*. San Francisco, CA: Mellen Research University Press, 1992.

Geschiere, Peter. "'Tournaments of Value' in the Forest Area of Southern Cameroon: 'Multiple Self-Realization' versus Colonial Coercion during the Rubber Boom (1900–1913)." In *Commodification: Things, Agency, and Identities*, edited by Wim M. J. van Binsbergen and Peter L. Geschiere, 243–63. Münster: Lit, 2005.

Giles-Vernick, Tamara. *Cutting the Vines of the Past: Environmental Histories of the Central African Rain Forest*. Charlottesville: University Press of Virginia, 2002.

Glassman, Jonathon. *Feasts and Riot: Revelry, Rebellion, and Popular Consciousness on the Swahili Coast, 1856–1888*. Portsmouth, NH: Heinemann, 1995.

Gordon, David M. *Invisible Agents: Spirits in a Central African History*. Athens: Ohio University Press, 2012.

Grant, Kevin. *A Civilised Savagery: Britain and the New Slaveries in Africa, 1884–1926*. New York: Routledge, 2005.

Gray, Richard. *Black Christians and White Missionaries*. New Haven, CT: Yale University Press, 1990.

Grenfell, F. James. *História da Igreja Baptista em Angola, 1879–1975*. Queluz: Núcleo, 1998.

Harms, Robert. "The End of Red Rubber: A Reassessment." *JAH* 16, no. 1 (1975): 73–88.

Hastings, Adrian. *The Church in Africa, 1450–1950*. Oxford: Clarendon Press, 1994.

Heintze, Beatrix. *Afrikanische Pioniere: Trägerkarawanen im westlichen Zentralafrika (ca. 1850–1890)*. Frankfurt am Main: Lembeck, 2002.

———. "As construções de parentesco e sua retórica na política da África centro-ocidental do século XIX." In *A África centro-ocidental no século XIX (c. 1850–1890): Intercâmbio com o mundo exterior, apropriação, exploração e documentação*, 39–99. Luanda: Kilombelombe, 2013.

———. "Der portugiesisch-afrikanische Vassallenvertrag in Angola im 17. Jahrhundert." *Paideuma* 25 (1979): 195–223.

———. "Luso-African Feudalism in Angola? The Vassal Treaties of the Sixteenth to the Eighteenth Century." *Revista portuguesa de história* 18 (1980): 111–31.

Herbst, Jeffrey. *States and Power in Africa: Comparative Lessons in Authority and Control*. Princeton, NJ: Princeton University Press, 2000.

Heywood, Linda M. *Contested Power in Angola, 1840s to the Present*. Rochester, NY: University of Rochester Press, 2000.

———. "Porters, Trade, and Power: The Politics of Labor in the Central Highlands of Angola, 1850–1914." In *The Workers of African Trade*, edited by Catherine Coquery-Vidrovitch and Paul E. Lovejoy, 243–67. Beverly Hills, CA: Sage Publications, 1985.

———. "Portuguese into African: The Eighteenth-Century Central African Background to Atlantic Creole Cultures." In *Central Africans and Cultural Transformations in the American Diaspora*, edited by Linda M. Heywood, 91–113. Cambridge: Cambridge University Press, 2002.

———. "Slavery and Forced Labor in the Changing Political Economy of Central Angola, 1850–1949." In *The End of Slavery in Africa*, edited by Suzanne Miers and Richard Roberts, 415–36. Madison: University of Wisconsin Press, 1988.

Heywood, Linda M., and John Thornton. "Central African Leadership and the Appropriation of European Culture." In *The Atlantic World and Virginia, 1550–1624*, edited by Peter C. Mancall, 194–224. Chapel Hill: University of North Carolina Press, 2007.

Higgs, Catherine. *Chocolate Islands: Cocoa, Slavery, and Colonial Africa.* Athens: Ohio University Press, 2012.

Hilton, Anne. "Family and Kinship among the Kongo South of the Zaire River from the Sixteenth to the Nineteenth Centuries." *JAH* 24, no. 2 (1983): 189–206.

———. *The Kingdom of Kongo.* Oxford: Clarendon Press, 1985.

Hochschild, Adam. *King Leopold's Ghost: A Story of Greed, Terror, and Heroism in Colonial Africa.* Boston: Houghton Mifflin, 1998.

Hunt, Nancy Rose. *A Colonial Lexicon of Birth Ritual, Medicalization, and Mobility in the Congo.* Durham, NC: Duke University Press, 1999.

Iliffe, John. *Africans: The History of a Continent.* Cambridge: Cambridge University Press, 1995.

———. *Honour in African History.* New York: Cambridge University Press, 2005.

———. *A Modern History of Tanganyika.* Cambridge: Cambridge University Press, 1979.

Isaacman, Allen F., and Jan Vansina. "African Initiatives and Resistance in Central Africa, 1880–1914." In *General History of Africa.* Vol. 7, *Africa under Colonial Domination, 1880–1935,* edited by A. Boahen, 169–93. London: Heinemann, 1985.

Jadin, Louis. "Les survivances chrétiennes au Congo au XIXe siècle." *Études d'histoire africaine* 1 (1970): 137–85.

Janzen, John M. *Lemba, 1650–1930: A Drum of Affliction in Africa and the New World.* New York: Garland Publishing, 1982.

———. "Renewal and Reinterpretation in Kongo Religion." In *Kongo across the Waters,* edited by Susan Cooksey, Robin Poynor, and Hein Vanhee, 132–42. Gainesville: University Press of Florida, 2013.

Jerónimo, Miguel Bandeira. "The 'Civilisation Guild': Race and Labour in the Third Portuguese Empire, c. 1870–1930." In *Racism and Ethnic Relations in the Portuguese-Speaking World,* edited by Francisco Bethencourt and Adrian J. Pearce, 173–99. Oxford: Oxford University Press, 2012.

Keese, Alexander. "The Constraints of Late Colonial Reform Policy: Forced Labour Scandals in the Portuguese Congo (Angola) and the Limits of Reform under Authoritarian Rule, 1955–61." *Portuguese Studies* 28, no. 2 (2012): 186–200.

———. "Searching for the Reluctant Hands: Obsession, Ambivalence and the Practice of Organising Involuntary Labour in Colonial Cuanza-Sul and Malange Districts, Angola, 1926–1945." *Journal of Imperial and Commonwealth History* 41, no. 2 (2013): 238–58.

Kirk-Greene, Anthony H. M. "The Thin White Line: The Size of the British Colonial Service in Africa." *African Affairs* 79, no. 314 (1980): 25–44.

Landau, Paul S. "Political Systems, African." In *The Princeton Companion to Atlantic History,* edited by Joseph C. Miller, 376–79. Princeton, NJ: Princeton University Press, 2015.

———. *Popular Politics in the History of South Africa, 1400–1948.* New York: Cambridge University Press, 2010.

———. *The Realm of the Word: Language, Gender, and Christianity in a Southern African Kingdom.* Portsmouth, NH: Heinemann, 1995.

Law, Robin, ed. *From Slave Trade to "Legitimate" Commerce: The Commercial Transition in Nineteenth-Century West Africa.* Cambridge: Cambridge University Press, 1995.

Lawrance, Benjamin Nicholas, Emily Lynn Osborn, and Richard L. Roberts, eds. *Intermediaries, Interpreters, and Clerks: African Employees in the Making of Colonial Africa.* Madison: University of Wisconsin Press, 2006.

L'Hoist, André. "L'ordre du Christ au Congo." *Revue de l'Aucam* 7 (1932): 258–66.

Likaka, Osumaka. *Naming Colonialism: History and Collective Memory in the Congo, 1870–1960.* Madison: University of Wisconsin Press, 2009.

Lonsdale, John. "The Moral Economy of Mau Mau: The Problem." In *Unhappy Valley: Conflict in Kenya and Africa*, vol. 2, *Violence and Ethnicity*, by Bruce Berman and John Lonsdale, 265–314. London: James Currey, 1992.

———. "Political Accountability in African History." In *Political Domination in Africa: Reflections on the Limits of Power*, edited by Patrick Chabal, 126–57. Cambridge: Cambridge University Press, 1986.

———. "The Politics of Conquest in Western Kenya, 1894–1908." In *Unhappy Valley: Conflict in Kenya and Africa*, vol. 1, *State and Class*, by Bruce Berman and John Lonsdale, 45–74. Oxford: James Currey, 1992.

Lovejoy, Paul E. *Transformations in Slavery: A History of Slavery in Africa.* 2nd ed. Cambridge: Cambridge University Press, 2000.

MacGaffey, Wyatt. "Changing Representations in Central African History." *JAH* 46, no. 2 (2005): 189–207.

———. "Dialogues of the Deaf: Europeans on the Atlantic Coast of Africa." In *Implicit Understandings: Observing, Reporting, and Reflecting on the Encounters between Europeans and Other People in the Early Modern Era*, edited by Stuart B. Schwartz, 249–67. Cambridge: Cambridge University Press, 1994.

———. "Economic and Social Dimensions of Kongo Slavery." In *Slavery in Africa: Historical and Anthropological Perspectives*, edited by Suzanne Miers and Igor Kopytoff, 235–57. Madison: University of Wisconsin Press, 1977.

———. *Kongo Political Culture: The Conceptual Challenge of the Particular.* Bloomington: Indiana University Press, 2000.

———. "Kongo Slavery Remembered by Themselves: Texts from 1915." *IJAHS* 41, no. 1 (2008): 55–76.

———. "Lineage Structure, Marriage and the Family amongst the Central Bantu." *JAH* 24, no. 2 (1983): 173–87.

———. "A Note on Vansina's Invention of Matrilinearity." *JAH* 54, no. 2 (2013): 268–80.

———. *Religion and Society in Central Africa: The BaKongo of Lower Zaire.* Chicago: University of Chicago Press, 1986.

———. "The West in Congolese Experience." In *Africa and the West: Intellectual Responses to European Culture*, edited by Phillip D. Curtin, 49–74. Madison: University of Wisconsin Press, 1972.

Mamdani, Mahmood. *Citizen and Subject: Contemporary Africa and the Legacy of Late Colonialism.* Princeton, NJ: Princeton University Press, 1996.

Mann, Michael. "The Autonomous Power of the State: Its Origins, Mechanisms and Results." *European Journal of Sociology* 25, no. 2 (1984): 185–213.

———. "Infrastructural Power Revisited." *Studies in Comparative International Development* 43, no. 3 (2008): 355–65.

Marcum, John. *The Angolan Revolution.* Vol. 1, *The Anatomy of an Explosion (1950–1962).* Cambridge, MA: MIT Press, 1969.

Martin, Phyllis M. *The External Trade of the Loango Coast, 1576–1870: The Effects of Changing Commercial Relations on the Vili Kingdom of Loango.* Oxford: Clarendon Press, 1972.

———. *Leisure and Society in Colonial Brazzaville.* Cambridge: Cambridge University Press, 1995.

———. "Life and Death, Power and Vulnerability: Everyday Contradictions at the Loango Mission, 1883–1904." *Journal of African Cultural Studies* 15, no. 1 (2002): 61–78.

———. "The Violence of Empire." In *History of Central Africa*, vol. 2, edited by David Birmingham and Phyllis M. Martin, 1–26. London: Longman, 1983.

Mbembe, Joseph-Achille. *On the Postcolony*. Berkeley: University of California Press, 2001.

Miller, Joseph C. *Way of Death: Merchant Capitalism and the Angolan Slave Trade, 1730–1830*. Madison: University of Wisconsin Press, 1988.

———. "Political Systems, Collective Consensual." In *The Princeton Companion to Atlantic History*, edited by Joseph C. Miller, 379–83. Princeton, NJ: Princeton University Press, 2015.

Moore, Barrington. *Injustice: The Social Basis of Obedience and Revolt*. London: MacMillan, 1979.

Moyd, Michelle. *Violent Intermediaries: African Soldiers, Conquest, and Everyday Colonialism in German East Africa*. Athens: Ohio University Press, 2014.

Newbury, Colin. *Patrons, Clients, and Empire: Chieftaincy and Over-rule in Asia, Africa, and the Pacific*. Oxford: Oxford University Press, 2003.

———. "Patrons, Clients, and Empire: The Subordination of Indigenous Hierarchies in Asia and Africa." *Journal of World History* 11, no. 2 (2000): 227–63.

Newbury, David. *The Land beyond the Mists: Essays on Identity and Authority in Precolonial Congo and Rwanda*. Athens: Ohio University Press, 2009.

Newitt, Malyn. *Portugal in Africa: The Last Hundred Years*. London: C. Hurst & Co., 1981.

Northrup, David. *Africa's Discovery of Europe: 1450–1850*. 3rd ed. New York: Oxford University Press, 2013.

———. "Freedom and Indentured Labor in the French Caribbean, 1848–1900." In *Coerced and Free Migration: Global Perspectives*, edited by David Eltis, 205–28. Stanford, CA: Stanford University Press, 2002.

Ochonu, Moses E. *Colonial Meltdown: Northern Nigeria in the Great Depression*. Athens: Ohio University Press, 2009.

Oliver, Roland. *The African Experience: From Olduvai Gorge to the 21st Century*. London: Weidenfeld & Nicolson, 1991.

———. *The Missionary Factor in East Africa*. London: Longmans, Green & Co., 1952.

Ortner, Sherry B. "Resistance and the Problem of Ethnographic Refusal." *Comparative Studies in Society and History* 37, no. 1 (1995): 173–93.

Osborn, Emily Lynn. "'Circle of Iron': African Colonial Employees and the Interpretation of Colonial Rule in French West Africa." *JAH* 44, no. 1 (2003): 29–50.

———. "'Rubber Fever,' Commerce and French Colonial Rule in Upper Guinée, 1890–1913." *JAH* 45, no. 3 (2004): 445–65.

Paquette, Gabriel. *Imperial Portugal in the Age of Atlantic Revolutions: The Luso-Brazilian World, c. 1770–1850*. Cambridge: Cambridge University Press, 2013.

Pélissier, René. *História das campanhas de Angola: Resistência e revoltas 1845–1941*. 2nd ed. Lisbon: Editorial Estampa, 1997.

Phillips, Anne. *The Enigma of Colonialism: British Policy in West Africa*. London: James Currey, 1989.

Pinto, Françoise Latour da Veiga. *Le Portugal et le Congo au XIXe siècle: Étude d'histoire des relations internationales*. Paris: Presses universitaires de France, 1972.

Porter, Andrew. "An Overview, 1700–1914." In *Missions and Empire*, ed. Norman Etherington, 40–63. Oxford: Oxford University Press, 2005.

Price, Richard. *Making Empire: Colonial Encounters and the Creation of Imperial Rule in Nineteenth-Century Africa.* Cambridge: Cambridge University Press, 2008.

Pritchett, James A. "Christian Mission Stations in South-Central Africa: Eddies in the Flow of Global Culture." In *Christianity and Public Culture in Africa*, edited by Harri Englund, 27–49. Athens: Ohio University Press, 2011.

Randles, William G. L. *L'ancien royaume du Congo des origines à la fin du XIXème siècle.* Paris: Mouton, 1968.

Ranger, Terence O. "Connexions between 'Primary Resistance' Movements and Modern Mass Nationalism in East and Central Africa." *JAH* 9, nos. 3–4 (1968): 437–53, 631–41.

———. "Europeans in Black Africa." *Journal of World History* 9, no. 2 (1998): 255–68.

———. "The Invention of Tradition in Colonial Africa." In *The Invention of Tradition*, edited by Eric Hobsbawm and Terence Ranger, 211–62. Cambridge: Cambridge University Press, 1983.

———. "The People in African Resistance: A Review." *Journal of Southern African Studies* 4, no. 1 (1977): 125–46.

Redding, Sean. *Sorcery and Sovereignty: Taxation, Power, and Rebellion in South Africa, 1880–1963.* Athens: Ohio University Press, 2006.

Reid, Richard. *Political Power in Pre-Colonial Buganda: Economy, Society and Welfare in the Nineteenth Century.* Oxford: James Currey, 2002.

Reinhard, Wolfgang. *A Short History of Colonialism.* Manchester, UK: Manchester University Press, 2011.

Rockel, Stephen J. *Carriers of Culture: Labor on the Road in Nineteenth-Century East Africa.* Portsmouth, NH: Heinemann, 2006.

Rosenwein, Barbara H. "Problems and Methods in the History of Emotions." *Passions in Context* 1, no. 1 (2010): 1–32.

Rotberg, Robert I. "Plymouth Brethren and the Occupation of Katanga, 1886–1907." *JAH* 5, no. 2 (1964): 285–97.

Santos, Catarina Madeira. "Écrire le pouvoir en Angola: Les archives ndembu (XVIIe–XXe siècles)." *Annales: Histoire, Sciences Sociales* 64, no. 4 (2009): 767–95.

Scott, James C. *Moral Economy of the Peasant: Rebellion and Subsistence in Southeast Asia.* New Haven, CT: Yale University Press, 1976.

Setas, António. *História do Reino do Kongo.* Luanda: Editorial Nzila, 2007.

Slade, Ruth. *King Leopold's Congo: Aspects of the Development of Race Relations in the Congo Independent State.* London: Oxford University Press, 1962.

Spear, Thomas. *Mountain Farmers: Moral Economies of Land and Agricultural Development in Arusha and Meru.* Oxford: James Currey, 1997.

———. "Neo-Traditionalism and the Limits of Invention in British Colonial Africa." *JAH* 44, no. 1 (2003): 3–27.

———. "Toward the History of African Christianity." In *East African Expressions of Christianity*, edited by Thomas T. Spear and Isaria N. Kimambo, 3–24. Oxford: James Currey, 1999.

Stanley, Brian. *The History of the Baptist Missionary Society, 1792–1992.* Edinburgh: T & T Clark, 1992.

Steinmetz, George. *The Devil's Handwriting: Precoloniality and the German Colonial State in Qingdao, Samoa, and Southwest Africa.* Chicago: University of Chicago Press, 2007.

Thompson, Edward P. "The Moral Economy of the English Crowd in the Eighteenth Century." In *Customs in Common*, 185–258. London: Penguin Books, 1993.

Thornton, John K. "Afro-Christian Syncretism in the Kingdom of Kongo." *JAH* 54, no. 1 (2013): 53–77.

———. "Central African Names and African-American Naming Patterns." *William and Mary Quarterly* 50, no. 4 (1993): 727–42.

———. "The Development of an African Catholic Church in the Kingdom of Kongo, 1491–1750." *JAH* 25, no. 2 (1984): 147–67.

———. "'I Am the Subject of the King of Congo': African Political Ideology and the Haitian Revolution." *Journal of World History* 4, no. 2 (1993): 181–214.

———. *The Kingdom of Kongo: Civil War and Transition, 1641–1718*. Madison: University of Wisconsin Press, 1983.

———. *The Kongolese Saint Anthony: Dona Beatriz Kimpa Vita and the Antonian Movement, 1684–1706*. Cambridge: Cambridge University Press, 1998.

———. "Kongo's Incorporation into Angola: A Perspective from Kongo." In *A África e a instalação do sistema colonial (c. 1885–c. 1930)*, edited by Maria Emília Madeira Santos, 349–58. Lisbon: Instituto de Investigação Científica Tropical, 2000.

———. "Master or Dupe? The Reign of Pedro V of Kongo." *Portuguese Studies Review* 19, nos. 1–2 (2011): 115–32.

———. "Mbanza Kongo/São Salvador: Kongo's Holy City." In *Africa's Urban Past*, edited by David M. Anderson and Richard Rathbone, 67–84. Oxford: James Currey, 2000.

———. "The Regalia of the Kings of Kongo." In *Kings of Africa: Art and Authority in Central Africa*, edited by Erna Beumers and Hans-Joachim Koloss, 57–63. Maastricht: Foundation Kings of Africa, 1992.

Tilly, Charles. "The Modernization of Political Conflict in France." In *Roads from Past to Future*, 51–108. Lanham, MD: Rowman and Littlefield, 1997.

———. "Parliamentarization of Popular Contention in Great Britain, 1758–1834." In *Roads from Past to Future*, 217–44. Lanham, MD: Rowman and Littlefield, 1997.

Torres, Adelino. *O império português: Entre o real e o imaginário*. Lisbon: Escher, 1991.

Twaddle, Michael. "The Emergence of Politico-Religious Groupings in Late Nineteenth-Century Buganda." *JAH* 29, no. 1 (1988): 81–92.

———. *Kakungulu and the Creation of Uganda, 1868–1928*. London: James Currey, 1993.

Vanhee, Hein. "King Pedro VII of Kongo (r. 1923–55)." In *Kongo across the Waters*, edited by Susan Cooksey, Robin Poynor, and Hein Vanhee, 26–27. Gainesville: University Press of Florida, 2013.

Van Reybrouck, David. *Congo: Een geschiedenis*. Amsterdam: Bezige Bij, 2011.

Vansina, Jan. *Antecedents to Modern Rwanda: The Nyiginya Kingdom*. Oxford: James Currey, 2004.

———. *Being Colonized: The Kuba Experience in Rural Congo, 1880–1960*. Madison: University of Wisconsin Press, 2010.

———. *Kingdoms of the Savanna*. Madison: University of Wisconsin Press, 1968.

———. "Kings in Tropical Africa." In *Kings of Africa: Art and Authority in Central Africa*, edited by Erna Beumers and Hans-Joachim Koloss, 19–26. Maastricht: Foundation Kings of Africa, 1992.

———. *Paths in the Rainforest: Toward a History of Political Tradition in Equatorial Africa*. Madison: University of Wisconsin Press, 1990.

———. *The Tio Kingdom of the Middle Congo, 1880–1892*. London: Oxford University Press, 1973.

Vellut, Jean-Luc. "The Congo Basin and Angola." In *General History of Africa*, vol. 6, *Africa in the Nineteenth Century until the 1880s*, edited by J. F. Ade Ajayi, 294–324. Paris: UNESCO, 1989.

———. "La violence armée dans l'État Indépendant du Congo: Ténèbres et clartés dans l'histoire d'un état conquérant." *Cultures et développements* 16, nos. 3–4 (1984): 671–707.

———. "L'économie internationale des côtes de Guinée inférieure au XIXe siècle." In *I Reunião Internacional de História de África: Relação Europa-África no 3° quartel do séc. XIX*, edited by Maria Emília Madeira Santos, 135–206. Lisbon: Instituto de Investigação Científica e Tropical, 1989.

Vezzu, Rinu, and Francisco Ntanda. *O centenário: Resenha histórica da evangelização em Mbanza Kongo*. Luanda: Editorial Nzila, 2007.

Vos, Jelmer. "Child Slaves and Freemen at the Spiritan Mission in Soyo, 1880–1885." *Journal of Family History* 35, no. 1 (2010): 71–90.

———. "The Economics of the Kwango Rubber Trade, c. 1900." In *Angola on the Move: Transport Routes, Communications and History*, edited by Beatrix Heintze and Achim von Oppen, 85–98. Frankfurt am Main: Verlag Otto Lembeck, 2008.

———. "Of Stocks and Barter: John Holt and the Kongo Rubber Trade, 1906–1910." *Portuguese Studies Review* 19, nos. 1–2 (2011): 153–75.

———. "Slavery in Southern Kongo in the Late Nineteenth Century." In *Trabalho forçado africano: Experiências coloniais comparadas*, edited by Centro de Estudos Africanos da Universidade do Porto (CEAUP), 315–36. Porto: Campo das Letras, 2006.

———. "'Without the Slave Trade No Recruitment': From Slave Trading to 'Migrant Recruitment' in the Lower Congo, 1830–1890." In *Trafficking in Slavery's Wake: Law and the Experience of Women and Children in Africa*, edited by Benjamin N. Lawrance and Richard L. Roberts, 45–64. Athens: Ohio University Press, 2012.

Voyages: The Transatlantic Slave Trade Database. Accessed August 20, 2014. http://www.slavevoyages.org.

Waltz, Heinrich Jakob. *Das Konzessionswesen im belgischen Kongo*. 2 vols. Jena: G. Fischer, 1917.

Wamba-dia-Wamba, Ernest. "Bunda dia Kongo: A Congolese Fundamentalist Religious Movement." In *East African Expressions of Christianity*, edited by Thomas T. Spear and Isaria N. Kimambo, 213–28. Athens: Ohio University Press, 1999.

Watts, Michael. *Silent Violence: Food, Famine, and Peasantry in Northern Nigeria*. Berkeley: University of California Press, 1983.

Wheeler, Douglas L. "Nineteenth-Century African Protest in Angola: Prince Nicolas of Kongo (1830?–1860)." *African Historical Studies* 1, no. 1 (1968): 40–59.

Wheeler, Douglas L., and René Pélissier. *Angola*. London: Pall Mall Press, 1971.

———. *História de Angola*. Lisbon: Tinta-da-China, 2009.

Willis, Justin. "'Men on the Spot,' Labor, and the Colonial State in British East Africa: The Mombasa Water Supply, 1911–1917." *IJAHS* 28, no. 1 (1995): 25–48.

———. "The Nature of a Mission Community: The Universities' Mission to Central Africa in Bonde." *Past and Present* 140 (1993): 127–54.

———. "Violence, Authority, and the State in the Nuba Mountains of Condominium Sudan." *Historical Journal* 46, no. 1 (2003): 89–114.

Willis, Justin, and Suzanne Miers. "Becoming a Child of the House: Incorporation, Authority and Resistance in Giryama Society." *JAH* 38, no. 3 (1997): 479–95.

Young, Crawford. *The African Colonial State in Comparative Perspective.* New Haven, CT: Yale University Press, 1994.

UNPUBLISHED DISSERTATIONS

Afonso, Camilo. "O contributo da tradição oral no estudo da história de Angola: Caso dos Bakongo." Licenciatura, Universidade Agostinho Neto, Lubango, 1991.

Broadhead, Susan Herlin. "Trade and Politics on the Congo Coast: 1770–1870." PhD diss., Boston University, 1971.

Cleveland, Todd Charles. "Rock Solid: African Laborers on the Diamond Mines of the Companhia de Diamantes de Angola (Diamang), 1917–1975." PhD diss., University of Michigan, 2008.

Coghe, Samuël. "Population Politics in the Tropics: Demography, Health and Colonial Rule in Portuguese Angola, 1890s–1940s." PhD diss., European University Institute, 2014.

Kiala, Luzolo. "Comércio e sociedade: Subsídios para a história dos Bazombo, c. 1880–c. 1925." Licenciatura, Universidade Agostinho Neto, Luanda, 2005.

Pires, Ana Flávia Cicchelli. "Comércio e trabalho em Cabinda durante a ocupação colonial portuguesa, c.1880–c.1915." PhD diss., Universidade Federal Fluminense, 2010.

Schrag, Norm. "Mboma and the Lower Zaire: A Socioeconomic Study of a Kongo Trading Community, c. 1785–1885." PhD diss., Indiana University, 1985.

INDEX

Page numbers in italics refer to illustrations.

AFRICA AND THE DIASPORA
History, Politics, Culture

SERIES EDITORS

Thomas Spear
Neil Kodesh
Tejumola Olaniyan
Michael G. Schatzberg
James H. Sweet

Printed in the United States
By Bookmasters